WITCHCRAFT

WITCHCRAFT

The Heritage of a Heresy

HANS SEBALD

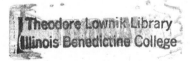

Elsevier · New York
NEW YORK · OXFORD

ELSEVIER NORTH HOLLAND, INC.
52 Vanderbilt Avenue, New York, New York 10017

Distributors outside the United States and Canada:
THOMOND BOOKS
(A Division of Elsevier/North-Holland Scientific Publishers, Ltd)
P.O. Box 85
Limerick, Ireland

Library of Congress Cataloging in Publication Data

Sebald, Hans.
  Witchcraft: the heritage of a heresy

  Bibliography: p.
  Includes index.
  1. Witchcraft—Germany, West—Franconia.
  2. Franconia—Religious life and customs.
  I. Title.
BF1583.S42   200'.943'3   78-10441
ISBN 0-444-99058-5 cloth
      0-444-99059-3 paper

Manufactured in the United States of America

Designed by Loretta Li

to
my clans,
THE SCHNEIDER
AND THE KLOPPERER

Contents

Acknowledgments

I am grateful for the 1975 Arizona State University Faculty Research Grant #981755 that partly supported the field research in Franconia; the 1977 sabbatical leave granted by Arizona State University that enabled me to complete research in European libraries and archives; the advice, information, and logistics provided by members of my clans, the Schneider of Sachsendorf and the Klopperer of Tüchersfeld; and particularly for the generous help extended by cousins, Karl Eckert, Adolf and Georg Sebald. Of the Catholic clergy in the area, Fathers Fischer of Pottenstein and Luchesius Spätling of Gössweinstein were as gracious as they were informative. Mr. Josef Singer, principal of the school in Gössweinstein, and Mr. Broda, vice principal, gave valuable advice and arranged introductions to members of the community who told me about their experiences with witchcraft. Mrs. Reta Arnold, on the staff of the Gössweinstein community government, guided me to literature on Franconian witchcraft and folklore. My cousin, Karl Eckert of Waidach, and photographer, Karl Reckziegel of Selb, assisted me in subject-related picture hunting.

A number of persons helped in literature research and the technical development of the manuscript, and I would like to thank Professors John M. Johnson of the Arizona State University, John Kunkel of the University of Western Ontario, Margarita Kay of the University of Arizona, Gerhard Wurzbacher of the Institut für Soziologie und Sozialanthropologie in Nürnberg, Mr. Erwin Honig of the Volkshochschule Selb, Gabi Welsch in East Germany with access to the vast *Deutschen Bücherei*, Petra Bauer in West Germany consulting government archives, and my American helpers Becky White, Jo Hall, Jim Canino, Alan Austin, Denise Armstrong and Sandi Ranahan.

My particular appreciation is reserved for all those villagers who confided in me and told me about their beliefs and, in some instances, practices and participation in witchcraft. They are the ones who made this study possible.

HANS SEBALD

At the Superstition Mountains,
Arizona, 1978

I

The Setting of

WITCHCRAFT

So deeply rooted are some errors that ages cannot
remove them. The poisonous tree that once overshadowed
the land may be cut down by the sturdy efforts
of sages and philosophers; the sun may shine clearly
upon spots where venomous things once nestled in
security and shade; but still the entangled roots
are stretched beneath the surface, and may be found
by those who dig.

CHARLES MACKAY

The Contours of Witchcraft

Witchcraft is a version of an awesome human venture: the pursuit of magic. Recognizing magic as the vital ingredient of witchcraft reveals the true meaning of the black art and defines the central purpose of this book.

Man's search for magic is ancient, and at its core lies his attempt to master life's dangers and vicissitudes by commanding the service of supernatural powers. While this attempt is the primary reason for many people's infatuation with witchcraft, it is not the only motive; this book explores a colorful range of purposes for which witchcraft has been exploited. These chapters discuss a number of fundamental questions: What is the essence of witchcraft? What is behind the timeless pursuit of magical power? Why do humans linger in a magical cosmos? What is the role of witchcraft in the daily life of certain people? What are the differences and similarities between witchcraft, religion and mysticism?

These questions have greater than merely historical value. Witchcraft is "alive and well" on planet Earth. Today, as during past ages, witchcraft is significant to many people. The reasons for this amazing longevity—if not immortality—are mirrored in the answers to the above inquiries. These answers disclose a variety of intense human needs—needs that are never outmoded and offer a constant invitation to witchcraft. Some are deeply grounded in the individual and are expressed through the quest for knowledge, explanation and, most importantly, personal power. Other concerns are inextricably anchored in the human community and manifested through the demand for distinction between good and evil and a sanction system punishing the deviant.

Witchcraft has been viewed as an alternative search for knowledge and the pursuit of power over life's adversities; however, on numerous occasions it has also been cast into the deadly role of crime or mental illness. In fact, the interpretation of witchcraft as a vicious perversion or weird pathology, including the possible role of psychedelic drugs, is common today.

No discussion of witchcraft is complete without going into some details of history. The story of witchcraft continues through many pages of mankind's diary—often written in blood. It is the blood of a motley crowd, and no one can be certain to fully understand the motives and meanings of the victims of the witch-hunt; neither do we fully comprehend the persecutors and executioners. To shed light on these obscure issues, I will briefly sketch the evolution of the witch from the pre-Christian period through the Christian era into the modern era, and examine the role of Christian theology and cultural symbolism of Western civilization as they influenced the rise of one of the most stupendous mass manias of all times. A rudimentary understanding of certain facets of the traditional Christian creed is indispensable for grasping the evolution of witchcraft as we know it in the Western world.

The witchcraft described in these pages is a direct historical continuation of the folk magic of past centuries, rooted in the Middle Ages, even Antiquity. It is a heritage slightly frayed, showing signs of strain and stress in logic, but a heritage nonetheless. The central figure is the witch, the latter-day heiress of a tradition that, from a superficial and sentiment-hungry point of view, appears romantic. And to many modern individuals, who feel like lost children in an alien urban-industrial jungle devoid of a reassuring philosophy, magical esoterica lure with promises of meaning and personal significance. But in the frantic search for beatific promises they confuse a tradition of madness, inhumanity and deranged minds with a godsend. It seems that the ignorant in historical matters naively bask in romantic mysticism.

This book has little to do with the mimicry of witchcraft found in contemporary covens. Modern urban witches all too often have the qualities of hothouse plants. If they were plucked out of their pseudomystic gregariousness and left to their own spiritual devices, they would rapidly succumb to the cosmic meaninglessness that is ever-present behind their occult facades. Indeed, modern-day meaninglessness is the motive that drove them into the arms of the contemporary covens in the first place. Play-acting the satanic disciple affords them social satisfaction that is essentially the same they would have derived by joining the nearby Community Church, neighborhood synagogue or the Rotary Club.

The focus of this discussion is the heiress of witchcraft as she maintains the Faustian dream, stands alone, and is her own demonic authority.

Witchcraft, or the pursuit of magic in general, is a dynamic phenomenon and has proceeded through history in many different forms. Magical beliefs change like the brilliant designs of a kaleidoscope. The incessant human renditions of magic are discussed to cast the whole of magical creed and practice into a time perspective. It appears, for example, that the young generation of today's Western world stands at the crossroads, skeptically judging the objective consciousness of our scientific world view and courting the promises of the occult.

However, as we shall see, in certain parts of the world the situation is reversed: the immediate descendents of witchcraft believers rebel against the "superstition" of their elders. Beliefs that once were meaningful are gradually vanishing, swallowed up by a demystifying technocracy that has penetrated into the most remote niches of Western civilization. The demystification of Western civilization is nearly complete. In fact, it is so complete that it has created an almost unbearable void. Signs of a remystifying process—attempts at reintroducing magic into daily life—can be seen everywhere in Western civilization. The so-called counterculture of the 1960s and early 1970s is a poignant reminder of the craving for the magical and mystical.

Among the last bastions of the ancient magical beliefs in the Western world to crumble before the inexorable onslaught of technocracy was the belief in the power of witchcraft among the peasants who live in a part of Bavaria called Franconian Switzerland (Fränkische Schweiz). A felicitous circumstance enables me to draw from the life-stories of people who believe in witchcraft and with whom I am intimately acquainted—indeed, related. The rural people of this secluded region, with their ancient beliefs and practices, serve as live material in the portrayal of witchcraft. These peasants provide the core example throughout this book. They are a source that has not been tapped previously, making an interesting comparison with such notorious events as the Salem witch-hunt and such famous studies by E. E. Evans-Pritchard among the Azande in Africa, Clyde Kluckhohn among the American Indians, and Bronislaw Malinowski among the Melanesian people. This book values cross-cultural comparisons and investigates how basic human conditions in different parts of the world are similarly, if not identically, distilled through the medium of witchcraft.

The concrete illustrations were gathered just before it was too late: one purpose of the book is to capture the evening glow of the belief in witchcraft and preserve the memory of the black art as it was practiced among the Franconian peasants. This is a semihistorical record, insofar as the belief is still alive. Members of the older generation participated in or witnessed witchcraft during their younger years (roughly during the first three decades of this century and told me about their experiences. But, their convictions no longer find credence among their offspring. They have no followers. Their belief is dying.

This is not a history book—neither arm-chair philosophy nor abstract library research. It deals with people directly, with their dreams, beliefs, and fears—mostly their fears. These people are alive; at least they were at the time I gathered the information. I collected material from peasants, mostly octogenarians, who vividly remembered witchcraft and other types of supernatural beliefs and practices in their villages. The field research, consisting of interviewing and observing, was completed during the past few summers. But the informal "research" dates back over many years—to my childhood.

My information was obtained by ethnomethodology. This means that the study was conducted more from the inside than the outside. My family background has its roots in the villages of Franconian Switzerland; I am known by my clan names (naming proceeds through the maternal as well as the paternal line, so that an individual is known by two clan names); I have access to a score of witchcraft-believing relatives who see me as a clan member instead of a *Fremden* (meaning either stranger or tourist); and finally I have the advantage of speaking their dialect. Therefore, it is somewhat misleading to label the method of collecting the data as "interviewing."

In fact, most of the old peasants whose acquaintance or reacquaintance I made were pleased to talk to me. Some of them knew me as a child and were happy that I had not forgotten them, had maintained respect for them and showed an interest in their lives. A typical example was an old man from the village of Bärnfels who recognized me, although we had never met, as the grandson of a folk healer of the village of Sachsendorf. He knew my paternal grandmother who was reputed as a healer and did not hesitate to tell me of his encounters with witches. After all, he seemed to reason, if a descendent of a healer does not understand such matters, who would?

I gathered the information by listening to relatives and village elders under a variety of informal circumstances: while they were conversing, reminiscing, feeling entirely at ease. I had meals with them; joined them at gravesides; asked them about a departed relative or friend; sat with them in the beer garden at the village inn; helped harvest the hay; worked at their sides tilling the fields; and walked with them to church.

Their innocent trust in their magical cosmos was left untouched. I neither asked intrusive questions nor showed skepticism under the guise of scientific objectivism, but carefully listened; showed acceptance of their way of life; and participated in their everyday activities.

So as not to offend or embarrass them, I refrained from using a tape recorder. In some instances I did, however, resort to quick pen-and-pad scribbling to record stories that were new to me. By "new," I am implying that I was already familiar with most accounts. I had heard these or similar stories since my childhood. As a child I was an awed and appreciative audience for the raconteur. So the field work during the past few summers was actually a sort of verification process—refreshing my memory with a systematic record.

The literature concerning witchcraft in Franconian Switzerland is scant. I found surprisingly little material apart from theological treatises and medieval and Renaissance records dealing with witch-mania. My time was more fruitfully invested in talking and listen-ing—especially listening—to the peasants.

My primary recording technique was to immediately withdraw into a quiet environment after listening and observing and to write down every detail I could remember. I am confident that by inte-grating my behavior into the lifestyle of the peasants I have achieved a fair portrayal of their belief in witchcraft. The source certainly is the purest: the direct expression of the believers and practitioners. And, considering their ages, it seems the source was tapped just in time.

This timing creates a semantic problem. Franconian peasant culture has reached the end of an era and is changing from folk magic to the objective consciousness of Western science and technology. But while the ancient supernatural beliefs rapidly vanish in the wake of time, there are still survivors of the more credulous generation. This small minority, while not exactly practicing, still believes in ancient traditions. When reporting about the waning beliefs, I am therefore faced with the question of tense. Should I use the present or the past? Neither accurately reflects the situation. I finally decided on the past tense. But the reader should be alerted lest he be misled and gives the entire report an historical frame. It is not yet history, though it soon will be.

This book, then, represents several things: It studies an ethnic group that gives it qualities of an *anthropological study*; it recaptures childhood impressions that provide it with the touch of *personal memoirs*; it probes the past of a part of Europe that gives it an *historical dimension*; it crystalizes the essence and meaning of witchcraft with the quality of a *functional analysis*; and finally, it traces the change from the magical world view to the objective consciousness (and possibly back to a form of magic) and therefore has a *perspective on social and cultural change*. To put it succinctly: this book is about an esoteric aspect of human nature; the problems arising from communal life; the vagaries of history; and how people try to control by magic the frailties of mind and body; the unreliability of the environment and the unavoidability of death.

The book is arranged in three major parts. Part I outlines the *setting of witchcraft*—locale, occult traditions and the witchcraft history of the Franconian region as it played a most atrocious part in the overall European witch-hunt during the Middle Ages and the Renaissance. This part also emphasizes the peasants' profound inclination to see their lives and the events around them in an aura of supernatural intervention. Their beliefs include a many-hued spectrum of presumably supernatural facts and events.

Part II describes the *working of witchcraft*—the witch in modern times, the healer as the white-magic counterpart, the fascinating role of a secret book, a collection of cases of curse and cure, and the extraction of the major dimensions from the beliefs and practices of Franconian witchcraft.

Part III delves into the *meaning of witchcraft*—witchcraft as a form of magic; comparison with religion and mysticism; the historical meaning; the functions of witchcraft as they appear to serve a number of individual desires and social needs; the question of witchcraft as mental illness and/or being drug induced, the power and contagion of cultural symbols as they fuel extraordinary delusions and stoke the madness of crowds; the theological underpinnings of witchcraft; and, finally, the fluctuations of magic as they can be observed over the generations.

The book ends on a note of irony and comments on social and cultural change. While some people exit from the magical stage to embrace the scientific and objective world view, others flock onstage to pick up the abandoned scripts. This epilogue attempts to cast the subject matter into a universal and historical perspective, showing the interminable gyrations of the human mind trying to achieve control over fate. If humans lose faith in the art of magic, they give science a hearing; and if science disappoints, they revert to magic. It is the drama—or comedy—of the endless search for power.

Land and People of Franconian Switzerland

Franconian Switzerland has enjoyed peculiar seclusion throughout history. Nature has tucked it into a relatively inaccessible area that has not awakened to the technocratic 20th century until recently. Belatedly, it is experiencing the end of an era and making the transition from the world of magic to the world of science and objective consciousness.

This region is the farthest northeastern spur of the Jura range consisting of wooded mountains extending from Switzerland through Swabia into Franconia, which occupies central Germany. So Franconian "Switzerland" is part of Germany and, as a name, has purely topographic and not political meaning. Its outlines can be visualized by drawing lines connecting the cities of Nürnberg, Bamberg and Bayreuth (see map). The resulting triangle (ca 40 by 30 by 40 miles) marks the boundaries of a territory whose topography originated from an ancient sea bottom. While millions of years have eroded coral reefs into verdant hills, the terrain still shows sharp contours. Limestone forms steep, almost canyonlike valleys; sculptures picturesque rock outcroppings; is rich in fossils; and opens to caves with bizarre stalactites and stalagmites. This landscape limits access and is mainly responsible for isolation that over the ages has been characteristic of Franconian Switzerland. No railroad or major highway crosses this land and the only public transportation is an occasional bus. Until recently, most villages could be reached only by dirt roads.

This seclusion helped to preserve ancient folk customs longer than in most other areas of Germany. The untouched character of

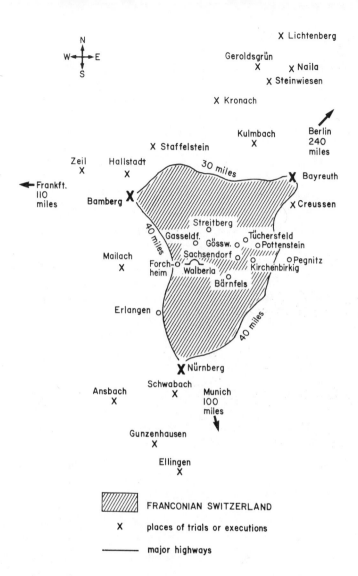

N
W ← + → E
S

X Lichtenberg

Geroldsgrün
X   X Naila
          X Steinwiesen

X Kronach

Kulmbach   Berlin
X Staffelstein   X   240
                              miles

Zeil   Hallstadt   30 miles
X   X   X Bayreuth

← Frankft.
110
miles   Bamberg X   X Creussen

40 miles   Streitberg
              Gasseldf. ○   Tüchersfeld
              ○   Gössw. ○   ○ ○ Pottenstein
Mailach   Sachsendorf ○
X   Forch- ○   ○   ○ Pegnitz
          heim   Walberla ○   Kirchenbirkig
                          ○
                      Bärnfels

Erlangen ○   40 miles

                      X Nürnberg

          Schwabach
Ansbach   X   Munich
X   100
                        miles
                          ↓

Gunzenhausen
X

Ellingen
X

///// FRANCONIAN SWITZERLAND

X   places of trials or executions

———   major highways

Franconian Switzerland was uniquely illustrated when I visited there in the early 1970s with Professor W. Mangold, Chairman of the Institut für Soziologie of the University of Erlangen-Nürnberg and mentioned to him my observations about witchcraft in the nearby province. He admitted that he had been unaware of folk magic being alive virtually in his backyard. As far as he knew, no scientific chronicler had ever gathered information among these peasants and no record preserved their vanishing beliefs.

The people almost exclusively pursued a peasant life, living off the land and dwelling closely together in small villages. The area

11

was, and is, relatively densely populated. But this is not noticeable since the villages are far apart and each is a tight cluster of small peasant homes. So the impression of the region is one of generous space with uncrowded woods and meadows.

While somewhat improved today, socioeconomic conditions used to be extremely harsh. The typical peasant family had two cows, two hogs, a small flock of chickens, a few geese and perhaps one or two goats. Cows were of greatest importance since they functioned as producers of dairy products and fertilizer and as beasts of burden (only the richer families could afford oxen or horses). The poverty of these peasants was extreme and the only way to survive was to work hard. All members of the family, from children to the old folk, shared in the daily chores. The warm months were filled with tilling and harvesting fields, the cold months with spinning, weaving, threshing grain, cutting wood, repairing and building stables and homes. The following description is a composite based on such reports as they came from my parents, grandparents and village elders, depicting a typical summer workday, and setting the time during the first two decades of this century. The conditions described therein are not altogether different from those I personally recall from my childhood during the late 1930s and 1940s.

During the hay season the peasants got up before sunrise, shouldered scythes and walked to often distant meadows to mow grass. It was important that the grass was mowed while still dew-moist, since dry grass thwarts a clean cut by the scythe. In the meantime, the womenfolk did the milking and other chores in the stable, prepared "coffee" made of roasted barley and carried a jug of it plus a few slices of dry home-baked bread to the men in the meadows. The peasants ate this breakfast standing up and went immediately back to raking the freshly mown grass to dry in the sun. Raking continued on other meadows to turn the grass cut on the previous day. By the time this was done, they returned to the freshly mown meadow to give that grass its first turning. By then the village bell announced noon and the workers returned to their homes for a simple meal, often consisting of only potato or bread soup. Immediately afterward, the peasants walked back to those fields where the hay was ready to be gathered up in big heaps and collected by a wagon pulled by cows. Loading the wagon required skill; weight had to be distributed evenly and the hay packed toweringly high, held down by the *Wischbaum*, a long pole tied along the length of the wagon atop a swaying mountain of hay. (Failure to load carefully could lead to an overturned wagon on the rutty, mountainous road that had to be traveled for miles.) Arriving at the farm, the peasants unloaded with pitchforks, tossing the hay into the hayloft. The hardest work was reserved for the person who tightly packed the hay in the loft, exposing himself to dust and temperatures ranging up to 120 degrees. Work was interrupted when the evening bell tolled for vespers and the peasants stood in silent prayer for a few minutes. After a light meal (resembling a lunch), the peasants took advantage of the evening dew and continued mowing until darkness put a halt to it. This was the routine day after day.

There were many hazards involved in this work. Someone, especially inexperienced youngsters, could fall from the wagon or the hayloft; a scythe might slip and cut a leg; the cows might shy and topple a wagon; a wheel might break; the *Kreuzotter*, poisonous viper of the region, might bite someone; and, more frequently, the weather might render all effort useless by raining and soaking the hay, by lightning and burning it or by hailing and smashing crops.

The well-being of the peasants was highly dependent on the weather. It sometimes happened that a peasant woman was caught in a rainstorm while on the road with her two cows pulling the wagon to a distant field where the menfolk were waiting to load hay. She, as well as her men, was soaked; the wet hay remained on the ground (diminishing in nutrition value); and late at night she returned home empty-handed. In addition, a cow might slip and hurt herself on the wet mountain road or a wagon might slide into the ditch. Moreover, the chilled cows might get sick and stop giving milk.

Sowing and harvesting crops were similarly laborious and hazardous. Sowing, weeding, cutting and gathering were done by hand. Weeds were saved as fodder for the animals; branches of the hazelnut and willow trees were used to tie sheaves; and during winter and late autumn the grain was threshed by flail. Threshing was evening or late night work, carried out on the barn floor by lantern light. Straw and chaff were manually separated and the grain sold to mills or breweries, again requiring long and cumbersome trips with the beast-powered wagon.

There was no insurance covering loss or theft of produce; loss or damage of buildings due to fire, flood or hail; damage of fields; disability or death caused by accident; or any other health problem.

13

When fate struck, the peasants had only themselves, kin and perhaps neighbors to rely upon. In misfortune, sometimes a field or two had to be sold to obtain the necessary money to pay for losses or accidents. If several strokes of fate coincided—as poor harvest, an accident, and sick or dying animals—it may have meant selling the farm which meant that the family members were to work the rest of their lives as day-laborers or farmhands.

Modern technology was slow in coming to Franconian Switzerland. The combustion engine, in form of the tractor, entered the history of this region in the late 1950s when it gradually began to replace cattle as agricultural work beasts. Likewise, rural electricity was not introduced until midcentury. At that time, water was also brought to the farm houses, which the peasants previously had to fetch from village wells. (I remember countless times when, as a child, I accompanied my grandmother to the well and pumped water with her supervising.)

Historically, Franconian Switzerland was ruled by oppressive landlords and the powerful Catholic Church. The peasants rarely owned the land they tilled; it was leased to them for exorbitant fees or for part of the crop (the tithing). While most of these arrangements have changed, vestiges of the robber baron system still exist.

Although most land is now owned by the peasants or leased to them for modest rates (large-scale land reforms, some of them as long ago as the Thirty-Years' War in the 17th century, have brought about these changes), arable land is scarce and farms have remained small—about 15–20 acres. In some villages, where the nobility was late in granting free peasant status (*Freibauer*), the average farm is noticeably smaller, approximating only 10 acres. Most leases are inheritable and stay in the family (*Erbpacht*), a custom dating back to medieval times when landlords leased meadows and fields to the families of serfs. This historical circumstance—peasants lease-inheriting small acreages—is probably the major reason why farms have remained small.

Two additional reasons should, however, be mentioned. One deals with the limitations that the region's topography imposes on farming. Miniature parceling naturally adapted itself to the rough contours of the land: steep valleys, narrow ridges, limited expanse between rivers and sharply rising valley walls and ubiquitous rock outcroppings. To this must be added the factor of dense population. The peasants raised large families and the continuous surplus of

14

births over deaths maintained pressure on the land. Although there was considerable country-city migration, it was never enough to make more room. As a custom, the oldest son stayed on the homestead and the younger siblings either married into other farms or moved to the city.

Another characteristic of farming in Franconian Switzerland was the lack of specialization. Because of the region's poor transportation, agricultural trading patterns remained limited and did not encourage specialization. For a farm family to be self-sufficient, it had to produce its own dairy products, grains, vegetables, meats and even goose down to fill bed covers.

This nonspecialization in production has had a number of peculiar economic and social consequences. First, it called for the villages to engage in parallel work. Each farmer needed the same implements and machinery as the other. While this sometimes led to borrowing of tools, it did not lead to cooperation in a collective sense. Property (tools or the fields) was sharply defined. With few exceptions, the only truly collective activities on a village or neighborhood basis consisted of the celebration of religious holidays.

Nonspecialized farming also necessitated scattered acreage. Since each peasant needed land suitable for such vastly different crops as wheat, potatoes and hay, the fields and meadows were never consolidated in one area. In other words, arable land was rarely contiguous by ownership. For example, the wet land along the stream in the valley was excellent for growing hay; the land on the mountain ridge was better suited for wheat or potatoes. Thus each farmer worked different pieces of land in different directions from the village. The government's attempt (*Flurbereinigung*) in the 1970s to change these time- and labor-wasting patterns by consolidating each farmer's lands was largely unsuccessful, first, because the peasants showed sentimental attachment to the fields and pastures that had been in their families for generations and, second, because consolidation of land would call for specialization, an agricultural innovation alien to these peasants. Finally, the farmer who envisioned all his land to be on the mountain feared the occasional drought that could wipe out the crops; the farmer who envisioned all his land to be in the valley distrusted the river that would occasionally flood and wipe out the valley crops. Consequently, scattered acreage appeared safer and remained the preferred mode of farming.

This custom depressed productivity and rendered the use of modern farm machinery unprofitable. Whatever farm implements have found their way to the Franconian peasants (and tractors have), their use has hardly diminished the excessive work hours. In sum, life has been and still is extremely hard work for the Franconian peasants.

The harsh conditions, combined with the close proximity of neighbors and their ubiquitous little fields, have had a decisive impact on the nature of interpersonal relationships and, as I shall point out later, on the nature of witchcraft as practiced among these peasants.

Generally, the character of the peasants of this area has always been strikingly peaceful. Perhaps it is appropriate to say that work was the opiate of these people. But there are additional reasons for this placidity. These peasants were deeply religious and their daily life was guided by their belief in supernatural powers. While most of their beliefs were consonant with Catholicism (the nearly exclusive religion of the region), in their daily lives they practiced an expanded version that incorporated significant elements of folk magic providing them with a set of guidelines for everyday life. Superficially speaking, these guiding beliefs might be called superstitions. Yet, the peasants' religious and magical imagination lent them the strength to carry on with the hardest work regime. It explained life's problems and hardships and, at the same time, provided a rationale, a consolation for them. In addition, their belief system played an important role in social relationships and provided the lubricant for working out interpersonal problems.

Crimes were (and still are) virtually unknown. For example, there still is no police officer in any of the villages.

In fact, there was little that attracted attention to this area, save for a limited tourist industry because of the charm of the land. But even in this respect, commercialism was kept at a minimum and there were few facilities for tourists in the villages. It was not until the past 10–15 years that a community effort was made to expand tourism which supplemented the peasants' income. The villagers were encouraged to renovate some rooms in their homes, setting them aside for tourist rentals. But tourists have never been cordially welcomed by the natives: they were regarded city-slickers and strangers to whom they could not relate. (Indeed, the word for tourist is "stranger," *Fremder.*)

16   The Franconian peasants still speak their ancient dialect, dis-

tinctly different from those of surrounding provinces. Their soft and melodious language bears little semblance to the harsher sounds of the rest of Bavaria, of which Franconia is the northern province. The warmth of the dialect is not limited to phonetics but also permeates the semantics that mellow communication with innumerable, endearing diminuitives. The softness of the language is in strange contrast to the harshness of the land and the austerity of the living conditions.

As emphasized earlier, the old Franconian culture is fading. A manifestation of the crumbling traditions may be seen in the fact that few peasant women continue to wear the ancient folk costume. Only at church can one spot an occasional long dark skirt topped by a longsleeved embroidered bodice; its wearer is invariably of the older generation. The men never wore conspicuous costumes—only plain black suits and black hats; again, only old men are seen wearing the traditional monotony today. (Groups of young people at folk festivals try to revive folk costuming, but it is no more authentic than the pageantry on a Shakespearean stage.)

For these peasants, the center of life was the family and the clan. This became particularly evident at harvest time when clan members helped each other, even if it meant traveling to distant villages. A person was known primarily by his or her clan's name—an unwritten name not found in the official registers. This name ascribed status, and depending on the prestige or reputation of the clan, conveyed negative or positive connotations.

The clan was normally characterized by internal cohesion. The security derived from this integration was badly needed. The threats to the Franconian peasants were many. They started with the possibility of droughts or floods wiping out their harvests and leaving them without food; continued with often poorly understood diseases among their farm animals; were concerned with other people and the fear of becoming the victim of harm or a hex; became particularly frightening when illness or death struck the family; and carried over to the supernatural realm, which was an inseparable part of the peasants' everyday lives.

Fears were basic components of their daily lives. And the most mystifying concerns derived from their beliefs in supernaturalism. Whether these beliefs originated from attempts to explain the world and its dynamics, or to console for many hardships and disappointments or a complex mixture of both, will be discussed later. Perhaps for ten supernatural beliefs that caused fear, ten others could comfort. One could logically argue that if the first set of ten were abolished, the second set of ten would no longer be needed. Possibly. But this is a purely theoretical proposition; reality, as the Franconian peasants knew it, was simply the way it was. Our task here is to convey a measure of understanding of their spiritual world.

This book focuses almost exclusively on the more fearsome elements of the peasants' life. It is an exercise in selectivity. Lest this create the impression of an unduly bleak social climate, I must add that this peasant culture was not devoid of a sense of humor, lustiness and frivolity.

The Supernatural—
Substance and Sustenance
to the Peasants

As mentioned in the previous chapter, the traditions of these peasants were replete with beliefs in supernatural powers. Poltergeists and the souls of the departed were visiting; apparitions were common; evil and benign spirits abounded; and the reality of witchcraft was beyond question. Indeed, the Franconian peasants' preoccupation with the supernatural covered the entire spectrum of the occult.

However, I must emphasize that the focus of this book is on witchcraft and that witchcraft is a distinct species of the occult. After this introduction to the occult cosmos of the Franconian peasants, the discussion will hew more closely to the subject of witchcraft.

Rather than presenting the occult tradition as made up of superstitions, I prefer to label it a system of beliefs. I hope the approach will thereby be more objective and nonjudgmental. I am following William I. Thomas' principle that reality to a person is his or her definition of the situation.[1] Whether this definition squares with an absolute, objective reality is not the question. The essence of an experience is what the individual believes about it, and the ensuing consequences are real for the believer.

It is quite possible that some peasants became so agitated with apprehension that they actually opened themselves to the risk of delusions and hallucinations. Delusions usually align themselves with specific fears and, for example, can symptomize themselves as "demonic possessions." In other words, demonic possession loomed as a potential reality to the Franconian peasants. Like Satan, who was viewed as a reality that could be personified, demons were real beings who assumed active roles in the lives of the people.

19

We can carry the implications of the principle expounded by Thomas a step further. The essence of the principle can express itself so powerfully that a bodily effect of a belief can sometimes be observed. I am referring to the physiological impact of a mental state, a process defined as *psychosomatic*: if people believe in the effectiveness of a hex (an evil spell or a curse) and expect to suffer ill health, reduced well-being or certain pain, it is possible that the believers will manifest these symptoms. Anthropologists have discovered evidence of the correlation between belief and bodily reaction around the world. The most extreme example is the role of the "dying person," the person who believes that he or she has been irrevocably cast into that role and will actually die—and, indeed, he or she dies without a discoverable medical cause.[2] Apparently a poorly understood neurological and endocrinological process complies with the believer's definition of the situation and successfully persuades the organism to function (or disfunction, as the case may be) accordingly.

It follows, then, that witchcraft is not just a harmless collection of unworkable spells and incantations employed by those who misunderstand the scientific principle of cause and effect, but that it and all things that are occult are real in the sense of having physiological effects on the believers. Therefore, I suggest that a person who claims a serious belief should be taken seriously. To him or her, the belief determines reality and he or she can often show the concrete results of the belief.

Based on the above premise, I shall focus on the *instance of a particular belief* and make it the basic unit of examination.

To grasp the essence of a supernatural belief and to distinguish between different types, I suggest that each belief be examined for certain qualities. To render homage to the truism that reality comes in hues and shades, each quality should be viewed in terms of degrees. For example, the beliefs of a person are in rare instances entirely unique, but are usually influenced by the surrounding culture of which he or she is a part. This means that a confrontation with the ghost of one's grandfather, who perhaps reveals a family secret, is unmatched and therefore unique. On the other hand, a person's sighting of a troll is less unique since "everybody knows" of their existence and may have "seen" them. The encounter can of course wax in uniqueness, depending on precisely what transpires during the event. (The troll may deliver an unprecedented message or behave in an unparalleled manner.) To determine the precise point on the unique-to-general range in a given situation is a question of refined sociometrics that would have to take into account statistical data concerning the proportion of the peasant population with identical experiences or identical beliefs. Such sophisticated measurements would exceed the framework of this book. I will indicate only estimates of the varied nature of the supernatural beliefs.

The evaluation should consider at least five qualities.

1. The **unique–general** dimension, illustrated above, deals with how common a supernatural belief is. One could also use the term idiosyncratic, i.e., how unique to one's temperament or experience a belief is, versus typical, how generalizable the belief is to the remainder of the populace.

    It is important not to confuse belief with one limited event. As we shall see, many people hold beliefs without being able to base them on actual happenings. The dimension of unique–general concerns *belief.* (One might, however, suspect a significant positive correlation between belief and corresponding occurrence: the self-fulfilling prophecy explaining the significant correlation.)

2. The **passive–active** dimension diagnoses whether a person is a passive party to a supernatural manifestation, or whether the person tries to introduce and manipulate supernatural forces. The passive stance is primarily resigned and explanation-seeking. Examples include the interpretation of such natural phenomena as lightning, rain, drought, death and disease. The active stance seeks to control and direct supernatural forces. Examples include incantations in voodooism, witchcraft and healing.

3. The **personal–interpersonal** dimension examines whether an individual views a supernatural episode as a purely personal matter or an interpersonal affair including a dispute, revenge or healing attempt. Personal examples are apparitions, visions, dreams and other isolated experiences that may be traumatic, horrifying, beatific or simply informative. Interpersonal examples assume that an individual engages supernatural powers for or against another individual, as typical of the witch or the healer.

4. The **legendary–experiential** dimension examines whether an individual believes in a supernaturalism because it is "popularly believed to have a historical basis, although not verifiable,"[3] or whether the person claims an experience. A legend can be exemplified by the belief in what is "popularly known," such as the existence of a ghost in a castle, but with the lack of personal testimony. However, an experiential claim would be based on a true encounter with the ghost.
5. Many beliefs draw from a mixed heritage. I therefore include the **pagan–Christian** dimension. This addresses the historical intertwining of pagan and Christian ideas. Each belief should be examined as to the proportion represented.

The five dimensions are primarily of comparative value. The reader may benefit by applying them to other beliefs in supernaturalism. Except for the pagan–Christian dimension, they can probably be applied universally to identify important elements in belief systems.

When we look at any one case of belief in supernatural power, we must henceforth remember that it is multidimensional. The different dimensions usually exist in complex and interwoven patterns. No dimension is exclusive of another. If we use witchcraft in Franconian Switzerland as an illustration, we find that its essence if *general, active, interpersonal, experiential* and *mixed pagan–Christian*.

With these guidelines in mind we are going to examine a number of supernatural beliefs prevalent among Franconian peasants. The reader will find it easy to apply the five dimensions and recognize the qualities that characterize each instance.

In this section, we sample the peasants' inclination to see and explain the world in a supernatural light. The examples illustrate the supernatural climate of the belief system among the peasants and set the stage for the discussion of witchcraft in subsequent chapters.

Most of the supernatural beliefs that were held by the Franconian peasants combined ancient pagan custom and Christian tradition. But in some of them one preponderated over the other. For example, the belief in the *Wütenker* seemed to derive from the ancient Germanic trust in Woden, the supreme God of the pre-Christian Germanic tribes, who was revered for his mercurial prowess.[4] The

Wütenker was believed to be an army of nightly riders striking terror into the hearts of the peasants. The phantoms roared through the skies with deafening screams, horrifying curses, blood-curdling cynical laughter, wild barking and cracking whips. They uprooted trees and bushes in their paths and punished humans who failed to immediately throw themselves to the ground and bury their faces into the dust. The roaring horde rotated around its own axis, creating formidable turbulence. Victims have allegedly been found lacerated, maimed, with hair torn out, torn limb from limb. The careless or obstreperous could be glad if all that happened was merely being defecated upon by horses and hogs that rode in the entourage of the *Wütenker*. Other reports told of children who had died and later were seen riding with the raging hordes. These children had died before they could be baptized—an interesting Christian element in an otherwise pagan plot. A similar adaptation was found in the story where a peasant on the way to poach a Christmas tree in the forest encountered the *Wütenker* who dropped an ax beside him. When he used it to fell the tree, he cut his leg. The wound would not heal. Finally, he went back to the forest, offered to return the ax to the phantoms, who appeared and accepted it; the wound healed miraculously.

Probably without exception, the older generation has heard of the phantom hordes, many claim to have had encounters and almost all believe in its reality. But the personal experiences are invariably dated. When asked why there were no recent (over the past 40–50 years) "sightings," the elders in all villages were as unanimous as they were laconic: "Because the *Wütenker* has been banned for 1000 years by the Holy Father in Rome." (A few respondents made it 100 years.)

Interviews with Catholic clergy of the area revealed that this belief has no official theological or encyclical basis. How this amazing unanimity developed among the peasants is a mystery to the priests and to me, as a researcher.

The independent folk theology spun the issue into further intricacies. Many of the older peasants debated with great seriousness the question of the identity of the members of the *Wütenker*. No unanimous opinion emerged. Some thought that they represented souls suffering a trying sojourn in purgatory or limbo and periodically unfurled their pain by sweeping through the skies. (This opinion would explain or reconcile two aspects of the belief: the presence of unbaptized children among the raging hordes, since, according to the traditional Catholic dogma, lack of baptism relegated a child to enternal limbo without hope of ever entering heaven; and, second, the assumption that through the mediation of the Pope, God would either redeem or restrain the souls pining in purgatory.) Other opinions held, however, that the hordes represented satanic forces. But no one spoke with certainty about one or the other interpretation. One notes the duality between the good (though anguished) and the evil (satanic) forces—a duality that will be rediscovered in many instances of folk belief and will be specifically discussed in the confrontation of the witch and the healer.

A brief evaluation of the belief in the *Wütenker* shows that it was highly general, the phantom horde existed for everyone, it was passively experienced and could not be conjured or manipulated; it had few if any interpersonal elements; it was of mixed Christian–pagan origin; and it was presumably truly experienced and not legendary.

While the origin of the *Wütenker* was primarily pagan, other traditions were more aligned with Christianity. One concerned the mysterious "little men with faintly glowing bodies," *feurige Männlein*, who would silently accompany a lone wanderer to help him or her find the way home at night. Their identity was unknown until the following story spread through the villages.

A peasant who frequented the village inn found a little translucent man each time waiting at the inn's gate to walk mutely with him to his home. Arriving at his house, the peasant always rewarded the mysterious creature with a coin and the little man would disappear with a sigh and a sad expression on his face. One night the peasant did not find a coin in his pocket and he regretfully addressed the small translucent companion, "May the Lord reward you this time." Whereupon the little man, normally mute, jubilated, "That's what I was waiting for!" and disappeared forever. Now the peasant understood that he had dealt with some "poor soul from purgatory" (*arme Seele*) who sought redemption, finding it through the peasant's pious words of thanks. They story spread and established the definition of the translucent beings.

Accordingly, the little shiny men were good (albeit tormented) spirits who would not harm anyone, but needed the help and prayer of humans. Many peasants thought that if a person did not know this, he or she might be unnecessarily frightened when encountering a little shiny man.

During a conversation, one elder speculated on whether the little translucent men might be stray members of the *Wütenker*, thereby suggesting that the raging hordes might be made up of "poor souls from purgatory." The occupation with such speculations betrayed the degree of seriousness with which the peasants viewed such matters.

This belief, again, reflected the duality theme. The peasants agreed that evil spirits (Satan himself or his representative) sought out *living* humans to reside in them. The souls of departed may be tormented but were never evil or in Satan's service. It was the witch who was Satan's firmest ally.

The belief in the "little glowing men" was general, since the creatures existed as a category and presumably could be encountered by anyone. The content of each event was less generalizable than that of the *Wütenker*, however, since the "little glowing men" were more selective than the blindly raging phantoms and were engaged in more unique interactions. The encounters also allowed for more active participation, since the person could actually (though largely unwittingly) influence the fates of the "poor souls." They were not truly interpersonal experiences, since the mysterious creatures were merely souls temporarily assuming human appearances, and the experiences had little if any bearing on the relationships with others in the village. It was, as described above, more Christian than pagan in origin. And it was an experiential account to which a member of the older peasants testified.

Another belief attached to an ailment called the *Gfrasch*. It struck infants and evidenced itself through convulsions, often resulting in death. Apparently it was the particular symptomatology of the spasms and convulsions that led the peasants to believe that evil demons possessed the child. They frequently also believed that these demons acted at the command of a witch. In order to exorcise the spell, the people preferred to call a healer from their own ranks rather than a medical doctor. (The latter was not available in the outlying villages, and there was none in the whole region before 1910.) If the child died—often in spite of prayers, rituals and medicinal herbs—it confirmed the uncanny power of the witch (who may have been "known" or merely suspected). Sometimes, however, it was simply attributed to the inscrutable "will of God."

This pre- or nonscientific explanation is, of course, increasingly replaced by medical insight. Although I witnessed at least one poignant example of this folk-magic interpretation among my relatives many years ago, the more recent diagnosis is acute calcium deficiency during teething. The baby's organism is deprived of vital nutrients and reacts violently. Not only has the interpretation changed, but also the frequency with which this condition occurs. The diminishing rate can be explained by improved nutrition over the erstwhile dismally inadequate nutrition of the impoverished peasants.

In the *Gfrasch* we again recognize a general supernaturalism, since it was believed that it existed as a type of demonic force that could strike any infant at will. Only insofar as it was sometimes attributed to a particular witch's evildoing did it assume a measure of uniqueness. The belief assumed a mixed passive–active character whereby one could try to counteract the evil forces at work, but was also ready to resign oneself to the inevitable. The condition had several interpersonal implications. First, it involved the relationship of parent and child. Many parents agonized why it was *their* child who was striken. (And further supernaturalisms proliferated on the basis of this question. Did a member of the family or the clan offend God? Was it the malice of a witch?) Secondly, it usually involved a healer (maybe a woman known for her healing power, or a clergyman or a medical doctor). The interpretation of the condition as a supernaturalism is a mixture with pagan–Christian origin. Finally, it was definitely experiential and not legendary.

Another medical phenomenon with supernatural interpretation, this one highly unique, occurred during the 1910s in the village of Tüchersfeld where a young girl, T. W., was believed to be tormented by demons. She would frequently throw herself on the ground, writhe and eventually fade into unconsciousness. While in retrospect the symptoms suggest epilepsy, the villagers did not perceive it as a medical problem.[5] The customary folk medicine showed no healing effect and, when she was a young adolescent, a number of village men got together and resorted to folk theology. They decided that the shroud customarily draped over the coffin at the occasion of the requiem mass in the nearby basilica of Gössweinstein would be instrumental in ridding the girl of the demons. This shroud was fetched one night (without the awareness of the clergy) and spread over the girl as she lay in an unconscious state. The assumption was that the blessed shroud would drive away the evil spirits. Since this procedure was in no way intended as "shock therapy" or to frighten the girl, it was spread over her body only after she had become unconscious. While the peasants believed that they noticed an initial improvement of the girl so exorcised, the dreaded symptoms recurred and the young girl died.

The basic element of this episode was the generalizable interpretation of demonic possession, which was nothing greatly unique in the Franconian peasant culture. But another aspect reflected a unique belief: the exorcising potential of the liturgic shroud—the use of which seemed to be limited to this one case. (The attempt to heal through sacred objects is as much Christian as it is pagan; in the latter instance we call it fetishism.) The event involved active participation and stimulated interpersonal relations because a certain amount of social structuring was necessary to organize the folk-exorcism. And the event was experiential, not legendary, having been reported to me by eyewitnesses.

While the accounts so far were characterized by a high degree of experiential quality, i.e., participants or eyewitnesses testified to their occurrence, some beliefs are based more on tradition than on personal report. This did not necessarily diminish the power of the belief in the alleged event: it only meant a shift in *how* the event was accounted for. The following lore reflects a belief, widely shared among the older peasants, for which none could render personal testimony.

As they will tell you, many years ago there was a large farm near Sachsendorf—large because an ancestor had moved deceitfully the boundary stone at the expense of neighbors. After the farmer died, his restless soul was seen every year on the night of his crime, carrying the heavy boundary rock in his arms from dusk to dawn. Whoever came near the place was asked by the ghost, "Where do you want me to put the marker?" But everyone so addressed bolted in fright without answering, making the sign of the cross to protect himself or herself against the tormented ghost who agonized under the heavy load.

One year, a shepherd new to the area, a crude and somewhat dim-witted fellow, walked through the pasture late at night. Suddenly, a wailing and lamenting figure approached him, carrying a large rock, and pleaded, "Where do you want me to put it?" Somewhat annoyed by the seemingly puerile behavior, the shepherd curtly replied, "Stupid, put it back where you found it." This straightforward reply delivered the tormented soul. The ghost disappeared with a joyful whoop and was never seen again. From then on, the boundary stone was in its rightful place.[6]

The theoretical evaluation of this account is interesting inasmuch as there was no personal testimony to its verity. It was an oral tradition. Yet, it was widely believed. Though it sounds like a unique event, it has a generalizable character since the role of the tormented soul who deceived neighbors by moving boundary markers was a common element in a number of stories. The prevalent tale was that the suffering soul could not rest until it rectified its wrong-doing—and could do so only with the help of the living. And to the extent that it required human cooperation, it obviously involved active participation and human interaction.

The Christian–pagan elements were again blended, since in both traditions the dead could return in some fashion—in Christianity as souls and in the pagan world as ghosts.

To contrast the previous story with a legend that was not believed to be true, here is the tale of the three nymphs of the Stempfermühle (a mill). The story goes that deep in the three springs rushing forth next to the mill and driving its big wheel lived the queen of the nymphs surrounded by many lovely attendants. Through the crystal waters, the nymphs emerged nightly to visit with humans. But the law of the springs was that they must return to their queen before the first crow of the rooster. Early one morning, a tragedy occurred. At the celebration of the betrothal of the lord of the Gössweinstein castle, three beautiful nymphs, who came to dance, failed to return to the springs in time. When they finally descended into the waters, blood welled up: the queen made them pay with their lives for breaking the law of the springs.[7]

Although this legend was widely known among the peasants, it was not taken seriously. It included active and interpersonal elements. It was mostly pagan in origin. The story focused on a unique plot, but drew from the generalizable element of nymphs who were known from many other stories—but hardly believed as real.

Barely believable to the peasants were the stories about the enigmatic *Holzfrala* (woman of the forest). She was sometimes described as a benign spirit who would reward virtuous behavior, and sometimes as a formidable spook who would haunt people. This spookish keeper of morals was particularly interested in children and would reward them with gifts if they were helpful to parents and neighbors, but would drag the incorrigible and lazy into a dank cave in the woods to detain them till they repented. The *Holzfrala* proved to be of service to the hard working peasants. She would stealthily visit at night and complete chores in deserving peasant homes, gardens, fields, and stables. But she has not been seen or heard of for generations. The reason for her disappearance, it is said, was the curiosity of people who sneaked up on her, teased her and played pranks on her. She, according to the story, left Franconian Switzerland—to be gone forever.

The *Holzfrala* stories were most understood as just that—stories. Most natives felt that they had been invented for children. But, then, there were peasants who felt that such creatures were common in ancient days. They helped in households and kept the young in their place. In general, however, the stories were accepted as legends.

Literary researchers assume that the legend of the *Holzfrala* derived from, or at least is parallel to, the old Germanic Goddess of the earth, *Holda* (the friendly one), who was wedded to Woden and was the divine guardian of domestic affairs, including marriage, fecundity, household chores and particularly weaving.[8] In a sense, she was the pagan counterpart of the Christian guardian angel who presumably watched out for children and well-meaning adults. Note, however that the *Holzfrala–Holda* type of guardian incorporated the punitive with the rewarding and protecting, while the Christian version is limited to the guarding and rewarding function.

The Franconian plethora of spooks and supernaturalisms presented also a male guardian who performed more limited functions than the *Holzfrala*. The *He-Männla* (*he* is German for hello; *Männla* means little man) lived hidden in the forest and guarded the woods against poachers and thieves. He therefore was of great value to proprietors of wooded land. From the tops of rocks or cliffs, he would watch over his domain and descend swiftly upon those who ventured into the forest to steal trees. With a shrill and interminable, "he, he, he," he would rush after the frightened intruder and not stop yelling and hollering until the would-be thief was well out of the woods.

Woe to those who dared to mock or repeat the "he, he, he" calls. Legend has it that a man once mocked the call and was nearly hunted to death by a thousand poltergeists who stormed after him and did not give up until he reached the door of his home.

Certain times of the year, the first few days of the Lenten season, for example, were particularly dangerous for wood thieves. At that time, so the rumor went, Satan himself dwelled in the forest, awaiting the unsuspecting. Not even the most experienced and intrepid poacher dared to enter the forest during that season.

The *He-Männla* enjoyed a somewhat higher credibility than the

Holzfrala. Many peasants suggested that this legend might be based on fact. The repeated comment was, "Yes, such things happened in the old days." Why they no longer happened in the modern days was rarely explained. At any rate, the *He-Männla* phenomenon was active and interpersonal, particularly alluding to the thief-proprietor relationship. It had the potential for uniqueness, since the encounters with the spook allowed for individual differences. The origin of the legend is obscure but it appears to be ancient and of pagan character.

The plethora of supernaturalisms also had room for the trolls. Legends told that in caves and ruins of crumbled castles dwelt an odd, dwarflike people, the *Hankerle*. These trolls, rumored to be rather ugly, guarded immense treasures of gold and precious stones. (There was rumor of much greater treasures in the region over which allegedly hovered fiery dogs or Satan himself.) The trolls denied approach to the hidden places and those who failed to heed their warning paid with their health or even their lives.

A story was told of a peasant from the village of Hungenburg whose greed got the better of his caution and who climbed into the labyrinthian canyon of the River Ailsbach to look for treasure. He was allegedly ambushed by a horde of dwarfs who stoned him with sharp rock crystals. Although escaping with his life, the man's eyes were so badly damaged that he went blind.

Most of the old peasants considered the story of the Ailsbach affair mere folklore. They hesitated, however, to write off dwarfs per se as legendary and again tended to put their trust in by-gone eras, allowing that such mythical beings existed in the area a long time ago. There are many Franconian stories dealing with dwarfs or trolls, and they invariably reflect a high degree of active participation on the part of humans. It is more difficult to recognize how dwarfs had an impact on interaction between humans. It is possible, however, that a villager's prestige or reputation was affected if he or she was suspected of contact with the dwarfs—especially if a transaction of gold or other treasures was surmised.

The origin of the *Hankerle* lore is entirely Teutonic.[9] Folklorists suspect the medieval peasantry of having believed that the first Slavic settlers of the area were subjugated by fierce Germanic tribes and that through long captivity they shriveled and became dwarfs. They ultimately withdrew to canyons and hidden caves. The lore distinguishes between the *Hankerle* dwarfs and the native dwarfs, the *Wichtelmännchen*—two different races. The cantankerous *Hankerle's* sojourn in Franconian Switzerland was not an enduring one and it is said that they left in recent history. No one knows where they went.

Many prominent features of the Franconian landscape are associated with, indeed identified by, a supernatural explanation.[10] It is told that many years ago a shepherd and his sheep were enjoying a lush green valley when a storm drew near. Soon the valley was hit by rain, sleet, thunder and lightning. The shepherd's anger against the nasty weather knew no limits and he shouted a sacrilege against God. No sooner had the oath passed his lips than a colossal lightning bolt struck him and his flock and cast them all into cold, hard rock. Though it is said that this happened hundreds of years ago, the rock formations can still be seen at the foot of the old fortress, Streitburg, where among scattered boulders the size of sheep stands a rock spire resembling a human figure. The peasants call it the "petrified shepherd," *steinerne Hirt*.

This story plainly carries Christian connotation. It shows a human who rebels against God and, in being punished, causes annihilation to his animals, too. It is generalizable and has an interpersonal quality inasmuch as it serves to warn others against sacrilegious behavior. The peasants accepted the possibility that God could punish in such manner and that He probably did so many times throughout history, although they were not certain whether the rocks at the Streitburg were a factual example.

We have now looked at a number of different beliefs. Some of them reflect human passivity in the face of presumably supernatural events, some depict humans as active agents, some give impetus to interpersonal relations, some describe beliefs attached to highly unique events and others confirm common beliefs; many have pagan origin and many share Christian background, but the vast majority blends both traditions.

Certain events enjoyed little credibility and were mostly relegated to the category of legends. Events in which the figures were ghosts or "poor souls" enjoyed a conspicuously greater degree of credibility than events animated by such universal and mythical characters as dwarfs and nymphs. Greater trustworthiness was apparently attached to the beliefs in the raging *Wütenker* and the meek *feurige Männlein*. To many peasants, these beliefs were based on factual accounts—accounts that enjoyed an amazing corroboration among the elders of different villages and reflected agreement in almost every detail.

It is important to realize that the corroboration was not influenced by literate sources. The only literary treatment that mentioned some of these beliefs and stories prior to the 1970s was by the Gössweinstein teacher, Karl Brückner, who, in the 1920s, published two books of legends from Franconian Switzerland. These books collected stories, but in no way influenced their origin that is ancient and preliterate. In fact, it may be safely assumed that no literary source has ever influenced the peasants' beliefs to the extent of causing them. For example, in my interaction with older peasants, I have not encountered one instance where Brückner's books were known.

Also, Brückner's writing tended to focus on what was established more or less as legend and shied away from those accounts that dealt with the personal experiences of the peasants. This tendency undoubtedly was a result of the author's desire to steer clear of personal beliefs and family affairs. At the time of his writing, witchcraft was still strong in many villages and certain persons were still known as witches or wizards. Writing about them might have caused unpleasant consequences for the author. As a result, Brückner wrote little about witchcraft.*

My reasons for presenting a cross section of the beliefs are (1) to convey a picture of the peasants' preoccupation with the supernatural; (2) to demonstrate how the five criteria elucidate the nature of a belief; (3) to facilitate the comparison of different beliefs; and (4) to facilitate a clearer recognition of what witchcraft is and how significantly it differs from other types of belief in the supernatural.

In the next chapter, I will concentrate on the queen of supernaturalism: the witch.

---

* In a few instances, I have referred to some of Brückner's stories which border between legend and belief. However, my work focuses strictly on accounts given to me by the peasants. When I refer to the folklorist's writings, it usually is to acknowledge his report of an account I was told directly by the natives.

4

The Witch—
Evolution of a Satanist

The nature of the witch is interpersonal. Unlike many other types of the occult where the individual stands alone facing the supernatural experience, the witch stands between the person and the supernatural power. During Antiquity, her supernatural mediation was considered benevolent, but during later historical epochs this mediation came to be thought of as largely malevolent.

The German word for witch is *Hexe*. (Although an almost identical word in modern English, hex, is more commonly used to describe the curse or spell that a witch casts; in dialects it has been used synonymously with witch.) The word derived from the ancient Germanic *haziz* or *hazus* via the Middle High German *hexse*. During the earliest Germanic era, the *hazis* was thought of as a woman related to the *Valkyrie* (honorable helper of Germanic deities, who accompanied the slain heroes to Valhalla) and revered as goddess of the forest. As time went on, the *hazis* lost her status and was feared and shunned.[1]

In a parallel fashion, the English word witch derived from *wikke* (Middle English from which wicked also derived), which in turn comes from *wicca*, an old Anglo-Saxon word. (Present-day "witches" in England and the United States claim that *wicca* referred to Celtic high priests and priestesses, but etymological dictionaries relate it to Old Norse *wiccian*—to cast a spell.) Just as among the Teutonic tribes the *hazis* became the *Hexe*, among the Anglo-Saxon tribes *wicca* became the *witch*.

Instrumental in these transformations was the rise of Christianity. The Christian authorities usurped the erstwhile pagan concept and twisted it into a Christian heresy in which Satan came to assume the central role.

Modern *white* witches reject this usurpation and claim their spiritual heritage not from *black* witches of the Church-dominated Middle Ages but from the mysticism of Antiquity.[2] This interpretation of the evolution of the witch currently has popular appeal and is compatible with Margaret Murray's famous theory of the Old Religion, a presumably pervasive pre-Christian pagan world view. However, there are modified theories on the anthropological market, such as the amplification of the role of the Diana cult during the early centuries A.D. (The reader will find further discussion of the roots of the witch in Chapter Eleven, Witchcraft in Historical Context.)

In any case, modern white witches disavow connection with the satanic witch of Christendom and see their roots in the ancient mystic Nature religion. They insist that the so-called witch of the Christian era should be called a satanist and that the term witch should be reserved for the followers of the Celtic religion, which they call *wicca*. Followers of the *wicca* deplore being mistaken for medieval witches. They are not satanists but are involved in the revival of the pre-Christian Old Religion. (This revival, in harmony with the current rise of the occult in general, may well pick up momentum and assume significant dimensions in the future.) But, to confuse matters, most contemporaries who call themselves witches do in fact prolong the Christian tradition and, in essence, are definable as satanists. As such, they have little or nothing to do with the ancient Celtic religion.

This book focuses on the Christians' witch. Although she might have been more properly called a satanist, I comply with the prevailing historical and literary custom of calling her a witch.

Witches were not persecuted until the Christian era declared them responsible for innumerable evildoings—among them, preparing magic potions and casting a variety of spells. As far as spells were concerned, the *Hexe* was held responsible for the mania of love or hate, incurable diseases, bad weather (droughts, floods, sleet, lightning), poor harvests, accidents and just about everything else that was undesirable and for which the peasants lacked a ready explanation. Central to the persecution of the witches was the Christian dogma charging them with alliance with the Devil. Unlike the pre-Christian sorceress, the medieval witch was defined as a heretic who was inextricably associated with Satan.

It is interesting to note that the attitude of the *early* medieval Church toward witchcraft contrasted sharply with that of the preceding pagan era. Whereas the pagan view held the witches' claims of metamorphoses into beasts, the transpositions into other places and nightly flights through the sky to be realities, the early Church Fathers psychologized the matter and pronounced such claims the result of dreams, delusions and trances. In the 5th century Saint Augustine interpreted the witches' claims (intercourse with the Devil, nightly cavalcades through the skies and so forth) as mere dreams or trances induced by the Devil. The medieval Church's opinion was spelled out in the 10th-century *Canon Episcopi*, which continued to guide Church policy for approximately 200 years.[3] This dogma defined the witches' claims as phantasms, delusions or dreams. But *late*-medieval and Renaissance thought regressed. A reality assumption was reintroduced according to which witches were believed to do the things they claimed they were doing. The early pagan premises were reinstated and the witch-hunt proceeded on the basis of them. Now the witches' claims of metamorphoses, their night flights, their attendance at witches' Sabbaths and other reported events were taken literally.

The regression is a poignant reminder that human history does not evolve in a consistent manner. This case illustrates how early Christianity often fought pagan views of reality and yet later periods re-embraced the earlier pagan belief.[4]

France was the first nation to commence the witch-hunt, with its persecution peaking in the last two decades of the 16th century when one prosecutor, Nicholas Rémy, boasted that he burned 900 witches in about 10 years. However, France was also the first to deplore the mania and Louis XIV abolished the witch-hunts in a 1682 edict.

The persecution spread from France to other parts of Europe and threw the public of the Renaissance and Reformation into a witch-hunting fever which continued for over two centuries. With misapplied erudition and logic based on contrived premises, the crime of witchcraft was defined in theological-judicial terms. Learned men spent their lives composing treatises on the problem. The *Malleus Maleficarum* (witch's hammer), completed in 1486, was probably the definitive work, consolidating and encouraging the process of recognizing and prosecuting witches. This book was the result of an evolutionary process of perhaps 200 years of theological-judicial writings on witchcraft, and it became the guide for ecclesiastical, as

35

well as civil, judges in the prosecution of witches. From then on, the flames of the pyres roared across Europe. While the living witch was thought of as utterly wicked, her ashes were used as a powder for healing and protection against Satan—a gruesome fetishism furnished by Christianity during its most perverted period.

The *Malleus Maleficarum* opened the door to almost indiscriminate persecution. It evolved into a deadly spider web that trapped any victim who came in contact with it. The third part of the *Malleus* dealt with the methodology of witch-hunting and can be roughly summarized. For a witch trial to commence it was sufficient that an accusation be leveled at an individual. The unproven denunciation of a zealous believer could start the proceedings or a vague rumor could prompt a judge to open a case. A child's testimony or an enemy's statement was accepted as evidence. The sentence was brief and final. The judge's powers were absolute and beyond appeal. He decided whether the accused was entitled to defense; he could limit the counsel for the defense with so many conditions that he functioned virtually as an additional counsel for the prosecution. Torture was employed freely, and if the accused would not "confess" even under duress, that could be attributed to the Devil's power over the accused. There was no way for the defendant to escape the sentence: the accusation *meant* guilt. Retraction and repentance were no means of avoiding the ultimate penalty. Those sentenced were handed over to the secular arm—if the trial was not conducted by the secular court in the first place— since witchcraft was a civil as well as a religious offense.[5]

The infamous treatise did not stop proliferation of further theological-judicial thought on witchcraft and sorcery. Another noteworthy work was published in 1580 by the renowned French lawyer and political writer, Jean Bodin. His abstractions led him to proclaim that the Devil is one and the same everywhere and that the witches' Sabbath, too, is everywhere identical. Moreover, a witch could be in two places at the same time: she could be seen at home while simultaneously attending the witches' Sabbath. The ingenious judicial implication was, of course, that no normal alibi could help defend a person accused of being a witch.

But, mostly, Bodin favored theological speculation. His writings were representative of the fanatic climate of his time, and he is responsible for imputing that witches are guilty of fifteen sacrilegious crimes. They were

1. Denial of God.
2. Cursing God and other blasphemies.
3. Worshipping the Devil and bringing him sacrifices.
4. Dedicating children to the Devil.
5. Murdering children before they were baptized.
6. Pledging to Satan children yet in the womb.
7. Converting people to the satanic cult.
8. Honoring oaths sworn in the name of the Devil.
9. Incest.
10. Murdering men and little children to make broth.
11. Disinterring the dead, eating human flesh and drinking blood.
12. Killing by means of poisons and spells.
13. Killing cattle.
14. Causing famine on the land and infertility in the fields.
15. Having sexual intercourse with the Devil.[6]

There was generally little or no distinction made between witches and sorcerers. Both were believed to be anti-Christians who engaged in black magic, and were welcome prey for the inquisitors.

Yet a distinction can be made. Late-medieval witchcraft was an outgrowth of religion, i.e., a Christian heresy, and was limited in time and place primarily to Renaissance and Reformation Europe and to America. Sorcery, on the other hand, is universal. It is not limited in time to any special era nor has it necessarily anything to do with Christianity, as it existed prior to the development of the Christian theology. Sorcery is an attempt to control natural forces, either for good or evil purposes.[7]

Although the frenzy of witch-hunting largely obscured this difference, a fine theological distinction sometimes served to separate witches from sorceresses. It dealt with the *form* of calling on the Devil. If the Devil was simply asked to do what was in his power and given the command, "I order thee," no heresy was committed. And many sorceresses as well as witches were found guilty of this lesser offense. If, on the other hand, the Devil was approached in such obsequious terms as, "I beg thee," heresy was committed since it constituted a type of prayer and worship that acknowledged Satan's superiority.[8] This heresy was the mark of the true witch. As Sir Walter Raleigh fittingly remarked, "The conjurer commands, the witch obeys."

While sorceresses tended to be defined as the first type and witches as the latter, in the actual persecution, this distinction was rarely observed. For example, during the long reign of King Maximilian I of Bavaria (1597–1651), the royal edicts and laws allowed no distinction between the superstition of sorcery and the heresy of witchcraft. Every sort of black art was covered by his macabre edict of 1611: "All those who made a pact with the Devil should be punished with torture, death by fire, and confiscation of property."[9]

Witches (initially only female, but later male as well) were discovered in all socioeconomic classes and age groups. To illustrate the public witch frenzy, in the diocese of Würzburg, which borders Franconian Switzerland, 900 victims of witch trials were burned on the stake or died under the fiercest tortures imaginable within a period of less than ten years during the early 17th century.* The ruler of the bishopric, Prince-Bishop Philip Adolf von Ehrenberg (1623–1631), was well known as a hunter of witches. Among the victims were workers, peasants, government officials and the nobility; even priests were not exempt from prosecution. As an example, the Würzburg executions during a mere few months included a lawyer, a town mayor, a bailiff, three deacons, a number of curates at the cathedral, two pages and several children ranging in age from four to twelve years.[10]

The witch panic was well entrenched in the region of Franconian Switzerland and the record of Würzburg was closely rivaled by the Bamberg diocese of which Franconian Switzerland is a part. The fervor of witch persecution persisted for many decades, with Bamberg's most hysterical years occurring during the brutal reign of Prince-Bishop Gottfried Johann Georg II Fuchs von Dornheim (1623–1633), the cousin of the aforementioned notorious Würzburg bishop. The prince of the Church was responsible for the burning of a minimum of 600 persons, and he so zealously pursued witch-hunting that he ordered a special witch prison (*Drudenhaus*) to be built in Bamberg with room for about 40 prisoners. (Similar witch prisons were built in outlying towns of the bishopric.) The Bishop's penchant for witch-hunting was so keen that he was called

---

* The bishopric of Würzburg seems to have a stubborn affinity for medievalism. As mentioned in a footnote of the preceding chapter, Bishop Stangl approved the exorcism of a university coed in 1976. The girl was allegedly possessed by Satan, who tormented her and spoke through her body in the guise of Nero, Judas, Cain, Lucifer, and Hitler. The ritual ended with the young woman's death by fasting. The aftermath of the tragedy included a 12-count indictment against the bishop and two priests—with one count charging manslaughter.

the *Hexenbischof* (witch bishop). He was assisted by a secular council of doctors of law who supported his interest. One of them, Commissioner Dr. Ernst Vasolt, executed 400 who were denounced as witches. These lawyers often showed greater blood-thirstiness and inhumanity than the clergy who was involved in administering "justice."[11]

The speed with which the Bamberg witch tribunals proceeded destroyed every hope for justice and due process of law. A typical calendar is reflected in the case of a housewife, Mrs. Anna Hansen, in 1629:

> June 17, arrested and imprisoned on suspicion of witchcraft; June 18, tortured, but did not confess; June 20 tortured, and "confessed"; June 28, her "confession" read to her; June 30 "confession" confirmed and sentence pronounced; July 4, execution date announced; July 7, executed.

Bamberg acquired a reputation for skillful and liberal application of torture. Among the instruments and methods capable of extracting a "confession" from anyone were thumbscrews, leg vises (to break bones, etc.), flogging, strappado (hoisting the person by a rope and letting him or her fall the length of the rope), stocks (a block of wood with iron spikes), cutting through to the bone with a cord or rope, cold water immersion, feathers dipped in sulphur to burn under arms and groin, forcible feeding of salty substances and denial of water, baths in scalding water with lime added and other equally heinous means.

The condemned were not even safe from torture after sentence was pronounced and they were on the way to the place of execution. Final punishment could include hacking off the right hand and tearing the breasts of women with incandescent pincers.

Besides torture and execution, suspects were punished by total confiscation of their property. The lion's share went to the bishop; then the doctors of law of his infamous council received their shares, and the rest of the proceeds were used as fees to the various people instrumental in the prosecution and execution.

Some of the saner officials of Bamberg tried to check the hysteria. Their successes were either ephemeral or failed. Among the voices calling for humaneness and due process of law was a vice-chancellor of Bamberg, Dr. Georg Haan. His effort had a disastrous result: rebuked as a "witch lover," he, his wife and daughter were burned at the stake in 1628. Other public officials falling into disgrace with the "Nero of Bamberg" included a large number of *Bürgermeister* (town mayors), the bishop's own treasurer, various persons of nobility and several priests.

Many of these advocates of sanity and mercy fared badly. After they had spoken out against the slaughter of individuals they deemed innocent, they were accused of shielding witches against "justice" and became themselves suspect. Most of them were tortured into "confessions" and executed.

The inhumanity and flagrant disregard for due process of the witch persecution in Bamberg assumed dimensions that drew international attention. The Swedish king threatened to intervene militarily. The German emperor implored the prince-bishop to rein the zeal of his infamous tribunals. But it was not until the death of the rabid Prince-Bishop Johann Georg II in the mid-17th century that Bamberg became saner.*

Thus we see that the neighborhood of Franconian Switzerland has a lurid history of witch panic. Cultural history moves slowly and takes its time in healing vicious wounds, so it is not surprising to discover that the notion of the witch has lingered on—into our space age. While technologically we have achieved excursions into outer space, psychologically we have largely remained children of medieval mentality. While nuclear devices were invented and exploded, peasants pondered about Satan, his loyal witches and what perils might come from their existence. But let us return to our discussion of the Renaissance witch, the prototype of the modern witch.

The main thrust of the prosecution was to show that the accused had entered into a pact with the Devil; was his willing instrument; created harm and evil in the world; and participated in the nightly rendezvous of the brood of the underworld: the witches' Sabbath.[12] If the judges perceived any evidence that the accused had been involved in these things, or engaged in any of the 15 crimes mentioned earlier, he or she was labeled a witch and handed over to the torturers or executioners.

---

* The city's reputation lingered in history and the Englishman, Charles Mackay, writing in 1841, remembered it well. He included Bamberg in his list of the most witch-panicked places in Europe. I recommend his book, *Extraordinary Popular Delusions and the Madness of Crowds*, to all students of human behavior who are interested in understanding mass hysteria. (Mackay was a worthy forerunner of the famous French social scientist Gustave LeBon who, in the 1880s, wrote *The Crowd*, a sociological classic of mass behavior.)

The belief in the noctural bacchanalia of Satan and his witches deserves special description, since it was a widespread belief and a central item in the investigation of suspects. The presumed evidence of having witnessed a certain person participating in satanic orgies was often used to convict that person. (Even children's testimonies were acceptable.) The witches' Sabbath was believed to transpire usually on mountain tops to which the witches swiftly rushed through the night sky, riding broomsticks, gallowtrees or rakes. But before take-off, they never failed to anoint their bodies with witches' fat—a concoction prepared from the fat of cats or wolves, asses' milk and secret ingredients. The going ons at the witches' Sabbath—or the "Sabbath" as the Inquisition simply called it—included a night of feasting, dancing, fornicating and merrymaking by the witches and their demonic lovers.

Sometimes the diabolic orgy allegedly included the perverted and sinful ritual whereby the witch signified her devotion to the Devil: the *osculum infame*, the kissing of the Devil's posterior. Frequently, suspects were accused of having been observed rendering this infamous kiss and were even sentenced on the basis of such putative evidence.

How this belief in the witches' Sabbath was employed in accusing certain individuals of being witches is illustrated by a quasi-trial transcript.[13] The chronicler Godelmann of Frankfurt wrote (ca 1600) that a butcher, walking at night through a forest, heard sounds of laughter and lovemaking from a hidden grove. More curious than frightened, he approached the place and was able to see several figures (male and female) who immediately disappeared. They abandoned a table laid out for a lavish banquet complete with silver goblets for wine. To prove that what he had seen was not imagination, he picked up two of the goblets and took them to the local magistrate, reporting what he had witnessed. The magistrate was able to identify the owners of the goblets who assured the authorities that they had been stolen. They apparently convinced the investigators and the suspicion then turned to their wives. They were thrown into prison, accused of witches' crimes, and finally convicted.

Godelmann's report continued, showing that the evil spirits took revenge on the butcher. Some time later, when he was riding past the infamous place in the woods, he was attacked by a rider of fierce appearance and severely mauled. Furthermore, it was rumored that a prominent tree in the grove was hexed by the witches. The witches themselves had changed into animals to escape detection.

The same chronicler also reported that in some parts of Germany a raging nocturnal cavalcade of creatures, causing turbulence and making a formidable ruckus, were interpreted by a procession of witches on the way to their Sabbath. Since this phenomenon was called the *wütendes Heer* it is related in nomenclature to the *Wütenker* mentioned in the preceding chapter. But I noticed that the peasants of Franconian Switzerland make no connection between their version of the raging horde and the witch phenomenon. If there ever was such a connection, it was lost in history.

It is noteworthy that the contemporary belief in witches among the older Franconian peasants neglects the classical adjunct of the witches' Sabbath and the witches traveling on broomsticks through the air. However, even though they consider these aspects legendary, they persist in their belief in the rest of the witches' supernatural attributes and evildoings.

The medieval and Renaissance populace was easily taken in by the fantastic explanations and depictions of this supernaturalism and supported the witch-hunt with a vengeance. During the peak years of the hunt, virtually any disease, misfortune, accident or catastrophe could be blamed on a witch. Identification of the witch became a task in which almost everybody participated, since her destruction was thought to be for the good of everyone. The destruction of witches became a sordid community project.

In fact, the community's participation in identifying the witch was so zealous that the authorities at times were virtually coerced into a prosecution. They often hesitated to act on only one or two accusations but deemed it advisable to initiate action if three or more accusations were leveled against an individual. How the authorities were sometimes stampeded into the witch-hunt can be typified by this brief quote: "Although officials . . . had succeeded in suppressing popular desires for witch-hunts in 1612 and 1615, the power of all the surrounding examples of witch-panic finally infected Oberkirch too."[14]

To what pitch the frenzy could rise was vividly demonstrated by a neighboring town of Oberkirch, Oppenau. Oppenau had a series of trials from June 1631 through March 1632 during which 50 persons had been executed in eight separate burnings. During the same time, 170 other persons were denounced for witchcraft. "In a town of only 650 inhabitants one can easily imagine what suspicion on this scale would mean to social bonds of trust."[15] It seems that witches were hunted as much by the rule of the mob as by the rule of ponderous legal-theological authority.

This leads to the interesting sociological question as to how the hapless person accused of being a witch/wizard was detected. The spectrum of the potential victim was nearly limitless, since there were so many characteristics that created vulnerability.

Some researchers consider a person who occupies a noninfluential status in the community particularly vulnerable to such accusations. Anthropologist Lyle Steadman's contemporary data about the Samoan Hewa witchcraft seem to bear this out.[16] Historian Erik Midelfort also found that widows and spinsters were most commonly accused of witchcraft and sorcery. Their accusations were far out of proportion to their numbers in the community. In the later stages of witch-hunting, large numbers of married and young unmarried women were accused and convicted of witchcraft. Persons without families were unprotected and widows, in particular, seemed vulnerable until they remarried.[17] William Monter's historical investigation of the Jura mountains (between France and Switzerland) corroborated that most accused were poor and powerless: old women, especially widows, formed the largest single social block among the accused.[18]

A category of victims was probably made up of what we would diagnose in retrospect as mentally ill and deranged personalities whose conspicuous hallucinating was interpreted in a nonclinical, theological framework as evidence of Satan's presence.

On the other hand, many victims could have been as sane as anyone else. They were denounced by witnesses who were delusional. Persons stepping forward and accusing others of being witches, attending the Sabbath, riding through the sky on gallow-trees, having intercourse with the Devil and so forth may have been suffering from hallucinations and paranoid delusions. Researchers who tried to understand the mass hysteria over witches and why so many innocent bystanders were denounced coined the term, demonomania, the mania about demons. The situation thus created innocent victims through deranged witnesses and equally disturbed or misled judges.

Another category of victims was made up of those unfortunates who elicited repulsion and ostracism because of their physical ugliness, deformity or defect (hydrocephaly, epilepsy, skin diseases, paralysis and other medical problems). Charles Mackay recorded examples where ugly exterior turned into a fatal condition. He described how several women in England and Scotland became victims of the witch-hunt for no other reason than ugliness. All of them perished under the hands of either the jailer or the hangman.[19]

Others were the victims of envy or jealousy and suffered because, ironically, they showed qualities opposite to those in the previous category. This category included persons who were strikingly beautiful, extraordinarily successful or miraculously spared harm in an accident. Such features could be construed by the malicious, envious or overly credulous as signs of having entered into the service of Satan and benefitted from his powers.

Still others were the targets of political intrigue, where the unscrupulous took advantage of the popular paranoia to rid themselves of opponents and rivals. Similarly, business competition sometimes lurked behind a defamation and a number of examples are recorded in the court files of the Franconian town of Schweinfurt. Among them is the complaint of a saddlery master against a rival saddlery master (and his wife) who had defamed him as a sorcerer.[20] He complained that he lost business; people avoided him; and an able saddlery journeyman quit working for him because of the rumor. The slandered man was said to have in his possession a superstitious and heretical book on sorcery.

This, incidentally, is the only case I have come across where a *grimoire* played a role in witch accusation prior to modern time. Unfortunately, the complaint was undated and thus could have originated anytime between 1560 and 1682, the period covered by that specific file. The scarcity of witching, based on a formal *grimoire* during the 16th and 17th centuries, is corroborated by Monter who investigated the witchcraft history in another part of the Jura mountains. He discovered only one man, a doctor of law from the French-Swiss borderland, charged with having books on magic in his home (in 1606).[21] The situation changed when, with the gradual growth of rural literacy in the 18th and 19th centuries, popular witchcraft began to be influenced by printed texts.

Another category of the accused was made up of common criminals who, rather objectively, were found to have committed infanticide, poisoning and arson. Monter lists a number of French-Swiss examples from the Renaissance that include men and women who were convicted, in addition to these crimes, of highway robbery, sodomy, murder, incest, abortion and adultery.[22] The motive to these crimes was seen as evolving from alliance with the Devil and the method was defined as witchery.

Of particular interest are those individuals who actually believed themselves to be witches—who sometimes openly confessed to it. Whether we define such self-view as role-playing (after all, the expected behavior of a witch was thoroughly known and could therefore be easily imitated) or simply as a matter of sincere belief, may boil down to the same phenomenon: a person defining himself or herself.

Indeed, the irony of some witch trials consisted of the inquisitors having to reject an individual's claim of being a witch. The Spanish inquisitor, Alonso de Salazar y Frias, apparently more circumspect than his fanatic colleagues, exposed numerous cases of unsubstantiated claims. The girl, Catalina, for example, who claimed to have had sexual intercourse with the Devil and spoke of having lost a great deal of blood in the process, was found to be a virgin. Comparable claims of many other young women were disproven. One self-proclaimed witch had to retract her claim that the Devil had taken three of her toes, since examination proved her feet to have all of the digits.[23] Human nature includes a generous measure of the desire for public acclaim. In some individuals, the need to be recognized appears so overpowering that it apparently matters little whether they receive positive or negative recognition. Their leitmotif seems to be *"any* recognition is better than none." This theme can be observed throughout history, and it has waxed to the macabre in our own days. Almost invariably, after unsolved atrocities in late-20th century America—be it spectacular arson, robbery, kidnapping or mass murder—scores of impostors want to be recognized. After the Manson slaughters, for example, the authorities were nearly as busy disproving false confessions as they were finding the real killers.

Finally, the motive of maintaining status and making a living and a profit played a significant role in discovering and convicting witches. Those actively involved in implementing the *Malleus Maleficarum* (the judges, priests, court clerks, bailiffs, torturers and executioners) showed avid interest in bringing suspects to trial.

The clergymen's churchly pursuit of keeping their flocks safe from Satan blossomed into a grand business. The clergy's services were badly needed, and therefore handsomely recompensed. As Anton S. LaVey poignantly put it: "Satan has been the best friend the Church ever had, as he kept it in business all these years."[24]

Other profiteers of the witch-hunt were the torturers and executioners. Reports from the Bavarian region of Schöngau document that the public executioner, Jürg Abriel, grew powerful and wealthy, discovering witches all over the land. The fee for examining an accused to determine whether she bore the devil's mark, the *stigma diabolicum*, was two florins, regardless of the results. The case of a Bavarian woman may serve to exemplify the procedures. She was found to be "a true witch and therefore marked by the Devil with a small cut on the upper part of the middle finger of the left hand." ("Sie ist eine wahre Hexe und daher vom Bösen Geist mit einem kleinen schnittl on der linken Hand mittern finger vordern glits margiert worden.")[25] When Abriel failed to discover a mark on a suspect, he claimed that the person simply looked like a witch. Whereupon she or he was arrested and tortured for a confession. The fee for an execution was eight florins—with the result singularly uniform.[26]

The economic motive as the driving force behind the zeal of the prosecuting officials played an important role. Besides the substantial fees derived, the confiscation of the property of the convicted (frequently merely accused) furnished a handsome living. An entire "industry" of witchcraft was maintained by the vested interest of the prosecuting personnel. The "industry" was based on a simple syllogism: witch prosecution means profit; without witches no prosecution, without prosecution no confiscation, without confiscation no profit. Thus, witches were needed: the richer the witches, the fatter the profits.

This maxim was particularly respected in Bamberg and it paid off there. But it does not necessarily apply to other places. Midelfort's findings (earlier mentioned) seem to indicate that it usually were the poor and helpless who suffered the brunt of the mania and their persecution was relatively unprofitable. Profiteering partly explains why the witch frenzy was so acute and enduring. First, the rich in the community became vulnerable to witchcraft accusation. Second, males became as endangered as females since men usually were the legal owners of the household, properties and money. Women were meager trophies since they rarely owned much property. Though, according to witnesses, at early 17th-century trials of

Offenburg, care was taken to select for accusation "women of property."[27]

It is because of such economic circumstances that, with the ascent of the witchcraft persecution, increasing numbers of males were prosecuted. In many cases, care was taken to accuse both husband and wife so that confiscation could be carried out without complication.

The bishopric of Franconian Switzerland has a notorious history in this respect. Probably because of the economic benefits that accrued to the coffers of the prosecution during the reign of the Prince-Bishop Johann Georg II of Bamberg, an unusually large number of burgomasters were convicted. Burgomasters normally were not only responsible persons who felt they had to represent the interests of the townspeople and protect the innocent but they almost always belonged to the propertied class of the community. Their prosecution conveniently took care of two problems: it eliminated critics and allowed the confiscation of particularly attractive properties. Within a single year, a total of 720,000 florins was taken from accused witches in Bamberg.[28] In 1631, when terror was flagging, the Bamberg witch prison contained over 20 inmates, including the bishop's own treasurer. Their combined assets, already confiscated, were in excess of 220,000 florins—almost all of which went to the bishop.[29]

Interestingly enough, when the Holy Roman Emperor finally pressured Bamberg to lessen prosecution and forbade the confiscation of property, witchcraft arrests fell off sharply and almost stopped in the 1630s. One could, however, debate this explanation of the discontinuation, since at the same time Swedish military forces occupied the area, curbing Catholic fanaticism.[30]

The pecuniary motive in witch-hunting was much more rampant in Continental Europe than on the British Isles during those dark years. The reason for the difference can be found primarily in the restraints that the English law imposed on the prosecuting methods. For example, torture and confiscation of property were not allowed in England. By denying the prosecuting officials the economic bonus, the fervor in prosecution noticeably flagged and the English version of the witch frenzy never reached the heights of its mainland counterpart. In addition, reduction of the economic incentive caused the English to accuse and prosecute proportionately far fewer men than women.[31]

It is a temptation (to which some scholars have succumbed) to explain the entire witchcraft phenomenon by the vested interests of the prosecuting class. Some have viewed the extraordinarily vast spread of witchcraft as a contrived enterprise into which the prosecution kept blowing the breath of life to assure the continuation of a source of economic benefit. But the single economic motive is most likely insufficient to account for the rise and extent of witchcraft. Moreover, as hinted earlier, Bamberg is probably guilty of the most notorious financial exploits and may not represent the typical course of the witch craze. Although the economic motive existed, most witches were poor and confiscations were rarely lucrative. Fanaticism, rather than greed, seems to have been the principal motive— at least outside of Bamberg.

The prosecution of witches proceeded with a furious efficiency in Continental Europe. Since there were hardly any humane or legal restraints, the fate of a suspect was almost always sealed. Under horrendous torture, the desperate victim would confess to anything. Therefore, once the torture was under way, the townspeople started to build the pyre: the burning of the victim became a popular spectacle.

"Confessions" would often include the naming of other participants in the alleged act of witchcraft or the witches' Sabbath, particularly if the inquisitors made cessation of torture contingent upon such information. In this manner, the identity of the presumed members of an equally presumed coven was established.

According to the rules, confessions under torture had to be reaffirmed afterward by the accused. Also, torture was not supposed to be repeated; it could be "continued" indefinitely after interruption. And few accused individuals could persist in the denial of their "confession" after several sessions of torture.

To extort a "confession," the tribunal also resorted to spiritual threats. The court made "confession" a condition for receipt of the last sacraments to avoid eternal condemnation. Further, the accused were frequently promised pardon if they "confessed"—a promise that was rarely kept.

"Confessions" were publicly read at the time of the execution and distributed to the populace at large. By so doing, the prosecution effected a social psychological feat: it established the legitimacy of the trial and the execution and it reinforced the public's perception of the reality of witchcraft. Each time a "confession" was read, it confirmed the people's belief that there indeed were witches who flew at night, danced at the diabolic Sabbath and instigated harm and evil in the community. Thus, there was evil in the land and the authorities were more than justified in their attempt to stamp it out. The confession was one of the prosecution's means of keeping the witch panic alive.

The Renaissance, fertile as it otherwise may have been in regard to the arts and new ideas, was a deadly epoch that demanded the lives of uncounted numbers of innocent and confused people. According to modest estimates, this period claimed the lives of half a million persons who were accused of being witches. Other estimates put the figure as high as nine million.

It was not for many years that courageous voices dared to speak against the popular delirium in Germany and it was not until the Age of Enlightenment in the 18th century that victory was achieved by the opponents of the public mania; and even then there were lapses. The last officially recorded witch executions in Germany took place in 1749 in the Würzburg diocese when a 71-year-old woman (a nun for 50 years) was carried, because she was too frail to walk, to her place of execution;[32] 1756 in Landshut, Bavaria;[33] and 1775 in the Alpine city of Kempten. The last documented execution in Europe took place 1782 at Glarus in Switzerland. Some writers prefer to designate 1793 as the last European witch-burning when two women—because they had chronically infected reddish eyes and were suspected of continually hexing the animals of their neighbors—were burned in the Prussian city of Posen. This case, however, relies less on official records and more on apparently reliable verbal reports.[34]

With the last executions also ceased the legality of torture as an instrument of obtaining "confessions." King Frederick the Great of Prussia abolished torture in 1740; Empress Maria Theresia of Austria in 1776, and the kings of Bavaria delayed abolition till 1806.[35]

The discussion of the history of the witch mania has so far moved within the larger frame of Germany, if not Europe. I would like to draw a narrower focus upon Franconian Switzerland for a moment. How did it fare throughout the era of the witch-hunt? It came as a surprise to learn that the heart of Franconian Switzerland (the rural hinterland between the peripheral cities of Bamberg, Nürnberg and Bayreuth) apparently escaped the violence of official persecution. I could not find a recorded case of arrest, torture or execution. The witch frenzy raged around this region like a stormy sea around a quiet island. And, indeed, the nature of the topography warrants this metaphor: mountainous Franconian Switzerland stood out of the surrounding flatlands like an island, with all major traffic—today as in ancient times—bypassing these Jura heights. Violence did not enter into the secluded villages, although we may assume that the belief in witches and the practice of witchcraft prevailed in these villages as much as in the surrounding areas. For reasons we may only guess—perhaps the remoteness of the villages, the utter poverty that made prosecution appear unprofitable; the preoccupation with heresy in the adjacent larger towns and cities; the peculiar docility of the peasants of this enclave—Franconian Switzerland was spared the carnage.

This bucolic tranquility did not exist in the southwestern Jura which Monter studied. During the era of the witch frenzy, the Republic of Geneva's trials "both began and ended in her rural hinterlands . . . Geneva's rural territories, which contained about one-fifth of the Republic's population, produced roughly half of her witch trials."[36] In Franconia, the major front of the battle against the witches was in the cities and towns, particularly in the bishop-ruled cities of Bamberg and Würzburg and such affiliated towns as Hallstadt, Kronach, Steinwiesen and Zeil. Monter's explanation of Geneva's remarkably low rate of convictions focuses on Calvinism. Genevan judges, if given any reasonable grounds for doubt, preferred to leave suspects to the judgment of God by expelling them—not executing them.[37]

But Monter warns against generalization to all Protestant areas since evidence indicates a generally harsher treatment of suspects in the Protestant zones of French Switzerland and their milder treatment in Catholic areas.[38] Since this book is not a historical analysis of the Franconian witch-hunt, but merely offers some historical information as backdrop to the more contemporary observations in the next part, I am not certain how Franconia compared with the French-Swiss borderlands during the Renaissance. Monter prepared a meticulous demographic evaluation that allows comparison between Protestant/Catholic and rural/urban areas. I did not intend this type of historical analysis and therefore speak somewhat impressionistically when I say that Renaissance Franconia seemed to place the brunt of its persecution on cities and towns and probably divided its fervor equally between Protestant and Catholic domains. If we have not heard much about the Protestant side of Franconian persecution, it is, first, because there were relatively small Protestant pockets in the area—which, however, participated diligently in the witch-hunt, and, second, because in this report I focus on all-Catholic Franconian Switzerland, an east-central region of Franconia.

My discussion of the history of official persecution is limited to the adjacent areas of Franconian Switzerland, whose most prominent location is Bamberg. The other large city is Nürnberg. Compared with Bamberg, the old Imperial city has a modest record of witch persecution.[39] It started in 1300 with the banishment of sorcerers, the 1469 torture of a sorceress, culminated in a wave of trials and hearings during the early 17th century, ending in 1659 with the execution of two witches. The executions were carried out more humanely than elsewhere and Nürnberg has no record of live burnings. The city fathers resented the 1627 attempt by the Bamberg *Hexenbischof* to distribute his *Trudenzeitung* (a news bulletin reporting on the state of witchery and its persecution in Franconia) to stimulate greater zeal among the Nürnbergers to prosecute their witches. The bulletin was prohibited in Nürnberg, since it was feared that it might fan a mass hysteria identical to the one in Bamberg.

The other major city lying at the edge of Franconian Switzerland is Bayreuth. This city, currently famous for its Richard Wagner festivals, was one of the few anomalies in an otherwise prevailing Catholic Bavaria: it was Lutheran and belonged to the counts of Brandenburg in northern Germany. The records show only one witch trial in 1654. But a hasty conclusion that this moderation might have been due to its Lutheran rule is untenable. Also along the edge of Franconian Switzerland was a second Brandenburgish principality, Ansbach, equally Lutheran but fully participating in the witch mania of the era. As early as the last quarter of the 16th century, Ansbach commenced to torture and execute numerous suspects. And as late as 1691, the Lutheran abbot M. Adam Francisci issued *Generalinstruktion von den Trutten*, his own version of the *Malleus Maleficarum*, in which he assured the reality of witches and the necessity to exterminate them. In the same year, 22 witches were burned in this Brandenburg county.[40] The counts of Brandenburg basically relied on their *Constitutio Criminalis Brandenburgica* which, ironically, was an almost unchanged version of the infamous *Bamberger Halsgerichtsordnung* (penal law) of 1507

51

that had become the basis of the Imperial law, the *Constitutio Criminalis Carolina*, issued in 1532 and finding wide application among the inquisitors of the Catholic Church.

Other nearby towns with records of witch persecution include Creussen, which tortured and reprimanded a sorceress in 1569; Schwabach with seven witch burnings in 1591; Kulmbach with one witch trial in 1591; Naila, Geroldsgrün, Lichtenberg, Ellingen and Gunzenhausen with trials in 1590. Towns and communities that were under the direct sway of the bishop of Bamberg experienced greater activity. Along the northern edge of Franconian Switzerland, such towns as Kronach, Hallstadt, Steinwiesen and Staffelstein accumulated a total of 102 witch executions in 1617[41] (see map, Chapter Two).

Witch persecution abated toward the end of the 17th century. With the 18th century, official witch-hunts generally ceased and the public squares were no longer filled with hysterical masses watching the pyres. But the psychological tradition did not end. The common folk—as well as the not-so-common—continued to believe in the existence of witches.

While the law throughout the European countries relented and treated witch pretenders just as that—pretenders who were mentally ill or relatively harmless delinquents—informal tradition perpetuated the fear of witches. At times the fear burst into hatred and mob lynching occurred. One such memorable event took place in France as late as 1818.[42]

Instead of judicial persecution, alleviation from demonic powers was now sought through purely religious measures. Exorcism and an array of folk magic—with the figure of the folk healer playing a prominent role—resumed where the witch tribunals left off.

The region of Franconian Switzerland retained a remarkable affinity to the occult in general and witchcraft in specific. It is a striking example of the survival of old witch beliefs into the modern world. Without the late medieval and Renaissance backdrop, the lingering of these supernaturalisms would be difficult to understand. The purpose of this chapter was to provide that background. The next chapter will focus on the more recent past and to some extent on present conditions.

A strange encounter at the occasion of a wedding: The Meddler matriarch (*left*), reputed for her witching, ignores the camera and challenges the Schneider matriarch (*right*), esteemed for her healing (1920s).

Backofen—Oven for baking bread or drying fruit.
Disputes over usage resulted in vengeance witchery.

Orchard in Kirchenbirkig, issue in witchcraft battles between neighbors.

The farm of the Reject matriarch in Sachsendorf being renovated in 1977.

Old peasant women were often suspect as witches.

The site of an accident was usually marked by a religious symbol.

Traditional Franconian peasant house; left door leading to animal quarters, right door to human quarters, and manure pile in front of house (1970s).

Peasants used cattle as beasts of burden (Tüchersfeld, 1950s).

Only wealthy farmers could afford horses as beasts of burden;
others had to manage with cows (1950s).

Peasant women sickled
grass and carried it home
in large baskets (Tüchersfeld, 1950s).

II

The Working of
WITCHCRAFT

Ancient superstitions, after being steeped in human hearts,
and embodied in human breath, and passing from lip to ear,
in manifold repetition, through a series of generations,
become imbued with an effect of homely truth.

NATHANIEL HAWTHORNE

We find that whole communities suddenly fix their minds
upon one object, and go mad in its pursuit;
that millions of people become simultaneously impressed
with one delusion, and run after it, till their attention
is caught by some new folly more captivating than the first.

CHARLES MACKAY

Nun ist die Luft von solchem Spuck so voll,
Dass niemand weiss, wie er ihn meiden soll.

GOETHE, FAUST II

A community is subject to the truly magical power
of words; they can evoke the most formidable tempests
in the group mind, and are also capable of stilling them.
Reason and arguments are incapable of combating
certain words and formulas.

And, finally, communities have never thirsted after truth.
They demand illusions, and cannot do without them.

SIGMUND FREUD

5

The Witch in Modernity

The end of the official trials against witches did not signify the end of the belief in them.

In fact, with the Age of Enlightenment, during the 18th century, and the following Age of Romanticism, during the late 18th century and early 19th century, a general tolerance of witchcraft ensued. Witchcraft went unchallenged particularly during the period of Romaticism, since it was accepted as part of the newly valued genre of the occult. Occultism, in the form of a revitalization of such old themes as mysticism, spirits of the dead, reincarnation and witchcraft, redeveloped partly as a reaction against the abstract spirit of Enlightenment rationalism.

Witchcraft became a more or less acceptable folk magic and lost the stigma of the punishable heresy. It was no longer subject to official persecution, secular or ecclesiastical. And as such it lingered among many peasant cultures.

Thus the belief in witches and their evil work continued through the 19th century and in secluded areas, such as Franconian Switzerland, well into the 20th century. Today's village elders, grey octogenarians whose youth was spent around the turn of the century, are therefore in a position to report the historic supernatural atmosphere that included the belief and practice of witchcraft.

Before I turn to specific experiential reports of the modern period, let me add remarks about general attitudes toward witchcraft during the 19th century. Most of these attitudes are embedded in oral traditions only, and assume the character of folklore.

The primary reason why the accounts of the 19th century are

relatively unrecorded is the lack of witch trials from which transcripts could have been derived. And social scientists were highly selective in what to commit to paper when the topic was witchcraft. It was a matter of prudence. Though anthropologists studied and recorded the supernatural beliefs of many other cultures during that time, to do so in their own backyard was another matter. They might have invited lawsuits had they named certain persons witches. Folklorists and chroniclers may have shied away from the topic for the same reason.

There is at least one grand exception. The English scholar, Charles Mackay, who published his splendid *Extraordinary Popular Delusions and the Madness of Crowds* in 1841, fearlessly exposed the legacy of the witch mania in various European countries. In fact, some of the descriptions, taken primarily from the English countryside during the early decades of the 19th century, resemble the Franconian witch duels I will describe in later chapters.[1] Mackay wrote at a time when official prosecution had ceased. The last executions took place just before his lifetime. During his life, the prevailing law treated pretenders to witchcraft, fortunetellers, conjurers and their occult entourage more as a nuisance than as criminals. They were liable to the common punishment accorded to rogues and imposters, which usually meant imprisonment or the pillory.

Likewise, accusers of witches became vulnerable to punishment and libel suits could be filed against them.

In fact, a number of Franconian peasants remembered a lawsuit, filed shortly after the turn of the century, where a man was accused of having called a woman a witch. The slandered woman had chased his straying cow off her property when he, angered by her action, hurled the expletive at her. Since the woman's reputation of practicing witchcraft was based on community consensus, the judge tried to provide the accused with a way out. He asked the man with persuasive intonation, "Now, you meant the *cow* when you said 'witch,' didn't you?" Instead of taking advantage of the diplomatic question, the man blurted out, "No. I meant the woman!" Verdict: guilty and a hefty fine for slander.

For whatever reason, there is a conspicuous absence of information concerning Franconian witchcraft during the 19th century. Even the aforementioned Karl Brückner, who was a native of Franconian Switzerland and collected its folklore in the 1920s, treated the matter with caution. Only in the most general terms did he admit that these beliefs and practices still existed in his contemporary villages.[2]

This book thus represents one of the few attempts to capture the vanishing beliefs of the last survivors of an era of folk magic. And, it seems, this attempt was made in the nick of time. The young of Franconian Switzerland not only do not know, they do not want to know. Caught up in the modern objective consciousness, they refuse to have anything to do with what they perceive as an absurd and embarassing superstition.

The oral tradition that gives us an idea of what the beliefs in witchcraft were during the 19th century, right up to and around the turn of the century, includes many of the medieval formulations. It includes, for example, the suspicion that particularly foul weather may be the doing of a witch. This inclination is signified by the old German term *Hexenwetter* (witches' weather). Franconian folklore knows of a rainstorm so vicious that it threatened the inundation of the town of Forchheim. The frightened populace went to the monastery and asked the Franciscan monks to say special prayers. At the first blessing, so the story goes, a woman fell from the rain-heavy clouds into the courtyard of the monastery. The monks recognized her as one of the most dreaded witches of the town. Since they feared the woman might be harmed if turned over to the townspeople, they provided her asylum until tempers calmed and the matter was forgotten.[3] Records show that one of the earliest witch killings took place in 1090 in the Bavarian town of Freising where a lynch mob beat and burned to death three women held responsible for causing bad weather and diseases.[4]

Strong, gusty winds were suspected to be the *Hexenwind* (witches' wind) in the village of Kirchenbirkig and surrounding settlements. This turbulence frequently swept across the land, flattening entire fields and destroying crops. Ominously, it sometimes picked up bundles of grain or stacks of hay, carried them high into the sky, scattering them over distant acres. Conjectures about the identity of the witch who caused the disturbance followed on the heels of such events, and the ownership of the land on which the crop dropped was often considered a significant clue.

As in many other instances of magical disasters, folk tradition suggested an antidote. The peasants believed that the witch's power could be broken by throwing a sickle into the heart of the turbulence. (The sickle was an ubiquitous tool, carried by the peasant women when they worked in the fields.) Stories said, however, that the peasant might lose her sickle in the process; sometimes the sickle failed to fall back to earth. The disappearance was interpreted as the witch traveling in the turbulence snatching the tool and carrying it away. The usefulness of the folk antidote was thus tempered by the fear of losing one's sickle.

The Franconian witch has also been dreaded as an incubus who plagues people by the *Hexendrücken* (witches' pressing). She would steal into a bedroom at night and descend on the helpless sleeper, sit on his or her chest and prevent the terrified person from moving. A person was susceptible to this visitation if he or she was careless enough to talk about witches or refer to them in conversations during the day. The prudent never made references to them. It was believed that when the *Hexendrücken* struck, the victim could find relief by quickly throwing the big down-stuffed pillow on the floor. The witch was then obliged to sit on it and was unable to proceed with the hexing. If, while throwing the pillow on the floor, the would-be victim had enough presence of mind to call out: "Hex, morgen kommst, was zu borgen" ("Witch, come tomorrow to borrow something"), the identity of the harrassing witch could be learned the next day. The first person to knock at the door in the morning asking to borrow something was the witch.

The incubus phenomenon was not unique to Franconia. Oppressive nightmares were similarly interpreted in Silesia. The incubus weighed on the victim's chest to make breathing nearly impossible. If he succeeded in grabbing the incubus, he only found a straw, an apple or a catlike creature in his hands.[5] The incubus therefore was believed to have the ability to change its appearance—typical of witches. There often arose a definite suspicion as to the identity of the incubus. Certain women were suspected; they were either known witches or had their personality attributes, such as reclusiveness. The Silesian incubus was connotative of the witch (the experience could be explained in different ways), whereas the Franconian incubus was denotative.

The incubus nightmare is not unique to modernity. The *daemon incubus* has a long history. The Sumerian *lilitu* of the second millennium B.C. was the prototype of the Hebrew *lilith* and reappeared in the Latin *lamia*—incubi who roamed at night and seduced sleepers and slayed children.[6] The demons had definite sexual meaning, forcing the succubus to have sexual intercourse.

It is interesting to note that the sexual motive is absent from the Franconian—or, in general, German—incubus phenomenon. There it was understood as a vicious prank, punishment or a terror assertion on the part of the witch. The asexual meaning (at least in its overt description) was brought out by A. Wittmann's examination of the role of the witch in German sagas. He found that the Germanic *Hexendrücken* was usually explained on the basis of women's souls entering at night into bedrooms through cracks or the key hole and, in various metamorphosed disguises, sitting down on the chests of sleeping persons to frighten and immobilize them, but refraining from any sexual contact.[7]

A number of peasants advanced a fascinating theory—a mixture of pagan and Christian assumptions—to explain the origin of some witches. My Bärnfelser informant, a representative believer of his generation, related the once common belief that a witch could create another witch. To accomplish this creation (or miscreation), it was necessary for a witch to contact a newborn baby before it was baptized. If she succeeded in feeding the baby (usually some sort of mash), the baby was spiritually hers and was bound to become a witch. Sometimes the mere touch of a witch would suffice to destine an unbaptized baby to become Satan's accomplice.

Knowing this danger, mothers of newborn babies would observe extreme caution to keep strangers or suspect persons at a distance. To afford reliable protection, they would hasten to have the baby baptized as soon as possible. Such protectionism is not unique to Franconians. Sephardic Jews from Turkey settling in the United States have exhibited similar fear of demonic dangers to their babies, especially during the first eight days after birth.[8] Speedy baptism to avoid a witch's ominous contact with the child was practiced among East Prussian peasants. If an unbaptized infant developed a salty forehead, which could be tested by the mother licking her child, it was taken as a sign that a witch had placed a hex on it. Likewise, the violent crying of a baby was understood as a hex.[9] More recent research in northern Germany has indicated that this interpretation still exists. Johann Kruse cites the case study in which a baby screamed without fail every night at 11:00. There was no discernible cause for the distress and it was concluded that a witch was responsible for it. Suspicion fell on a certain woman. To verify the suspicion, someone sneaked up to the suspect's window at exactly 11:00 and allegedly witnessed the woman spanking the bare bottom of a doll to transfer the pain to the child.[10]

Widespread belief has it that witches are out to hurt children, putting on a kindly facade. They offer to tie loose shoe laces, give a piece of cake or candy, and in the process give them the evil eye or take their handkerchief to gain power over them.

Doing business with a witch was believed to have dire disadvantages. When you bought something from her, the newly acquired property (a tool, a plot of land, a farm animal or whatever it might be) seemed to return eventually to the witch. And those careless enough to sell her something would suffer the loss not only of the money the witch gave them, but also the money with which the *Hexengeld* (witches' money) came in contact. It was considered the duty of a responsible family man to see to it that the witch's money left the house as soon as possible and that, until that time, it was kept separate from other money.

The witch's money was feared to cause accidents or family disasters that would lead to expenses—and it was through these expenses that the witch would eventually get her money back.

One of the most widespread beliefs about witches' habits concerned their annual gathering on the Blocksberg (a prominent mountain in northcentral Germany). The belief that the witches assembled for a grand orgiastic festival during the Walpurgis Night (the eve before May Day) far exceeds the boundaries of the Franconian region. (Historians trace its origin to the ancient Germanic belief in the annual meeting of the Valkyries on the Blocksberg.) The tradition described the witches traveling in droves to the meeting place the night of the last day of April; they would anoint themselves with witch fat and ride through the air on gallowtrees or sticks, forming long processions that included animals symbolic of demonolatry (he-goats, cats, pigs and lambs).

The animals sharing the witches' airborne itinerary were called *familiars*, believed to be physical representations of demons and Satan, and suspected of committing sexual perversions with the witches. The sin of man-demon bestiality had entered Christian theological considerations as far back as the teachings of St. Augustine and was repeated by Thomas Aquinas (1225–1274) in his *Summa Theologica*. [11]

The concept of the familiar can also be found in non-Christian cultures. The Pondo people of Africa, for example, believe that familiars are always the opposite sex to the witch, can assume the form of a beautiful girl or boy, and have exaggerated sexual characteristics.[12] Among the Congolese, the pig was the favorite familiar of witches and sorcerers.[13]

In this connection a sad epitaph must be inserted for the millions of innocent felines who were hated, hunted and killed.[14] The humble house cat was without doubt the most persecuted animal on earth. Throughout most of the world, including Europe of past centuries, this animal was depicted as a minion of demons or the Devil. In some paintings of the Last Supper, the "bad cat" of Christendom sits at Judas' feet. It was particularly unfortunate if the feline was black. There were instances where black cats, just as witches, were burned alive. Even today, without necessarily thinking of it as a demon-creature, superstition is widespread and many people believe it a bad omen if a black cat crosses their paths.

Another animal associated with the witch was of even greater significance. The goat in medieval tradition was often believed to represent the Devil, reign over the witches' Sabbath and receive the blasphemous *osculum infame*. The goat as chthonic symbol has a long history; it appeared in Hebrew demonology by the end of the Apocalyptic period and in the fertility rites of Dionysus, who was sometimes called, "He of the black goat."[15]

Peasants feared that the demonic cavalcades of witches and familiars could harm fields, crops and homes during their journey, and it was an old Franconian custom to seek protection against the traveling witches through the *Hexenausknallen* or *Hexenauspatchen* (witch whipping). The young and the old of the village would get together the night before the first of May and, starting at dusk, crack whips and even shoot into the air to make certain that none of the witches would dare to descend in or around their village. At such times it was not advisable for old women who resembled the stereotype of the witch—big-nosed, toothless, stooped, and red-eyed—to be seen on the village street.

Similar practices were reported from Tirol, Upper Bavaria and Switzerland. In some of the regions the vigorous ringing of big cow bells was believed to drive the witches away since they presumably could not stand the noise.[16]

An old chronicle reported that some citizens of a small town suspected the cause of a large fire that consumed many homes to be witches' arson. This arson, they reasoned, could only have been accomplished because the townspeople failed to carry out the *Hexenausknallen* thoroughly enough during the Walpurgis Night.[17]

In one of the major valleys of Franconian Switzerland, the scenic Wiesent River Valley, it was the custom of the peasants to attempt to protect their fields and meadows against the traveling witches during the Walpurgis Night by sprinkling holy water and making the sign of the cross three times at each corner of their properties.

The old peasants of the village of Buckenhofen remembered a 19th-century oak tree called the *Hexeneiche* (witches' oak) on which the witches were said to rest on their way to the Blocksberg. The branches could presumably be seen swaying back and forth from the weight of the witches, even though there was no wind and the leaves of surrounding trees were not stirring.

Besides the Walpurgis Night convocation on the Blocksberg—the national witches' convention, as it were—there were minor regional gatherings. Certain prominent landmarks, usually mountain tops, were suspected sites of frequent witches' meetings. For example, the Walberla Mountain near Kirchehrenbach, the Spornagel Mountain near Kirchahorn, and the Schiess Mountain near Eggolsheim were said to serve witches of the region as frolicking grounds several times a year, but these times were never exactly known.

The tradition of the *Hexenausknallen* has largely disappeared. Where it has continued, it has lost connection with the witches' journey during the Walpurgis Night, and to the village youth, it is now merely annual merrymaking without an occult meaning. The disconnection between the witches' Sabbath and the villagers' noise-making during Walpurgis Night began a long time ago. Old peasants told of their participation in the village's *Hexenausknallen* when they were young, during the 1910s and 1920s, but did not recall that the reason for doing it the night before the first of May was the witches' annual flocking to the fabled Blocksberg. Notwithstanding their historical amnesia, the peasants trusted (and those interviewed still believe today) in the effectiveness of the whip-cracking practice in keeping the Devil's accomplices away from their villages and homes.

The Franconian witch whipping has equivalents in other regions. During a 1977 visit to East Germany, I learned about a colorful ritual annually performed by the Sorbs of the Lausitz area near the Polish border. The rural Sorbs are descendants of an old West-Slavic tribe and practice *Hexenbrennen* (witch burning) the morning after Walpurgis Night. The witch is represented by a life-sized doll, locked up in jail overnight, led to the public square in the morning, exhibited to the crowd, accused as a witch and then burned on a pyre. Accusation is carried out by different members of the community who approach the "witch" and accuse her of all the evil that has happened in the village during the year. Most poignantly, she is given a name—the name of the woman who currently enjoys the worst reputation in the community. The burning is a symbolic substitute killing, and the fiery death of a figure is equated with the deliverance from evil in the village.

A Franconian peasant's livelihood depended on the health and productivity of the farm animals. How the farm animals were tied up with the lives of their owners was manifested, almost symbolically, by the fact that both humans and animals lived under the same roof—literally. From the central, often cobbled hallway of the farmhouse you would turn to the right and enter the kitchen or living room, turn to the left and enter a room where the cows munched, slept and were milked. The stable thus was part of the living quarters. Animals and humans entered and left the house through the same front door. (It was not until the 1950s that the combined human–animal shelter changed and most peasants moved their animals to outbuildings.) Also, each cow was known individually; had a name; and its life history was part of the family history. For example, when I was a child, my grandmother's two cows were called *Weisse* and *Rote*; they seemed to live forever, as if immutable parts of the old farm house, and their markedly different temperaments were taken into consideration when assigning tasks. (For example, *Rote's* impatience made her a poor candidate for pulling the plough, and you had to watch out for an occassional kick at milking time.)

Even honeybees played an important role in the lives of the peasants. Many of the farmers kept hives in their orchards, not far from their houses. How much they were esteemed and considered part of the household was demonstrated by an old ritual. When the man of the house died, his death was announced to his bees. It was the custom to knock three times at the hives and each time call out: "Der Herr ist tot!" ("The master died!") This tradition was still observed in the 1920s, when at the death of my grandfather, my grandmother sent the oldest son to the hives to perform the ritual.

Given the importance of farm animals and the sternness of the supernatural cosmos of the Franconian peasants, it was understandable that they dreaded the malevolent powers a witch might marshal

71

to harm animal cohabitants and dry up their source of sustenance. The concern was so acute that the peasants envisioned specific types of witches, each specializing in defrauding certain aspects of the stable.

One of them was known as the *Milchhexe* (milk witch) who presumably had the uncanny ability to milk any cow in the village she could set her eyes on. It was believed that she could empty the udder of the selected cow by sheer power of magic while sitting at home and "milking" the corners of a kerchief or table cloth. Particularly reckless milk witches were suspected of milking a cow in this fashion so often that the animal ultimately perished from being overmilked.

If there was a surplus of milk produced by a peasant household suspected of including a witch, the milk was never mixed with the milk from other peasants. Pooling milk was sometimes done in order to wholesale it. The participants conspired to leave the milk from the ill-reputed farm in separate containers, making it appear coincidental.

The witch's milk-stealing reputation was so widespread throughout rural Europe that the concept of *Milchhexe* was almost universally accepted. Johann Bächtold refers to so many studies and examples in his comprehensive reference works of nine volumes that they become repetitious. For example, reports from Silesia, Tirol, Thuringia, Austria, Swabia, Bavaria, Switzerland, Bohemia, Westphalia, ethnic German settlements in the United States, and even Norway, Sweden, Yugoslavia and many other regions show great similarity with the Franconian version. The method of telekinetic stealing differs only insofar as the witch might milk the edges of some fabric, as in Franconia, or the handle of a knife or ax stuck in the door frame, as, for example, in parts of Austria. In other regions, rats or cats, held to be witches in disguise, are suspected of sucking udders.[18] Inquiries in northern Germany by Johann Kruse revealed the witch milking the handle of the bread knife stuck in the door jamb.[19] My personal inquiries, in 1977, among older peasants in the Upper Palatinate revealed similar memories about the milk witches. Refugees from rural Prussia (now under Soviet sovereignty) told me of identical practices.

The concept of the milk-stealing witch has also been developed among people culturally unrelated to the Franconians. For example, the Nyakyusa of Africa believe that witches in their dreams are able to steal milk by sucking the udders of cows. They also believe that cows so victimized dry up and later abort.[20] Another feat of telekinetic magic by this subspecies of witches was to make butter disappear from a peasant's butter barrel and reappear in the witch's. This belief helped explain why some peasants, in spite of prolonged churning, would be unable to produce butter.

A related category of witches was the *Stallhexe* (stable's witch) whose intent was to sicken cows, calves and hogs. Probably the most frequent complaint about this witch concerned her hex that made cows give bloody milk. Bächtold catalogs numerous cases, covering just as much territory as with the concept of *Milchhexe*. And, here again, the testimony of contemporary East Prussians and people from the Upper Palatinate verify the ability of the stable's witch.

Some peasants interpreted blood-milking as a result of a witch's procuring the milk (i.e., the doing of a *Milchhexe*) and leaving only blood for the owner. Thus a utilitarian motive might be ascribed to the witch's action. However, most people thought she did it out of malice alone.

Indeed, the cows frequently did show traces of blood in their milk and to the Franconian, it was a witch-induced curse. Today, the "curse" is revealed to be a relatively simple veterinary problem. (More about this in the functional analysis in a later chapter.)

A particularly mischievous version of the stable's witch was the *Pferdehexe* (horse witch). Her mischief was aimed at horses, terrifying them until they became sick or even died. Since only a minority of the peasants possessed horses, the menace was limited. But those who had horses could never discount the peril and had to be prepared to find their horses in the morning with manes and tails braided into countless fringes—the unfailing sign of a horse witch's visitation during the night. The animals would pant, perspire heavily and lose weight. If a witch repeated the prank a number of nights in a row, the horses might die of terror and exhaustion. Accounts of *Pferdehexen* came from Gössweinstein and Kirchenbirkig, but the menace was known throughout Franconian Switzerland and beyond. For example, my informants from Protestant East Prussia reported the same phenomenon of braided horse tails and the identical interpretation of a witch at work.

But the peasants were not helpless when confronting the wickedness of this witch. The Franconian tradition was full of protective customs. For example, the peasants believed that if they tied three

73

large *Kletten* (a type of burr) into the horse's tail, the witch would leave the animal alone. But the moment one of the burrs was lost, the mischief might start anew.

Rose hips were used to protect the stable. They were buried underneath the threshold of the stable door. No prudent witch, it was assumed, would dare to step through a door protected in this fashion. Many peasants believed that you could cause pain, injury and even death to the sorceress who had placed a curse on their cows by whipping the afflicted creature with switches from the thorny *Bocksdorn* bush. Regular use of a *Bocksdorn* switch on the cows was recommended for making the stable "witchproof."

Franconians put their trust in the tradition of burning wormwood (vermouth) in the stable to keep witches from entering and harming livestock. Witches, it was said, could not tolerate the smell of the herb.

A commonly practiced witch deterrent in Franconia was the pitchfork or broom that leaned next to the door or in a corner of the stable with the prongs or bristles pointing up. Particularly circumspect peasants recommended a combination of the broom/pitchfork method with defecation in front of the stable door, for they believed that it would sharpen the deterrent effect.

Two of the oldest witch deterrents known among the Franconians were the *Drudenfuss* (witch's foot) and the *Drudenstein* (witch's rock). The former was a figure composed of two superimposed and inverted triangles whose original meaning is lost in Antiquity. During the Middle Ages it was carved into the threshold, and it was believed that a witch seeing it would turn around, for crossing it would mean harm to her. The *Drudenstein* was a round river rock with a natural hole through the middle. (They were usually water-carved limestone.) A witch's rock was treated as a gem, placed above the door or cemented into the wall next to the door, and was believed to keep witches from entering the house.[21] The uses of the witch's rock and the witch's foot, however, are ancient rituals, and I encountered few peasants who were familiar with them.

The peasants' protectiveness toward their farm animals extended beyond the stable. In or around villages were small natural ponds where peasants often stopped to water their animals. In order to keep witches and demons away from these places, many villagers followed the old custom of arranging rose hips in the form of a cross at the edge of the pond. It was important to perform this ritual the night before the first of May when witches were believed to be swarming about in droves.

The Christian tradition added several antiwitch rituals to the repertoire of Franconian methods of keeping animals safe from witches. Certain herbs and flowers blessed in church on the day celebrating Mary's assumption to heaven (15th of August) were dried and kept until Christmas, then cut up and mixed with the fodder. After eating this mixture, the animals were thought to be immune to hexes for some time. Another religiously inspired prophylaxis was related to me in Sachsendorf where table salt, blessed in church on the eve of the Epiphany (5th of January), was used during the remainder of the year to keep witches away from the stable. The salt was sprinkled at such critical occasions as calving or at Christmas Eve and New Year's Eve. This practice is a holdover from the early Middle Ages when the ecclesiastical authorities introduced a comprehensive range of formulas designed to obtain God's blessing for everyday activities. The most common ritual was the benediction of salt and water for the health of the body and the expulsion of evil spirits. Theologians, as well as laymen, regarded this liturgy as possessing a power which was more than merely symbolic.

Other regions had their own protective equivalents. Bächtold refers, among other examples, to northern Germany where blood-milking was counteracted by speaking the name of Jesus over the milk bucket, sprinkling holy water over it and making the sign of the cross. Additional formulas had to be spoken—importantly, in the northern German dialect. There were many different methods of countering the stealing of milk. Examples: (1) overboiling some of the afflicted cow's milk so that it would run into the fire and burn—it would simultaneously burn the witch; (2) beating the boiling milk with certain plants was the equivalent of beating the witch over the head; (3) beating the hexed cow with juniper branches; (4) sprinkling holy water, and (5) in Silesia, ornamenting stable doors and windows with oak leaves and simultaneously saying certain formulas.[22] Prussians recognized hexed cows by excessive perspiration, trembling limbs and the smell of cow manure in the milk. They counteracted these hexes by stirring the milk with a broom, hanging the broom in the chimney to dry, then burying it under a pile of manure. It was believed that the witch would vicariously experience the same treatment. Another Prussian recipe called for the boiling of the milk over open fire until evaporated, cutting a cross into the residue while saying a prayer to the Holy Trinity, placing the vessel on a fence pole to be picked clean by wild birds, and making certain that no pets or other domestic animals would eat from it.[23]

Kruse's examination of witchcraft practices in northern Germany discovered an extreme countermeasure to the witch's evil. The revenger had to catch the witch's cat and stab it with an incandescent iron or fork. A strange cat would suffice if addressed with the name of the witch and then killed identically. An alternative killing was achieved by obtaining sand from the witch's foot tracks and sticking the nail of a coffin into it.[24] These measures were said to be fatal to the witch. I have not found an equivalent of such murderous magic in the traditions of the Franconians.

This extreme suggestion may be extraneous to the oral folklore of the German peasants and derived from arcane books. Kruse points out that the belief in and the use of various books of magic, offering hex formulas as well as antihex seals, have been widespread during the past few decades.[25] Among the antihex (thus, presumably, *white* magic) literature were *Das Wunderbuch, enthaltend grosse Geheimnisse früherer Zeiten, Das Romanusbüchlein, Ägyptische Geheimnisse, Der magisch-sympathetische Hausschatz* and *Formeln der magischen Kabbala*. Best known of this category was the so-called *Sixth and Seventh Books of Moses*. Many people believed that this volume was meant to counteract the *Black Bible*, a Satan-inspired book, and that Moses delivered it to provide power over the hexes of a witch. This book, allegedly authored by Moses, showed widely different content depending on the date of its edition. While the seals, in order to be effective, were to be spoken in Hebrew, someone familiar with the ancient language could recognize that the characters were jumbled together meaninglessly. More *black* than white magic could be found in the book *Geheimnisse der Nigromantiae und Beschwörung deren bösen Geister*. Another manual of magic, *Der feurige Drachen oder Herrschaft über die himmlischen und höllischen Geister*, suggests seals, talismans and pieces of paper with characters to be borne on the person, and gives directions to summon Lucifer and other demons. While these books pretend to afford protection against witches, they actually advance the practice of witchcraft by disseminating seals and formulas for commanding demons, and thus create more anxieties than they claim to avert.

We have so far dwelled on the safety of the peasants' livestock. But, of course, the peasants' greatest fears concerned their personal safety. Most firmly belived that the witch's major goal was to harm their bodies and souls.

One of the milder pranks a witch could play was to afflict a person with lice (*Läuse-Anmachen*). An individual would suddenly find himself or herself the center of attention of armies of voracious body lice. The only deliverance for the tormented victim was to go to the person who had cast the curse and beg to be forgiven for whatever had aroused his or her ire. The hex of lice can be found in most German regions, as well as beyond. For example, A. Macfarlane reported a similar belief in England.[26]

Far graver than this affliction, as repulsive and uncomfortable as it must have been, was a curse that could lead to illness or death. These ailments were of a nature that, at the time, defied medical diagnosis. Peasants were inclined to think they suffered from witch-induced ailments when they came down with an unknown ailment. With modern medicine progressively penetrating the rural area and providing more doctors, hospitals and labs, the proportion of ominous ailments has sharply declined over the past few decades. The increase in natural explanations of hitherto obscure diseases has resulted in the decrease of suspicions and accusations of witchcraft.

Peasants believed a witch must first acquire some personal belonging before casting a hex on anyone. Consequently the villagers took pains to avoid the witch's getting hold of a personal item. The fear of the witch obtaining a piece of their property, and thus being able to loose evil spirits against them, bore heavily on their minds. If such acquisition occurred through one's own default, a substantial frustration was added to the anxiety. Parents reminded their children not to wander off with tools or toys. A forgetful child could open the door for the witch to practice her black art. Kruse found the Franconian concern shared: northern German peasants also believed witches gained power in this manner.[27]

Because of the desire to steer clear of the witch, peasants wanted to know who among the villagers was a witch. One could never be quite certain. After all, one could learn to become a witch virtually overnight by reading certain forbidden books and entering into a pact with the Devil. There was therefore always the possibility that a person not a witch today could be one tomorrow. However, the possibility of mistaking innocents for witches was limited, since Franconian witches usually had a family lineage that seemed to establish their identities. William Monter, the historian, studying the witchcraft history of another segment of the Jura mountains, corroborates this feature. "Since very few classes were immune from suspicion, one's family lineage was almost as important as one's social rank in creating a reputation for witchcraft. Some Jura families . . . produced suspected witches over a long span of time."[28] Kruse discovered a similar family-gravity in northern Germany: "Families still today have the reputation that the black art is hereditary with them."[29]

But even when family reputation established the individual's reputation, reconsideration was possible and a previously dubious person could regain a measure of trustworthiness by consistently being honest and leading a Christian lifestyle. In any case, a margin of uncertainty remained, and the social bonds of the villagers were perennially frayed with distrust.

Yet, humans desire certainty and prove to be amazingly inventive, as well as bizarre, in achieving it. Though never totally alleviating wariness, they reduce doubt by applying certain tests. In other words, they want to see signs that tell them who is and who is not a witch. This effort can be observed wherever there is fear of witches.

I have already referred to at least one Franconian method of identifying a witch: the incubus. The method in the case of the milk witch is more elaborate. It was believed that a faithful Christian kneeling on a special footstool during the midnight mass on Christmas Eve would be bestowed with the divine grace to recognize a witch when he or she looked at one. This gift lasted only as long as the inquisitive person knelt on the stool. Recognition of witches was therefore limited to those witches who were attending mass. (The peasants apparently reasoned the incongruence of a Satan-allied witch attending church as a sly device to keep her true identity unsuspected.) The temporary seer of witches would be able to recognize them by certain farm implements or symbols floating above their heads. A typical *Milchhexe* would be recognizable by the milk bucket or the butter barrel above her head, and all were recognizable at the moment of transubstantiation when they turned ashen and turned their backs to the alter. This *Hexenstuhl* (witch's stool) was a low footstool that had to be carpentered from nine different types of wood and its manufacture was accompanied by a number of occult ceremonies. The effectiveness of the *Hexenstuhl* in exposing witches was believed in many villages, particularly in Kirchenbirkig, Weidenhüll, Kühlenfels and Elbersberg.

The belief flourished in spite of the clergy's condemnation of the practice. The Church's disapproval of the "superstition" was poignantly brought home in one case when members of the congregation smuggled a *Hexenstuhl* into the midnight mass and caused a noisy breakdown of the contraption when one of the more weighty conspirators knelt on it. The priest condemned the incident as a sacrilegious abuse of the house of God, levied special prayers of penitence on the sinner and warned the congregation against further attempts of that sort.

Bächtold collected numerous examples of methods of recognizing milk witches in other regions. It is interesting that the *Hexenstuhl*-method is identical in Lower Bavaria (specifically in the area of Landshut) and the Upper Palatinate, including the detail that the stool had to be made from nine different types of wood.[30] An Austrian version required that an unaware person attending the midnight mass at Christmas Eve had to be slipped a four-leaf clover. The person was then enabled, probably to his astonishment, to recognize witches by the milk buckets on their heads. In Lutheran Ansbach, bordering Franconian Switzerland, three grains of wheat found in bread had to be carried on your person during Walpurgis Day to recognize milk witches in church by the milk implements over their heads. In Silesia, the peasant had to milk through a wreath of *Gundelreben* (ground ivy, *Neptea hederacea*), then wear it on the head and so recognize witches.

Another Franconian method of "seeing" the witch was to hold a mirror over the exact location of a witch-induced tragedy. The mirror would reflect the face of the witch. One of my uncles assured me that by this method he once identified a witch who had caused an accident on the farm.

Besides these widely shared beliefs in signs revealing the witch, there were numerous idiosyncratic signals that could confirm one's suspicion. For example, a peasant told me that she saw a *Wischbaum*, the long pole fastened on top of a wagonload of hay to hold it down, soar through the air and disappear into the chimney of the house of an ill-reputed family. The insinuation was that the pole was used for the witch's nocturnal junket.

The last three chapters have shown that a pervasive fear of the supernatural permeated the cosmos of the Franconian peasants.

They harbored a peculiar apprehensiveness about the wickedness of the witch and saw hexes as the seeds of disasters and diseases. As among humans everywhere, overwhelming fear stimulated inventiveness to reduce mental torment. Some inventions became assuaging institutions. Just as the witch was the nefarious queen of their supernatural world, the woman (in rare cases a man) who was skilled in the *Anfangen* became the rival to check the power of evil.

Next I will introduce the black witch's counterpart—the white witch who represented hope and healing to the frightened peasants.

6

The Witch and the Healer

Identification of the evil-doer was not the only weapon the peasants could marshal against the witch. Indeed, there was a far more effective avenue. After all, identification of the witch by means of the *Hexenstuhl* or the mirror image merely amounted to ex post facto recognition of the witch but not to protection or relief from her hexes.

Over the ages, a beneficial counterpart to the witch evolved among the Franconian peasants. It was a woman who was adept in doing the *Anfangen* (the beginning, the commencing). She was supposedly allied with the good spirits; able to tap divine grace; and knowledgeable in secret prayers and rituals that would shed this grace on the less fortunate. This woman allegedly had the knowledge as well as the personal charisma to administer effective rituals; in other words, she was a mistress of good (white) magic.

I must insert a modification at this time. In one account I heard that the person skilled in the *Anfangen* was a man. He was a well known healer from the village of Rabeneck. His reputation was somewhat tarnished by the rumor that he occasionally stepped outside the Christian tradition to effect a cure. In other words, some people thought him a sorcerer—but not a witch. Apart from this exception, all individuals of whom I heard that they did the *Anfangen* were women, usually older ones. I shall therefore generalize and refer to this type of healer as a woman skilled in the *Anfangen*.

The peasant dialect curiously lacked a name for this woman. The imposition of a noun to identify this person would be tantamount to a violation of the world view of these peasants and would fail to correctly reflect the meaning they had in mind. For example, in High German there exists a concept that apparently is closely related to this healer. The word is *Gesundbeterin*, the woman who heals through prayer. Other nouns that could possibly, however more remotely, have been used to refer to this woman are *Heilerin* (healer woman) or *Zauberin* (sorceress). But these terms were never used to refer to the woman doing the *Anfangen*. Without exception, reference to this woman was *eine Frau die das Anfangen kann* (a woman who knows how to do the beginning).

I asked elders and village priests about the origin of this awkward phraseology but none could give an adequate answer. Those who attempted an interpretation thought that the phrase referred to a woman who could effectively commence the healing process, but had to leave it up to God, good spirits or Nature to complete the task. She could only initiate the process.

Like the witch, the woman who knew how to do the Anfangen was largely a Christian invention. She usually functioned within the confines of the Christian dogma, assuming that God could be approached through special prayers and rituals offered by qualified persons (those touched by divine grace) and that God's merciful response would result in averting or in healing a witch's curse.

The Church held no official stock in the woman skilled in the *Anfangen*. She was thought of as practicing an informal folk custom that was not a legitimate function of the church. The Catholic clergy took no official stand concerning this folk curer and offered neither condemnation nor endorsement. In some instances where peasants specifically approached the priest for advice or counsel about the *Anfangen*, the priest made it clear that there was nothing wrong in praying to God to ask Him to heal sick members of the household, either human or animal. In addition, the clergy traditionally gave in to the wishes of the peasants who asked for blessed objects from the plethora of the Church's liturgy, such as candles, blessed herbs, crucifixes, blessed grain and eggs and so forth. Often, these items were used in the process of doing the *Anfangen*.

Here we see an interesting dualism: the concept of the evil woman, the witch, and of the good woman who knew how to do the *Anfangen*. The Judeo-Christian dualism thus had its counterpart among the Franconian peasants.

A peasant in trouble had therefore a choice either to turn to a witch for help or ask for the service of a woman skilled in the *Anfangen*.

As an example, a man who suspected witchcraft as the cause of his piglets' ailment could have approached either someone who was known to have the secret books on magic (and ipso facto a reputation that smacked of witchery) or a woman with the full reputation of being a witch. It is noteworthy that almost all peasants believed the witch could not heal the piglets or prevent their dying, but could only respond with a hex on the stable of the offending witch (or "layperson" who dabbled in witchery) to coerce her to withdraw the curse.[1]

The process of countercursing commenced with the task of identifying the person responsible for the hex. Various methods were used. One was the detection through mirror reflection at the location of the trouble. Another was through the *Hexenstuhl* at midnight mass on Christmas Eve. But since this carried an obvious time condition, probably it was seldom applied. (After all, who wanted to wait until Christmas when one's piglets got sick in May?) Still another method was to wait three days and see who would be the first to knock at the door and borrow something. (This incidentally, is the same detection process described earlier in the case of *Hexendrücken*.) But most of the time, identification of the curser was done on the basis of reputation. One simply "knew" who would do such a thing.

Once the evil-doer was identified, a witch could put a countercurse on her person, home or farm animals. This revenge could dry up a fruit tree, command legions of tormenting body lice, or sicken and kill farm animals. It was conceivable that a battle could then ensue between witches, for each was her own authority—an isolated magician, not subordinate to a coven. The purpose of the counterhex was to persuade the witch, or the "lay person" dabbling in sorcery, to lift the hex. If this was achieved, the consultant witch likewise withdrew her hex. In the end she was rewarded with gifts and matters settled back to normal—at least for a while.

It must be emphasized, however, that a confrontation between witches was more theoretical than real. If the hex came from a real witch, the affected person would most likely turn to a healer or seek deliverance through miscellaneous semi-sacraments of the Catholic Church. Only if the hex came from someone not really a witch but merely experimenting with the magical *Sixth Book of Moses* might the afflicted peasant turn to the services of a witch. We must also note that, though the witch could withdraw her own hex, she had no power to withdraw or deactivate a spell cast by another witch.

Thus the lifting of a hex depended either on the witch who cast it or on a person skilled in the *Anfangen*.[2]

A healer never dabbled in witchcraft or cast hexes, but had the charismatic power to lift a hex and to cure the damage. To continue the above example, the peasant with the sick piglets could have asked the healer to come to the stable and perform the arcane rituals. This included praying, applying various sacred objects and sometimes having the animals eat blessed herbs—all without an audience. After the curer emerged from her private sojourn with the animals, she was thanked and given gifts of farm produce, and then she departed, leaving behind a family assured that the worst was over and the spell broken. She never asked for money, but accepted a return favor or an occasional gift.

The curer doing the *Anfangen* usually left protective directions with the family. Normally they specified the following three days as being critical and that care had to be taken to prevent a reversal of the healing process. The thrust of the directions usually was the admonition to refuse to accept any object from a suspicious person for the next three days. All a person—allied with evil demons or the Devil himself—needed to do was to transfer a personal object to the victimized peasant in order to regain the power to renew the hex. Likewise, the healer would warn against giving a personal item to a suspect, since thereby the witch could recast the spell. In other words, the witch could gain or regain power through the transfer of a personal item *to* or *from* the victim.

Those skilled in the *Anfangen* were in high esteem among the villagers. They usually came from families known for honest work and faith in the Christian belief. They were also consulted when problems arose that were not classified as having a supernatural origin; they functioned as midwives, served as paramedics and were favored in instances of such childhood diseases as the measles, mumps and chicken pox. Also, they were effective veterinarians. In short, they were practitioners of folk medicine requiring extensive knowledge of peasant remedies and medicinal herbs and berries. But the interpretation of an out-of-the-ordinary event or of an unexplained disease as a supernatural phenomenon was never remote. The women who knew the *Anfangen* were competent in helping in natural as well as supernatural problems. Their roles were in line with the ancient magico-medical tradition of healers and sorceresses.

Besides medical and spiritual problems, they were favored as counselors, and their opinions at the time of making important decisions were highly valued. In this context, these Franconian healers carried out to some degree—atrophied as it might have been—the function of the oracle: predicting events and revealing divine insights.

In sum, then, the woman skilled in the *Anfangen* was a curious mixture of Christian prayer healer, ancient sorceress, practitioner of folk medicine and oracle.

On the other hand, the witch's activities were not associated with healing. Her deeds were restricted to the black art of witchery, and no one would think of consulting her in matters of medicine or prophecy.

This limitation is not universal, however; in some parts of the world the witch also functioned as a practitioner of folk medicine. Reports of witchcraft in Spain, dealing roughly with the same turn-of-the-century era as these Franconian reports, point out that the witch was also known for selling curative philtres.[3] (Her recipes were, however, found to be notoriously feeble.)

Witches of the Middle Ages were known, among other things, for herbal medicine and were reputed to possess charms for curing diseases (especially of cattle) and promoting fertility. But it seems that over the ages, particularly with the degrading influence that the Church exerted over witches and sorceresses, witches tended to specialize in the black art as opposed to the helping white art. A polarization evolved, with the classical sorceress transformed into opposing figures: the black witch practicing satanism and the white witch practicing healing, *magia naturalis*. Opposed as the figures appear, they were complementary in the larger context of the community. There was demand for the services of each. But the realms were sharply divided. Each magician practiced her occultism within her proper field of power and rarely, if ever, trespassed into the purview of the other.

It is important to recognize the woman competent in the *Anfangen* as a part of the Christian heritage. Her work was anchored in the dogma of the medieval Church, characterized by the other-worldliness of that era and replete with saints, angels and other benevolent spirits. And yet there was another element involved. She expressed the age-old individual claim on magic that asserts authority on the basis of personality and not on the basis of a formal institution, such as the Church. Insofar as she was her own magical authority, she perpetuated an element of the pre-Christian sorceress. But insofar as she aligned her autonomy with the Christian belief in good spirits and a supreme deity of whose power she can partake, she was relatively acceptable to the religious authorities. All the while, a part of the sorceress of Antiquity survived in the woman who knew how to do the *Anfangen*.

But, just as the witch, this healing woman became the victim of the advancing objective and scientific consciousness. She has now become a historical figure, and, as far as I could determine, none of the contemporary Franconian villages claim to have a folk healer anymore. Some of my conversations with village elders reminded me that one of the last women known to be skilled in the *Anfangen* was my paternal grandmother, an esteemed figure of the Schneider clan. I was surprised to discover that the knowledge of the Schneider's healer woman still exists among old peasants in remote villages. In fact, my clan membership and the relation to a healer helped to open the doors and mouths of village elders. The aura of association created the impression among them that I was trustworthy, an insider and a believer.

I should emphasize that a family's reputation of being involved in witchcraft mainly depended on the peasant wife's reputation. Similarly, a family's reputation of being knowledgeable in the *Anfangen* depended on the wife's ability. (We shall, however, note at least two exceptions in the cases presented later; in one case a man was skilled in the *Anfangen* and in another, a man was known as a sorcerer.)

In the realm of the supernatural, whether witchcraft or healing, the wives were usually active and the husbands passive. This, however, is not to say that the Franconian peasant culture followed a matriarchal system. On the contrary, it had a patriarchal slant, although not as pronouncedly as can be found among many other peasant societies. The aggressivity of the women in the area of the supernatural can possibly be explained by the greater emotional leeway, the more overt nurturing function and the more expressive role enjoyed by Franconian women—elements of the feminine role certainly not unique to the lifestyle of this peasant society. In addition, the origin of the sorceress in Antiquity may have been connected with the greater mystique that women have enjoyed (and recently loathed) and may thus have prepared the women's special place in the supernatural cosmos.

The seemingly impeccable duality of healer/witch was at times tarnished in Franconian Switzerland by an ambiguous third figure who seemed to roam the no-man's-land between the two. It was the *Hexenmeister* (wizard or sorcerer). Apparently there were very few of them in the region and I am familiar with only two cases. This type of person (always a man) was ostentatiously available for the *Anfangen* and white magic, but invariably enjoyed a mixed reputation and was suspect of being willing to also cast hexes. He basically was an opportunist—a businessman up for hire. He, unlike the women who did the *Anfangen*, would expect to be paid in cash for his services and cleverly played the field of the occult to his financial advantage. While the witch and the healer were believers who took their missions seriously and paid little attention to remuneration, the *Hexenmeister* impressed me as a charlatan who took advantage of people in need.

This type of pseudohealer is well known in other regions of Germany; in fact, outside Franconian Switzerland, his activities have continued, if not increased, over the past few decades. In contrast, this pseudosorcerer has disappeared, along with the witch and the healer, from the villages of the Franconian region. This man is known in the rest of Germany as *Hexenbanner*, a sort of equivalent of the witch doctor or "cunning man." Kruse, with almost personal vindictiveness, has tried to expose the shady business of the *Hexenbanner* in various parts of Germany, mainly in the north. His efforts extend from the 1930s into the 1950s. He found veterinarians who bitterly complained that these quack magicians were undermining their business by selling "teletherapy," high-priced powders for the cure of sick animals. In many cases, Kruse discovered the clientele's stubborn adherence to quack magic; when the prescribed cure failed to lift the hex and the disease progressed, the client, instead of consulting a regular veterinarian, would look for a different *Hexenbanner*.[4]

Kruse and others perceive the industry of the *Hexenbanner* as a danger to the welfare of the community. It perpetuates anxiety about possible supernatural harm; threatens legitimate business; financially and emotionally exploits the gullible; and, most seriously, casts certain helpless members of the community into the role of witches. These communities also have the healer woman, called *Gesundbeterin* (faith healer). The nomenclature referring to the woman who does the *Anfangen* apparently is not known outside of the Franconian realm. In any case, Kruse draws the conclusion that the activities of the *Hexenbanner* perpetuate a healer/witch duality that he finds socially and emotionally unhealthy and which is being unscrupulously exploited by the quacks.

The Franconian setting of past generations bears some resemblance to the situation exposed by Kruse in other parts of Germany. The only modification I would add is that I have learned of only two quack *Hexenmeister* in the entire region and that the healer/witch duality existed undiluted in most villages of Franconian Switzerland.

The duality of magic is part of the tradition of many, if not most, peoples, including related as well as unrelated cultures. East Prussian peasants observed an identical dualism of witching and healing individuals. The culture of the *shtetel* (the Jewish community of Eastern Europe) has the *obshprekher*, a sort of interdenominational healer, who was consulted to charm and chant against witches, the "evil eye" and other sorts of evil.[5] England had the witch doctors or "cunning man" whom Charles Mackay described as "quacks who pretend to cure diseases inflicted by the Devil."[6] The witch/healer dualism is not unique to the Judeo-Christian tradition. The Azande witch doctor was just as juxtaposed to the witch as the Franconian healer.[7]

Enough about the duality theme. This and the earlier chapters have sketched a general picture of the supernatural universe of the Franconian peasantry and have outlined the place of the healer and the witch in it. In the next chapter we shall come closer to the description of the actual working of witchcraft and discuss two important prerequisites for the enactment of witchery.

7

The Book and the Devil

There were two conditions the peasants of Franconian Switzerland had to meet before engaging in witchcraft. One was the consultation of a secret book that taught the skill to practice witchcraft. The other condition was entering into a pact with the Devil—similar to the age-old story of Faustus aspiring to power and forbidden knowledge through a diabolical covenant.

Whoever appeared to have fulfilled these two conditions was considered a witch. The wicked power of the secret text could be awakened only if the person committed himself or herself to Satan. That, of course, was the sine qua non of witchcraft. Thus, the folk logic had it that the two basic elements, the book and the satanic commitment, were inextricably connected. One would not work without the other.

The commitment to the master of the underworld and the use of the book added up to a permanent lifestyle for some individuals and a temporary Faustian arrangement for others. Certain peasants resorted to the book only rarely to punish a neighbor or take revenge for an offense. Such "amateurs" rarely possessed the evil book but were able to borrow it—frequently from a relative with the reputation of a witch. These "part-time witches" incurred a bad reputation when their sorcery-dabbling became known, but they were not necessarily defined as witches. The permanent label of witch was reserved for those who possessed the book, used it habitually and made witchery central to their lifestyles.

The infamous book is known among these peasants as the *Sixth Book of Moses*.

In an effort to identify this book, I consulted the Catholic clergy of the region. These officials agreed that the book made its appearance in Franconia many generations ago; the priest of the hamlet of Pottenstein, who is an avid scholar of ancient scriptures, indicated that his research showed the book prevalent already during the Middle Ages. However, other experts would find this an exaggeration and place its appearance sometime after the 1640 publication of the so-called Weimar Bible that allegedly included the basic material now found in the magic manual.[1] It actually consists of two books in one, more accurately titled the *Sixth and Seventh Books of Moses*. This *grimoire* (manual of magic) was expanded at a later time and a sequel appeared, consisting of the alleged 8th, 9th and 10th Books of Moses. But the peasants spoke in the singular, always referring to it as the *Sixth Book of Moses*.

Virtually all scholars agree that these books were neither authored by the Biblical Moses nor represent a true continuation of the first five books of the Old Testament, also understood as the Torah, which is sometimes called the Books of Moses. Scholars disagree as to the true authorship of the books or the date of their creation. Some assume that the magic books are a spin-off from the Kabbala. In fact, this claim is actually made in the foreword of the *Sixth and Seventh Books of Moses*

The Kabbala reflects the ancient mystic philosophy of the Jewish people and was an effort to spiritualize formal Judaism. It probably was written during the early medieval period by a so-called Moses de Leon who used as his source the *Sefer Yezirah* (Book of Creation) and the *Zohar* (Splendor), which he attributed to the rabbi, Simon ben Yohai, of the second century. Most believers in the Kabbala feel that these ancient records report the verbal communication given by God to Moses on the Mountain. Presumably, Moses received these divine revelations in addition to the laws engraved on stone. However, there are diverse opinions among the believers as to exactly how, when and where these divine mysteries were communicated by God.

The question is: Are the magic books of Moses offshoots of the Kabbala? I consulted rabbis, well acquainted with ancient scriptures, and found that they vehemently objected to the idea that the voodoo-like *grimoire* has anything to do with the true Kabbala. They see the manual of magic as a fraud and consider as an insult the insinuation of its Judaic heritage.[2]

In any case, the *Sixth and Seventh Books of Moses* indeed

describe the skill of sorcery. The medieval Church recognized them as heresy and as eminent danger to the spiritual welfare of Christians, and the Holy See placed them on the famous (or infamous, as it may be) *Index Librorum Prohibitorum*, the list of prohibited books. (An individual's reading of a book so placed used to incur the condemnation of the Church and could mean, among other penalties, excommunication.)

It is this ambiguous piece of writing that played a central role in the practice of witchcraft among the peasants of Franconian Switzerland. That the books were placed on the *Index* was known to virtually all peasants and increased the awe with which they were regarded. That a piece of obscure writing should be dignified with this supreme condemnation also was proof to many that there must have been good reason for doing so—that witchcraft was something real and could be learned through Moses' magical books. In fact, traditional Catholicism (as well as fundamentalist Protestantism) viewed, and still views, witchcraft as real. Suppression of the witching books was meant to reduce the practice of the black art. However, the attempted suppression failed dismally.

While almost all of the older peasants know of the book (I use the singular since in the minds of the peasants it is one book), few have seen it. I have met only one person who admitted to having seen—indeed used—the book. It belonged to her relatives, was never shown to outsiders, and its possession was as secret in a village of approximately two dozen peasant families as a house on fire. The family who owned the book was reputed to include witches.

The elusiveness of the book as a physical phenomenon among the Franconian peasants can be partly explained by the Church's relentless persecution and destruction of it. All copies found were destroyed. The destruction did not stop with the cessation of the official book-burning crusade. Surviving copies were often destroyed by family or clan members who opposed the presence of the evil book. Since possession of the book was considered a mortal sin by many theologians and priests, many obedient Christian relatives took it upon themselves to destroy it. So, over the ages, copies were decimated and I could not find a family that had (or would admit having) the controversial scripture. Apparently this book is also absent from official libraries of the region, since the powerful authority of the Church has permeated public life in Franconian Switzerland since before the invention of printing.

91   The underground popularity of the book was not limited to

Franconia. The geographic parameters of the book probably covered all of Germany and regions beyond. My interviews with elders verified that the book was used by peasants in East Prussia, the Upper Palatinate (along the Bohemian border) and Saxony. In the latter province I discovered an interesting side aspect. A children's game existed as late as the early 1950s wherein youngsters gathered around a tub or bowl of water with one older child asking, "Do you know *The Sixth Book of Moses?*" (My informants could not exactly recall whether the word was "Sixth" or "Seventh.") If a child answered "no," the "ignoramus' " head was dunked into the water. The game apparently continued to work, since a novice was always found. The young adults who had played this game as children in the 1950s had not the slightest idea about the nature of the book to which they referred in their game.

How widespread is this *grimoire*? Anti-Sadducee Summers answers, and if we weed out his theological prejudice (that witchcraft is real and a worldwide Satanic conspiracy), his historical information appears quite valid. He reminds us at the outset that there are numerous *grimoires*; that some overlap in certain regions; usually ascribe authorship incorrectly; and have obscure dates of origin. The *Sixth and Seventh Books of Moses* are unknown in Scandinavia, France and most Slavic regions. The Scandinavian witches follow a manual dubbed, *Book of Cyprianus.*[3] In France, the "most famous, or infamous," of all printed *grimoires* are *Les admirables Secrets du Grand Albert* and the collection known as *Le Petit Albert.*[4] Both are (most likely, but falsely) attributed to Albertus Magnus (1206–1280), the *doctor universalis* who taught Thomas Aquinas, and who passed into history with the reputation of a magician. These two texts are extensively employed and, according to Summers, the most mischievous today. Editions and reprints of the two manuals vary widely in content since their first publication in the 16th century. Joined publication of the two texts occurred in 1885—which represents the most commonly used edition in France today.[5] Monter verifies the use of these manuals in the French-Swiss borderlands and he describes them thus:

> If we examine a best-selling *grimoire* like the *Marvellous Secrets of Natural and Cabalistic Magic of Little Albert*, we can see that it has many aspects in common with 15th-century witchcraft. Its first eleven recipes deal with types of love magic worthy of the most famous sorceress in Renaissance literature, La Celestina; the twelfth tells how to remedy the

charm to make men impotent, the *aiguillette*; and the next one even describes how to make an *aiguillette* . . . . The *Petit Albert* is full of drawings of magic pentacles; of methods for many kinds of divination; of magical cures for various illnesses; of ways to raise spirits; and even of recipes for making oneself invisible or resisting torture.[6]

Other magical texts used in France include *Le Dragon Rouge*, *Le Dragon Noir* and *La Poule Noire*. Summers repeats superlatives and describes them as *grimoires* of the worst type, even furnishing necromantic evocations.[7] Will-Erich Peuckert systematically compared *Le Dragon Rouge* (also called *Le véritable Dragon rouge*) with the *Sixth and Seventh Books of Moses* and discovered striking similarities, concluding that both texts must have a common ancestor.[8] Among other *grimoires* is the widespread, nearly international *Key of Solomon the King*, which allegedly was found in the king's tomb, rescued by a Babylonian and passed on in Hebrew, Latin and Greek versions to be translated into English and published in 1889.[9] In Germany, the literary basis of witchery has primarily remained the *Sixth and Seventh Books of Moses*, with a shelf of other manuals following as distant seconds.

The absence of *grimoires* in most Slavic regions has been convincingly explained to me through personal communication with Professor Ludwig Traut-Welser, one of Germany's foremost experts on the cultural history of southeastern Europe. The Eastern Orthodox Church, always strictly New Testament oriented, bristled with hostility against the intrusion of Jewish elements. This was particularly true for 15th- and 16th-century Russia where a theocracy evolved that combined feudal system with priestly hierarchy. The regime protected its lordly reign by, among other measures, suppression of those Biblical sources, especially the prophets, who suggested a separation of state and church, since such separation would have threatened their rule. The authorities so severely persecuted and eradicated heretics, especially members of the sect that tried to introduce Hebrew ideas, that such mystic and magic thoughts as emanated in the West from the Kabbalistic tradition had no chance of evolving in the East. Even the Old Testament was perceived as an anarchistic threat and the early Muscovite rulers suppressed it. Under such conditions, the magic books, especially those that might have derived from the Jews' Kabbala, failed to enter the folklore of magic and sorcery in most Slavic regions, excepting some Catholic zones in Poland, the Ukraine, Bohemia,

Slovenia and Croatia. Moreover, in Eastern Europe, peasants were less literate than in Catholic or Protestant regions—thus, how could they use *grimoires*? Illiteracy and the suppression of magical literature resulted in an Eastern witchcraft phenomenon that generally was far more subdued. Eastern Europe had witchcraft beliefs and resulting trials, but none comparable to the West's witch mania during the Renaissance.[10] The Slavic rulers nipped witchcraft in the bud when they eliminated the early sects that tried to spread Hebrew ideas.

The *Sixth and Seventh Books of Moses* are far from being an Antiquity. They are very much alive in parts of Germany. While they have virtually disappeared from our Franconian area, they have been printed and reprinted a number of times in other parts of Germany. Each edition altered the style and content. In the 1930s, for example, Buchversand Gutenberg, a publisher in Dresden, produced a substantially purged edition of this *grimoire*. "It was a revision that adapted to modern conditions, in part borrowed from scientific literature and thus succeeded in making an authoritative impression on the superstitious."[11] During the 1950s, the Planet-Verlag of Braunschweig in northern Germany printed and sold 9000 copies of the *Sixth and Seventh Books of Moses*, and in addition, the 8th, 9th, 11th and 12th books allegedly also part of Moses' sequences.[12]

This particular publication of the *grimoire* did not go unchallenged. Johann Kruse, a teacher from Schleswig-Holstein whose mother had been slandered as a witch in his native village, became a self-appointed folklorist who set out to combat the spread of witchcraft. He became founder and director of the Archives for the Investigation of Contemporary Witchcraft Superstition in the Federal Republic of Germany at Hamburg. This man made it his personal vendetta, though ultimately unsuccessful, to have the book suppressed. He saw the book as an instigator of illegal, if not outright murderous, behavior. He referred to one of the seals (magic formulas) in the book that promises that he who kills nine persons may expect a large fortune through magic means. Kruse was able to point to a case in the 1920s when a man by the name of Angerstein, proceeding with the demonic instructions, was arrested just before he could carry out his ninth killing. He was convicted on eight counts of murder and sentenced to die.[13] On a less extreme tangent, Kruse held the book, and consequently the publisher, responsible for stimulating the exploitation of superstition for profit, causing antisocial behavior and slandering innocent persons as witches. He cited 56 lawsuits that involved the book since 1945 and police statistics that, in 1950, an estimated 10,000 *Hexenbanner* were plying their trade in West Germany.

Kruse sued Planet-Verlag. A 1956 court hearing exhibited two opposing teams of experts: on one side, Professor Prokop to speak for Kruse's cause; on the other side, Professor Peukert to testify for the defendant. The court's verdict found the publisher guilty of deceit and "harmful publication" and imposed heavy fines. However, the appeals court disagreed, rescinded the fines and Kruse lost the case. Kruse and Peuckert emerged from the controversy to remain irreconcilable opponents, if not personal enemies.

The record shows that Peuckert never forgave Kruse for "intrusion on his territory"—a domain he had staked out through many years of research, lecturing on the subject and functioning as court-appointed expert in trials involving the practice and criminal consequences of witchcraft. He found fault with literally everything that Kruse had advanced—his ideas, terminology, spelling and research procedure.[14] While I agree with Peuckert's criticism concerning some of Kruse's questionable research tactics and theoretical assumptions, I find his criticism of style unduly pedantic, as well as amusing. Peuckert's own writing reveals a convoluted style and often hides behind awkward grammar so that one can only guess at the meaning he intended. But more importantly, Peuckert finds Kruse ignorant of the larger context of magical literature, a genre with an impressive tradition that reaches back to ancient Roman, Greek and Egyptian ideas of healing and *magia naturalis*.

Alas, academic discourse is not free from emotional hexes.

The *Sixth and Seventh Books of Moses* are free to continue their journey through the 20th century and probably will triumphantly enter the 21st century. They have reached the shores of the New World and are selling briskly in the land of the Americans and can be bought for $2.00 in bookstores specializing in the occult. In fact, my later description of the *grimoire* is based on the American edition, claiming to be a direct translation from German.[15] It is noteworthy that this manual of magic is becoming popular particularly among black Americans. Many blacks claim that the books reveal a style of magic akin to that of their African ancestry. The irony of these books, then, is that they may be instrumental in the revival of voodoo in the United States.[16]

Now a closer look at the content of the magic manual. Some

parts offer biographical material about Moses and fault the Bible for withholding magic that Moses presumably learned from Jethro and/ or directly from God on the Mountain. In sum, the Bible is accused of failing to grant Moses his rightful place as history's greatest sorcerer.

But the basic purpose of the *grimoire* is to teach demonomagy: magic invoking the aid of demons to cast hexes and spells. Therefore, many parts of the book concentrate on a procedure that, for lack of better terms, could well be defined as voodoo. And, indeed, there is considerable similarity between the practice of vengeance magic among African tribes and the suggestions of the magic manual.[17] But to be fair, it must be pointed out that not all seals offered in the book have a negative and harmful intention. Peuckert reminds us, in his defense of the book's redeeming qualities, that the nature of most of the seals is "medical," followed by magic-medical, and that only a relatively small portion consists of formulas for harmful spells.

Regardless of the proportions of positive and negative seals, it must be understood that the Franconian peasants were highly selective in what they used from the *grimoire* and that they extracted mostly those aspects that dealt with certain interpersonal problems— theft, disease, death, vengeance and other harmful spells. The distillation of the *grimoire* through the psychological, social and natural problems of the peasants tinted the manual as exceedingly sinister, a characterization that is mainly achieved through selectivity. But since this was the slant of the peasant's usage of the book, this is the way I must portray it, otherwise I am not doing justice to the meaning it had among them.

With this in mind, here are a number of biased examples as they can be found in the magical sequels. Incidentally, a number of the examples deal with formulas that must be spoken in an ancient tongue, supposedly Hebrew. Rabbis consulting the book have recognized the language as mostly pseudo-Hebrew with faulty characters that smack of either invention or poor imitation. An elaborate seal promises, "That the Devil Shall Smite an Enemy." To implement this seal, the ritual demands, "Take a stone and throw it to a dog who shall bite it, and on it write these names and throw it in the house of thine enemy and thou shalt see wonders."[18]

Another seal is to be used to "Wreak Vengeance upon an Enemy." A certain emblem is written upon some surface. The drawing is then to be washed with water until the surface is again clean, " . . . taking the water thereof and sprinkle it in the house of an enemy on the second night of the week or fourth of the week at the seventh hour."[19]

To impose a certain dream (more appropriately defined as nightmare) on another person, an arcane text has to be written with a solution of myrrh on a "writing tablet." Then "a cat, black all over, and which has been killed" serves as the medium. The text has to be deposited in the mouth of the dead cat.[20]

To destroy one's enemy, "Take a laden plate and some of his hair and clothes, and say the 'Sword' prayer over them and bury them in a deserted house and he will fall down."[21]

Hexes are also available to satisfy amorous or possessive desires. "If thou wishest a woman to follow thee, take thy blood and write her name upon a newly laid egg and say toward her: RAMPEL."[22]

The catalog of hexes and spells is long and varied: to punish an enemy; to secure love; to satisfy lust; to gain riches; to restore health; to gain influential friends; to escape misery of all sorts; to achieve longevity; to discover treasures; to win quarrels; and so forth. In addition, wearing of magical seals in bed promises dreams in which a person will achieve any type of insight he or she desires.

Secret rituals are divulged which supposedly empower a person to summon, as well as dismiss, a vast assortment of spirits and demons. These entities from the spirit world are believed to serve the person performing the correct ritual. Among the demons is Mephistopheles (the personification of the Devil). He also provides the "familiars" (animals that accompany and assist the witching person) and brings treasures of gold from the depth of the earth.[23]

The central goals reflected again and again in these writings are health, longevity, fortunes and protection against enemies, which is, conversely, to say that the believers in witchcraft are most concerned with the problems of illness, death, poverty and dangerous enemies. These concerns mirror the essential sentiments underlying witchcraft as a form of magic: fear, revenge, hope and the desire for power. (More about the essence and the meaning of magic in Part III.)

The book is still ominous in the minds of many of the older peasants. This was manifested by the responses I received when I asked them why witchcraft and hexes have gradually disappeared during recent years. Many were quick to explain that no one has the book anymore and that without it no one can practice witchery. The logic is clear and simple: no more book, no more witchcraft.

Still today the book is seen in an aura of evil. And it makes us pause to ponder exactly who among these seemingly simple peasants had the temerity to place themselves outside their community's moral and religious conventions by holding on to the condemned book. The theological penalty was excommunication—the ultimate punishment to the religious populace. The exclusion from the ranks of the believers was tantamount to the exclusion from normal social life among the villagers.

Who would invite such ostracism?

From my observations, persons (or whole families) who risked theological and social exclusion were thoroughly estranged from neighbors and had arrived at a self-definition that at once accepted and confirmed their reputation: they saw themselves outside of the circle of Christian believers and fancied themselves in a pact with Satan.

It was role confirmation without reservation. Mostly, it had a simple pragmatic slant: they thought to be able to make more headway in this world and to effectively avoid disaster and pain if they entered into an agreement with the Devil. Again the Faustian aspirations. Except that, unlike its literary prototype, it emphasized the negative side, being more preoccupied with the avoidance of pain and misfortune than the attainment of riches and power. The Franconian witch had a thaumaturgical slant, i.e., she or he tried to perform miraculous feats to effect relief from immediate personal problems.

It is significant that fear of life's many dangers tempted some persons to choose witchcraft as an attempt to gain a foothold on a Faustian island amidst a treacherous sea. The same dangers led others to devise a set of different protections against the onslaught of evil. It seems that because of their bitter life conditions, the obedient Christians as well as the heretics among the Franconians were motivated to embrace their lifestyles because of anxiety and misery.

One more word about role theory. It is difficult to determine what came first, the reputation and then the confirmation of the role, or a relatively private decision to ally with Satan and then the corresponding reputation. From this point in history, it is almost impossible to answer the question. No records or oral traditions have reliably captured the social and psychological processes showing how the witch's reputation and self-definition interacted or which of the two aspects came first. It probably is one of those instances where we must futilely ponder the chicken-or-egg priority.

In any case, we can conclude that there were villagers who had the reputation of being witches and who identified with that reputation. These, then, were the persons who claimed to be custodians of magical power, confident of their ability to place curses.

8

Cases of Curse and Cure

"The heart has a longer memory than the mind.
That is why a story clings more tenaciously
to us than a statistic.
How much more so if the story happens to be true."

RABBI MORRIS N. KERTZER

The spectrum of the witch's wickedness extended from mischievous pranks to deadly malfeasance. This chapter samples the range, illustrating the generalizations offered in preceding chapters and, hopefully, adding substance and color to abstractions. The examples are based on primary sources: the reports of persons who claim they personally experienced or witnessed the events. The places of occurrence are the villages of Franconian Switzerland, and the time of the majority of these events ranges from 1900 to 1940. A few of them, however, occurred as late as the early 1950s.

We begin with examples of the prankish side of the witch and defer her serious malfeasance until later.

Hexes of Lice

The peasants entertained no doubt that the malicious imagination of the witch was boundless. Among the multitude of vicious pranks that might be expected of her was the hex of lice. The Franconians believed this retaliatory sorcery to be most widespread. The curse was highly personalized insofar as the body of a victim might virtually teem with the parasite, which, however, refused to transfer to another individual regardless of intimate physical proximity. This is a typical example:

One afternoon, a peasant boy surprised a number of unfamiliar chickens in the barn, while stealing grain from the freshly threshed crop. The ruckus resulting from the boy's chasing the birds from the premises brought the neighbor woman, the owner of the chickens, to the scene. She was irate and threatened, "You just wait, you'll pay for this!"

When the boy woke up the next morning, he found his body teeming with lice, while his brother with whom he shared the bed was not bothered by one. The agonizing visitation continued in this most exclusive manner for several weeks until, no longer able to stand the discomfort, the boy went for advice to the village shepherd. The man nodded knowingly and suggested that the boy go to the angry neighbor and beg for forgiveness. Without hesitation, the boy followed the advice and the lice vanished as suddenly as they had appeared.[1]

A peasant woman, the octogenarian Mrs. Bigfarmer* of Weidenloh, told me of an event she had personally witnessed. When a peasant let his cows graze on the *Rain* (a grassy strip marking the centerline between fields), the woman tilling the adjacent field reproached him and demanded that he immediately remove his animals. In revenge for not complying with her wish quickly enough, the peasant found his body invaded by legions of lice the next day. As in all lice hexes, someone in close contact (in this case his wife who shared the conjugal bed) was totally unaffected by the vermin. The man tried delousing chemicals which he bought in the apothecary of the nearby town, but discovered that they were absolutely ineffective. Suspecting what had prompted this peculiar torment, the peasant resorted to the only means that, according to folk tradition, was left to him. He went to the woman who scolded him and asked to be forgiven. She withdrew the curse and the peasant was quickly rid of the lice.

The setting of another case of a hex of lice was the village of Waidach where I was told that a woman from a neighbor village was punished for sneaking into a man's orchard and stealing plums and apples. One day, after again having stolen fruit, the woman was all of a sudden invaded by what seemed to be hundreds of head lice. Since the owner of the orchard was known to have the witching book, the logical assumption was made that he had placed a curse on the thief. The woman decided on the only possible remedy: to go to the man for *Abbitte*, to ask to be forgiven. She explained to the man the need and hunger of her family as the reason for her

---

* Pseudonyms, suggesting major attributes of the key figures, are used to protect the identities of persons and families. Names of villages and other places are authentic.

theft and begged to be forgiven. The man was agreeable, saying, "Go home, you're going to be all right." On the way home, the repentant realized that suddenly all lice had left her.

A Case of Hexendrücken

A form of incubus referred to as *Hexendrücken* was widely interpreted by the Franconian peasants as one of the witch's common pranks. (An explanation of the incubus phenomenon will be offered in Chapter Twelve.) Stories about the witch's nocturnal oppression were part of the regional folk beliefs and considered factual. Still today, older people speak of the frightening experiences and remember incidents.

An elderly peasant, Mr. Oldtimer from the village of Bärnfels, related a representative account of *Hexendrücken*. (This man was an excellent source of information on folk traditions, and his openness may have been prompted by knowing me as the grandson of a healer whom he had known personally.) One night, while half-asleep, the man heard steps ascending to his second-floor bedroom. The locked door opened, and the steps approached him. Suddenly he felt an immense weight descending on his chest. He gasped for air and tried to move, but found himself immobilized. After a seemingly interminable time of terror, the weight lifted, the steps went away, the door closed and he heard the steps descend the stairs.

This man was aware of the concept of a nightmare, and when asked whether he thought that his experience might have been one, he emphatically ruled it out, emphasizing that he was awake enough to clearly recognize it as it really was: *Hexendrücken*. He added that he clearly saw the door being opened from the outside though it was locked from the inside. He also maintained that he unmistakably heard the steps. Furthermore, he had a good idea of the identity of the witch: an ill-reputed woman of the village.

According to the folk belief, the identity of the witch could be determined by noting the first person who came to the house to borrow something within three days following the event. Sure enough, the day after the "witch's pressing," the suspected woman knocked at the door to borrow a tool. This confirmed the man's suspicion and settled the question of the identity of the nocturnal visitor.

Battles of Witchery between Neighbors

This report deals with a family chronically entangled in witch-craft. I was introduced to the family history by a woman, now in her 80s, whom I had known since my childhood. The woman was a daughter of the family under discussion, but had married into the Schneider clan and thus became a relative of mine.

The Meddler family, in which this woman grew up, had a reputation of frequent experimentation with witchery. In fact, the reputation adhered to some degree to the Meddler's daughter al-though there is no evidence that she personally engaged in the black art.

This family was one of the more well-to-do farm families in Kirchenbirkig and lived next to the Fruitgrower family, who also reportedly dabbled in witchcraft. Veritable witchcraft duels ensued between the neighboring households and my source related the following accounts from her youth.

During one season, the Meddler family experienced *Pech im Stall* (misfortune in the stable). Piglets died, the cows milked blood and the calves sickened. No natural explanation could be found. But soon the telltale sign of witchcraft was discovered; one morning the horses were found in their stalls with their tails finely braided. This was recognized by the peasants as confirmation that the Devil and his associates were at work.

After the horses' tails were unbraided and the customary protec-tion in the form of *Kletten* (large burrs) was tied into them, the Meddler matriarch insisted on a decision that her husband reluc-tantly accepted. The decision was to call on the service of a well-known healer from the village of Rabeneck. The husband's reluc-tance was due to the mixed reputation that this healer had; besides being known to be skilled in the *Anfangen*, which was an accept-able Christian folk tradition, it was rumored that he was more a sorcerer of kinds than a Christian healer. (Some called him a *Hexenmeister*—a wizard or sorcerer.) But his reputation of being eminently effective in lifting spells overrode the consideration of his other dubious skills.

The healer of Rabeneck apparently was sufficiently in line with the Christian tradition, since, after he arrived at the Meddler farm, he commenced with the *Anfangen*, a practice that would have been shunned by a true witch. The *Anfangen* must take place at the location of the disaster and proceed in absolute privacy. After the healer entered the stable and closed the door, the family was expected to stay in their quarters and wait for him to complete the ritual. My confidante was a young teenager at the time and her curiosity got the better of her sense of obedience. She defied the rule and sneaked into an outbuilding adjacent to the stable, found a knothole, and spied on the man. She saw him kneel, pray, make the sign of the cross numerous times, and light a blessed candle, the so-called *Waxstock*, that normally is used only at a requiem in church. After he had completed the ritual in the stable, he asked to see the butter barrel and proceeded to carve three crosses on the inside. This was to dispel the hex that presumably impaired this farm implement, as it had failed to curdle butter ever since the trouble began.

After the healer had finished the various rituals of the *Anfangen*, he reminded the family that they must not accept or lend any object for the next three days. He also announced that within these critical three days a person would come to the door and ask to borrow something. This person was the one who put the hex on the stable. After a gift of money (a rare form of compensation for such services) was given, the healer-sorcerer of Rabeneck departed.

The second day after the healing ritual, Mrs. Fruitgrower came and asked whether she could borrow the *Grasstumpf* (sickle), claiming she had left hers in the fields. The identity of the witch and the origin of the curse were now confirmed. (Under some plausible excuse, her request to borrow the tool was of course denied, since, otherwise, the hex could have been renewed.)

The *Anfangen* by the healer from Rabeneck was apparently effective; the animals recovered and the butter barrel again produced butter.

Now that there was no doubt about the identity of the evil-doer, the Meddler woman planned revenge. She took the initiative—her husband neither encouraged nor participated in the witchcraft activities—and secured the infamous *Sixth Book of Moses* from a distant relative who was a witch, a member of the Conspirator family of Kühlenfels.

The book specified how to cast a curse, and demanded as the first step that some object be acquired that was handled or owned by the person to be cursed. This turned out to be an easy task. The Fruitgrower woman had stolen some grass from the edge of a

104

meadow that belonged to the Meddlers. In the process of cutting it with the sickle and packing it away, some grass lay scattered at the location of the theft. Three blades of grass, thusly related to the thief, were taken to the house and with the help of the secret book, the demonic ritual was performed. In retaliation, the curse was to sicken the neighbor's animals that ate the stolen grass. Indeed, the neighbor's cows started to milk blood the very next day. (I was assured that no "trick," such as possibly adding chemicals or poisons to the fodder of the neighbor's cows, was used to effect this punishment. The method of the curse was limited to the magic ritual focusing on the three fateful blades of grass.)

As expected, the Fruitgrower woman soon came to the house to do *Abbitte*, but the Meddler's daughter could not remember whether her mother relented and withdrew the curse. In any case, the distrust toward the Fruitgrower family continued, and all members of the Meddler family carefully avoided vulnerability to the spells of the witch. The safest procedure was thought to be absolute shunning, avoiding even visual contact with the disreputable neighbor. (Here was one of the very few allusions to the "evil eye" that I encountered in Franconian Switzerland.) The avoidance procedure went so far as to avoid passing the neighbor's house. This caused considerable inconvenience since the village street went right by it. So, in order to get to the fields that lay on the far side of the village, the Meddlers engaged in time-consuming detours, using back roads to get to the other side of the village. Care was observed to keep the cows, when drawing the wagon to and from the fields, from inadvertently eating grass from the neighbor's *Rain* (grassy bank or border line of a field).

Children were reminded to stay off the neighbor's land and refrain from picking flowers in the neighbor's meadows. The coveted fat thistles that grew between the furrows of potato fields, normally picked by the children to feed the geese, were strictly taboo if they grew on land belonging to the dreaded neighbor. And, of course, no object whatever was to be borrowed from or lent to the neighbor. Exchanging personal items would make them vulnerable to hexes again.

It was during this period of strict shunning that the Fruitgrower woman bluntly requested the use of the Meddlers' *Backofen* (a masonry outbuilding used for baking bread) for drying fruit gathered from her orchard. Not every peasant household had its own *Backofen* as it was a relatively complex and expensive structure to build.

The Meddler matriarch did not grant the request. The refusal was primarily based on the fear of incurring spells if the witch were allowed to use the property. As an excuse, however, Mrs. Meddler announced that they needed to use the oven themselves, as it was the season to pick fruit and can or dry it for storage. The Meddler family had its own substantial orchard.

The refusal to let her use the oven apparently angered the neighbor into a plan of revenge. This, at least, was the interpretation of the Meddler people when all the fruit that they attempted to dry in their *Backofen* spoiled. Similarly, all the fruit on a fine pear tree shrunk and spoiled on the branches. The Meddlers, particularly the woman, were convinced: this was the result of another hex from the neighbor witch. And again there was talk of a revenge hex.

But this time the husband of the Meddler matriarch demanded a halt to the seesaw of witchery, insisted that the evil book be removed from the house and returned to its owner and that dabbling in witchcraft be stopped once and for all.

The *Sixth Book of Moses* was returned to the Conspirator people and peace lasted for a while. But new trouble arose. Sickness and death among the piglets of a litter of 16 were again interpreted as the signs of the witch's hex. This time, suspicion focused on a different source. The related Conspirator family of Kühlenfels, who on a previous occasion had supported the cause of the Meddler family, had since become alienated. The fault, it seems, lay with the Meddler family who had failed to live up to the traditional cooperation expected of kin. Ironically, however, it was the Meddler family who accused the Conspirator people of treachery and witchery, specifically of cursing their stable.

But the Meddler matriarch was in an awkward position. Although she burned with desire to put a retaliatory curse on the relatives, her lust for revenge was stalemated since the secret book—prerequisite to casting a spell—was in the hands of the very individuals she wanted to punish. So she forfeited vengeance and concentrated her efforts on deliverance from the curse. Unlike the earlier incident, this time the road to deliverance was a more institutionalized form of Christian healing and led to the Franciscan friars at the monastery in Gössweinstein. (Curiously, the chapel of this monastery was founded by the infamous *Hexenbischof* Johann Georg II of Bamberg who burned several hundred witches.)[2]

For three marks she received blessed herbs that she fed to the sick animals, who recovered almost immediately.

The Meddler woman had by then acquired an uncanny reputation, and many people believed that she knew more about witchcraft than a God-fearing Christian should. Rumors described her as being just as much a perpetrator as a victim of witchcraft. This reputation attracted as many as it repelled.

A number of acquaintances in trouble came to her with questions of witchcraft and she became a witchcraft consultant of sorts. A farmer from Gesee, for example, asked her advice about an ailing calf. She diagnosed the disease as having been caused by a woman visitor who stroked the calf's back with the intention of making it sick.

Witchcraft suspicions continued to be fueled among the Meddler people, and soon there was another series of events that, to them, justified apprehension. One morning they again discovered their horses with braided tails. The Meddler matriarch's daughter, who vividly remembered the incident, assured me that the intricate braiding was a stunning work of art. This sign of the Devil was immediately ascribed to the doing of the neighbor woman, the suspected witch of the earlier evil-doings.

The satanic braiding of the horses' tails continued several nights in a row. Apprehension grew to such a pitch that the family decided that something had to be done. A retaliatory curse was ruled out by the unavailability of the witchcraft book and by Mr. Meddler's unwillingness to employ witchery again. They decided this time to follow an old folk tradition. Peasant wisdom trusted that the witch could be kept away from the stable if one defecated in front of the entrance to the stable and leaned a pitch fork, prongs pointing up, in a corner of the animal shelter.

This earthy ritual was carried out and the result confirmed its validity to the people: the animals were no longer bothered and there was no more braiding.

The events taken from this family's history were not unique to the Meddlers. This kind of happening was known throughout the area and other families claimed similar incidents. The reason for my concentration on the Meddler family was the accessibility to information and its trustworthiness. Village elders corroborated the accounts.

The matter of corroboration surprised me consistently. It seemed that several persons supported every witchcraft report, and some claimed to have witnessed details of the event.

The affairs of the Meddler family call for a wistful epitaph. The villagers avoided the matriarch of the family as a spiteful person who begrudged good fortune to anyone. Of even greater significance to the villagers was her use of strange and demonic language, and it was whispered that she was in cahoots with Satan. (The "strange language" may have come from the Kabbalistic books from which she learned magical formulas to be chanted.) People suspected her of having evil books, including the *Sixth and Seventh Books of Moses*, and of dabbling in witchcraft. In fact, all the neighbors knew the latter habit—some only too well, as they at one time or another had been victims of her witchery.

Misfortune stubbornly pursued the family: a son died during childhood. Soon after the ill-reputed Mrs. Meddler died, a Maypole toppled and killed another son. The remaining sons married quarrelsome women who were known in the community as "no good." The only daughter established her own reputation of being meddlesome. When she married, she and her husband moved to the city, and many relatives were of the opinion that, had she stayed on in the village, she would have followed in the footsteps of her witching mother. Finally, the family homestead experienced financial ruin and fell into the hands of strangers—a rare occurrence in the region.

The villagers' supernatural interpretation of the misfortune was predictable. They believed that the family and the house had lost their blessings because of the matriarch's character. Many peasants believed that physical objects—such as a house, stable or water well—could be inhabited by demons. Thus, a house could lose its good spirits through the evil ways of its inhabitants and invite demonic possession. The belief in a demonized house is a form of primitive animism, i.e., it is the belief that natural phenomena and objects such as houses, rocks, trees and the wind are alive and have a soul—good or bad. This is an orientation found by anthropologists in many of the so-called primitive tribal societies.[3] It may come as a surprise to recognize traces of this world view in Europe during this century.

The Witch and the Soul of the Departed

A son of the Meddler family died during childhood. The death occurred at the exact moment when the neighbor, the witch-reputed Fruitgrower woman, squatted next to the *Misthaufen* (the traditional manure pile next to the stable) to defecate. (There were no indoor toilet facilities in the old Franconian farm houses until the middle of this century.) This woman claimed that at that instant she saw a white angel emerge from the Meddler's house, soar by her, and disappear in the direction of the village cemetery.

The report frightened the Meddler people, since, if a witch was able to see the soul of the departed, the soul was not in good repair. The family was gripped by fear of the departed child's ghost and took pains to keep all doors and windows tightly shut, lest the troubled soul try to reenter the house. In addition, for several months the family gathered every evening to recite prayers for protection.

A Case of the Anfangen with Humans

While most of the cases of Anfangen were performed on farm animals, a number of cures concerned humans.

One dealt with the Meddler's daughter when she was a young girl and suffered with an eye irritation. The cause was not known, but from the description it seemed to be a small particle lodged in the corner of her eye. Witchcraft was not suspected in this case. The irritation grew into a painful inflammation and the traditional herb remedies proved ineffective. So the mother decided to fetch the village woman known for her skill in the Anfangen. My octogenarian reporter remembered that the healer delayed her Anfangen since it would be effective only at the time of the declining moon. When the position of the moon was favorable, she returned, asked the patient to kneel, look across her right shoulder, and say the Lord's Prayer three times. At the same time, the healer prayed but the girl could not understand the words of the prayers. The Anfangen seemed successful and within a few days the irritation disappeared.

The Children and the Witch of Sachsendorf

The somnolent village of Sachsendorf offered a most incongruous neighborhood. Living within a stone's throw were the Schneider people with the matriarch known as a healer and the Reject people with their matriarch suspected as a witch.

While there was no animosity between the two families, the

Reject woman was shunned. Detours were made to avoid having to greet her or being addressed by her. Rather than animosity, the prevailing sentiment toward the woman was uneasiness. Most villagers "knew" her as an evil woman—an ally of Satan. And, of course, she was said to possess the fearful *Sixth Book of Moses*. The knowledge of the woman was pervasive throughout the village, and almost every instance of *Pech im Stall* was blamed on her. She was blamed for spreading misfortune, mostly affecting livestock.

The confidant who provided most of this account was (and at the time of this writing still is) an intimate source: my 87-year-old father who grew up on the Schneider's homestead. Before presenting his personal memories, I shall point out that he perceives witchcraft as a reality (unlike my mother who, though having grown up in the same environment, sees it as a delusion of a social psychological nature). His basic conviction can be summed up, "these things happened, they were real, they worked." He is convinced that the Reject matriarch's hexes had the power to affect animals and humans. He is also convinced that the people were powerless against witchcraft unless they went to the priest or called a woman who knew the *Anfangen*.

The village children, including the Schneider's, were often unmindful of the Reject woman's reputation and, when passing by her farm, would respond to her greeting. They would stop to talk to the woman and some of them accepted gifts that looked to them like ordinary medals bearing religious emblems or pictures, such as could be had from the monks at the monastery or cheaply bought from the Sunday street vendor in front of the basilica in Gösswein-stein.

The children normally did not tell their parents about the gifts, more because accepting a gift without a return favor violated the folkways of the Franconian peasants than because of the fear of being found having associated with a reputed witch. They did not yet fully understand the stigma attached to the woman. But the socialization process soon took care of the initial openness of the children. Once the parents realized the carelessness of the children and made the terrifying discovery that they were the naive carriers of ill-omened objects (albeit of religious appearance) into their homes, they put a halt to the practice. Soon the children behaved as stand-offishly toward the woman as the adults; she became isolated. Sometimes she would call to a passing youngster to stop for a chat or a gift, but the child would turn and run.

To wonder what the woman's motives were when she tried to approach the children leads to interesting speculations. Did she try to make friends with the children because they were the only ones who talked to her? Was it a simple case of a woman liking children? Did she, by giving away religious medals, try to tell the village that she was the good Christian she may have believed she was? Or did she indeed have a self-definition of a witch and try to use the children as carrier pigeons to transfer objects which, once in the homes of villagers, would give her power over their families? Obviously, these questions can no longer be answered. The Reject woman is long since dead, and only the memories of her younger contemporaries guide us in the attempt to understand the past. In the memory of most of those still living, she was a witch and the tragedies of the village (the occasional occurrences that are normal to village life anywhere: poor harvest, fire, trouble in the stable, disease in the family, and so forth) were ascribed to her hexes. It goes without saying that the accounts centering on the Reject woman yield absolutely no empirical evidence that the woman ever did any actual harm. But to the peasants of the early decades of this century she was an evil-doer.

This leads to the humanistic question whether we are not confronting a completely unfounded defamation of an innocent character who desperately attempted to reach out for acceptance and friendship. If so, the situation reflects a colossal inhumanity: the tragedy of a human being reaching out and being scorned.

Misfortune befell the Reject family. The son died at a relatively young age from what, in retrospect, must have been cancer. The son of this man also died young, succumbing to war injuries at the age of 25. The losses of a son and a grandson so early in their lives were ominous events to the villagers and confirmed their belief that something was wrong with the family. As one old villager told me, "The son and the grandson had to pay for the sins of that woman." In other words, the peasants understood the untimely deaths as punishment for or redemption of the witchery of the old woman.

The Fraud of Rabeneck

It seems that the traditions and beliefs of the Franconian peasants were not safe from abuse. (Exploitation through cultural hoodwinking is probably a universal phenomenon—the shadow side of just about every culture.) To be a healer and skilled in the *Anfangen* was considered a gift esteemed among peers, but it could be exploited for lucrative purposes.

The innkeeper of Rabeneck cultivated the reputation of being a sorcerer and knowing the *Anfangen*. (As far as I could ascertain, this was the same man who had been fetched for the *Anfangen* by the Meddlers.) He created a clientele of persons in trouble who turned to him as the presumed trustee of supernatural forces. This man impressed the public with a sorcerer's quality that has not received much attention in the other case reports: clairvoyance.

He awed the individuals who came to him by already knowing, in detail, their problems. Unfailingly he would tell the visitor at first meeting, "I know you wonder what caused two out of your three cows to milk blood. Isn't that what you came to ask me?" Each time the visitor was overwhelmed by his clairvoyance and, naturally, would be equally impressed by the explanation that the innkeeper gave to the matter. Undoubtedly, such talent was entitled to exceptional compensation, and the innkeeper would usually make a handsome profit from the consultation: either farm produce, money or dedicated patronage of his beer mugs.

Many profitable years passed until the innkeeper's talent was finally revealed a hoax. His scheme was utterly simple. When a guest approached the inn, the innkeeper would hide in the kitchen adjacent to the public guest room and open a connecting window just a crack to hear his wife welcome the arrival and ask about his or her troubles. The guest was made comfortable under the excuse that the innkeeper was out of town but would be back in an hour or so. While waiting, the guest usually divulged all the information that the innkeeper needed. After having absorbed the information, the charlatan would steal out a back door, make a detour around the house, and emerge at the front door as if just returning from a trip.

He then commenced to impress the victim with his prescience by telling him what would happen and advising him what he should do to alleviate the problem. He made ample use of the idiom of the region, told them what they usually wanted to hear, and hewed closely to the beliefs of the folk culture. For example, he might diagnose the disease of a calf as a witch's curse and offer some sacred herbs to be put into the fodder. Additional directions were given about how to lift the hex. And he never forgot to mention the critical three days during which the cure could be reversed if by mistake a personal object were transferred into the hands of the witch. There was always a convenient explanation if the cure failed, and in such cases the victim was made to believe that he, probably inadvertently, neglected some aspect of the directions. (Thus, the pseudosorcerer was covered in any event.)

I have few reports indicating that the fraudulent innkeeper made "house calls" and actually officiated the rituals of the *Anfangen*. Either the man deemed it an unnecessary bother to leave his home, since he could do a profitable business right there, or else he had scruples, feeling that doing the actual *Anfangen* ritual would exceed his stamina for sacrilege and deceit.

The discovery of his fraudulence reached the public through vague rumors, which did little to undermine the peasants' belief in the effectiveness of the cures he prescribed. So not much in terms of a scandal or punishment followed the rumor—except that suddenly the innkeeper dedicated himself more to such mundane matters as selling beer and less to selling supernatural yarn.

Intrafamily Witchery

The idyllic village of Kühlenfels was the home of a family torn by attempts to manipulate supernatural forces. Two brothers, the sons of the Smallfarmer family, were pitted against each other. When the younger son married, he and his wife were invited to live in the old farmhouse. This was a relatively unusual arrangement, since the older son customarily stayed on the homestead. Apparently because the older son married later, the younger son and his immediate family gained priority. When the older son married, the land of the homestead was divided; a small house was built directly against the side of the old house, and he and his wife became intimate neighbors of the extended family next door. The newlyweds started to till their own land and to raise their own livestock, and things seemed to be in the best of order.

But the older brother and his wife, Hilde, soon became concerned about her brother-in-law's reputation of having the magic book of Moses and of "knowing how to do uncanny things." Her apprehension grew into fear when she noticed that the chicks, which she tried to raise, died one after the other. She blamed her brother-in-law for having cast a spell. She also ascribed the rapid dwindling of her potato stock, stored in the cellar for the winter, to his thieving or to his magical power to make them disappear. To verify her suspicion, she spun hair-fine threads under rows of potatoes. Her control device checked out positively. The threads were visible the next time she checked, and she then knew that her potatoes were being stolen. Since she was certain that the man had not been in the cellar in person, she assumed that the potatoes were removed by sorcery.

Seeing the theft as a work of magic was not an unusual inclination; indeed, it was consonant with the belief of many, if not most, Franconian peasants of past generations. (The events of this case, however, represent some of the latest witcheries reported and happened as recently as the 1950s.)

With the suspicion confirmed, she refused her brother-in-law entry into her house, and the relationship with her inlaws deteriorated. Ultimately, all contact between the two households was severed. Borrowing or lending was discontinued, since, as Hilde feared, satanic power could be acquired through the transfer of personal belongings.

Hilde made frequent pilgrimages to the monastery at Gösswein-stein to consult the Franciscan abbot about the uncanny happenings. According to witnesses (her children and other relatives, who related their observations to me), she returned with blessed medals and a new determination to ward off evil by prayer.

The severance of contact between the two households was complete, since Hilde's husband apparently believed his wife's interpretation and ceased to speak to his brother and his parents.

A common backyard extended behind the two adjoining houses and served as barnyard and playground for the children. Hilde and her husband, who by now had two little girls, strictly observed a centerline, instructed the children not to cross it, and forbade them to as much as greet their relatives next door. The children were warned that their neighbor-relatives had the "bad book" and knew how to practice witchcraft. Finally, a sturdy fence was erected along the centerline.

The situation did not improve. As the years passed, quarrelling ensued between the brothers over what belonged to whom. (I could not determine how the quarrel began without the parties talking to one another.) And further misfortune in the stable was blamed on the witching neighbor-relatives, such as the mysterious sickening of a sow that had to be emergency-butchered. The outcome of the intrafamily deterioration was Hilde's and her husband's decision to give up their house and move to another community.

An Exchange of Fetishes

There was an additional episode of supernaturalism that, although only indirectly related to the intrafamilial problems described in the preceding account, included a main character of that setting.

Hilde, the wife of the older son of the Smallfarmer family, was visited by a gypsy belonging to a band of gypsies roaming the countryside. The distraught peasant woman felt the pressure of the intrafamily witchery at the time and sought advice and comfort from the stranger. Specifically, she desired protection against the witchery of her brother-in-law. That she would consult a gypsy in these matters signified how acutely distressed she must have been, since gypsies were suspected of sorcery and witchcraft and usually avoided.

The gypsy convinced the woman that she knew ways to keep evil spirits away and reintroduce safety to home and stable. She had Hilde insert a charm into her hair (which she wore in a bun), and made her promise not to remove it for three days. The itinerant occultist did not depart without first talking Hilde into surrendering a considerable sum of money and the best food in the house.

Soon after the "house call" of the peripatetic magician, Hilde developed second thoughts and removed the talisman from her hair. As the occult believer she was, she must have done so with extraordinary trepidation, for she had been warned that premature removal would mean harm to her health, possibly even death. The charm consisted of a piece of paper. No one in her family was ever told what the paper said, or whether it said anything. However, it was suspected that it was covered with occult (Kabbalistic?) characters. In any case, Hilde ran in terror to the monastery. She talked to the monks, but what transpired during that consultation was never revealed. One thing was certain: she paid money to the Franciscan abbot for special prayers and a holy mass in her behalf. She also brought home a blessed medal that the monks gave her to counterbalance whatever demonic threats might hang over her.

The interpretation of what really happened is difficult. Soon relatives, those suspicious of the validity of occult interpretation in general, thought that the gypsy had practiced hypnotism to extract money and property from Hilde. They felt that Hilde, a true believer of the occult, was an ideal medium for manipulation, easily susceptible to hypnotic suggestion. The action of the abbot in giving a blessed medal and assuring its beneficial effect can be interpreted either as practicing psychotherapy or practicing medieval theology. (Some observers understandably fail to see the difference between the two.)

Anyway, the exchange of fetishes was effective: the one of the gypsy caused anxiety and the one of the monk appeased. To Hilde and her immediate family, these things and the powers they stood for were real.

The Blacksmith of Gössweinstein

The events surrounding the blacksmith of Gössweinstein are of older vintage than the preceding two accounts and took place during the first two decades of the century. However, his notoriety as a sorcerer and witch had been indelibly edged into tradition and virtually every member of the older generation in the region is familiar with the blacksmith stories. To them, they are not stories but true accounts.

It is interesting to speculate what would happen to these accounts if they were not written down (as they are hereby) during the lifetime of witnesses who actually knew the blacksmith, had dealings with him and still swear to the verity of his supernatural capacities. Without such documentation, the stories would most likely metamorphose into folklore. Later generations would probably never think twice before they discarded them as bizarre fairy tales.

Yet, there are reasonable persons, among them my father, an aunt and an uncle, who are convinced of the blacksmith's nefarious character and his evil deeds. They have known the blacksmith; swear to have made extraordinary observations; and related the following accounts.

To begin with, the blacksmith enjoyed a dubious reputation. Most people "knew," through rumor, conjecture or alleged personal observation, that he was a wizard, was possessed by the Devil and, of course, perused the books of Moses the Magician. He was also known to go into stables at night, cast spells and leave his telltale sign: braided tails and manes on feverish horses. He was feared by virtually everyone. And he was one of the few persons who reputedly had the "evil eye," although this concept is generally not a significant part of the occult folklore of the area.

Yet, people needed his business. The region's other blacksmith was in a remote town, too far for most to handle their business. Nevertheless, some of the more cautious and some who thought they had experienced detriment through their contact with the man preferred the inconvenience of traveling far to the risk of having their home or stable exposed to a curse.

One of the peasants, an uncle of mine of the village of Geiselhöhe, regularly had work done at the smithy. There were braces to be fitted to the wagon, horses needed shoes and a wheel needed fixing.

The misfortune was not long in coming. My uncle claimed that after each visit to the smithy there would occur misfortune in the stable. Cattle sickened, hogs died, cows either stopped giving milk or milked blood. This *Pech im Stall* became so regularly associated with visits to the Gössweinstein blacksmith that such happenings seemed predictable to my uncle and his family. Therefore, they finally stopped patronizing the ill-omened smithy and either did their own smithery (they went to the trouble of buying expensive equipment) or made the trip to the more remote, but safe, blacksmith. Thereafter, I was assured, *Pech im Stall* ceased.

Others' testimonies have it that once in a while a peculiar puff of black smoke could be seen shooting from the blacksmith's chimney. Whenever this happened, the blacksmith was allegedly found lying unconscious or in a trance in his home or in the smithy (residence and place of work were combined in one building). In the minds of the believers there was no doubt about the meaning of this portentous sign: when Satan temporarily left the blacksmith, he created a void that rendered the man dead—or at least unconscious. As soon as Satan entered the man's body, the man was revived.

Individuals who observed or experienced more than one of these symptoms—the misfortune in the stable, or the Devil's exit through the chimney—did not doubt that the blacksmith had entered a covenant with the Devil and was a wizard.

Hexes on the Stable

I listened to numerous accounts of curse and cure centering on farm animals. The more involved cases were discussed in the preceding pages. But some of them are so simple that they can be briefly summarized.

A peasant near Kirchenbirkig discovered that clover had been sickled off the edge of his pasture. He and his family thereupon consulted a witch who had the magic book. She asked for an object that had been in contact with the thief, and the family produced cloverleaves assumedly lost by the thief next to the pasture. With the leaves in hand the witch was able to focus her voodoo spell. A few days later, a repentant peasant came to the door of the family for *Abbitte*. His cows had started to milk blood and he begged that the hex be lifted. This was done, but not until he agreed to pay a minor retribution for the theft.*

An interesting aside to this report consisted of the answer the peasants received when they asked the witch what was written in the forbidden book. The witch would not reveal, but told them this much: "In Gottes Namen geht's nicht an, aber in drei Teufels Namen." ("It does not commence in God's name, but in the name of three devils.")

Another peasant explained the sickness of his pigs by the potatoes he fed them. The potatoes came from a neighbor who was known to have the forbidden book of Moses and who now was suspected of "having done something" to the potatoes. After the hog raiser switched to a different farmer for feed potatoes, the animals recovered.

The matter of protecting livestock against hexes was a concern so serious to the peasants that the most innocuous situation was apt to grate their sensitivity. A pastoral vignette illustrates it well. A peasant couple, wife and husband, working in front of the barn, became involved in a conversation with a woman living down the road who happened to be walking by. When disclosing with considerable satisfaction that one of their cows had just had a fine calf, the visitor expressed a desire to see it. This caused uneasiness, since the woman was a relative of the ill-reputed blacksmith of Gösswein-stein. Reputation ran by family, and the reputation of the black-smith spilled over on the visitor. The couple experienced a conflict.

On one side, they feared for the well-being of their new calf, on the other side, they were embarrassed to deny a modest request to a person about whom they had no evidence of witchery.

Hard pressed, but trying not to show it, they guided the woman into the stable and showed her the calf. With increasing apprehension, they witnessed how the woman caressed the young animal. Not knowing what to do or how to stop her, they suffered silently. But as soon as she said good-bye and was gone, they called on a woman known for her skill in the *Anfangen*. As a precaution against the possible condemnation by demonic spirits that the visitor might have introduced, the healer went through the secret ritual.

In numerous reports, peasants assured me that faith in the *Anfangen* had paid off. Most of the problems dealt with sick sows, dying piglets, dry or blood-milking cows, abnormal calving, diseased calves and dying chicks. In the few cases where they admitted that the *Anfangen* was unsuccessful, they had a simple explanation: the fault always lay with the failure to heed the admonition of the healer to refrain from borrowing or lending for three days following the ceremony.

Another vignette commences with a rather romantic scene. Two young lads made use of the age-old custom of *Fensterln*, wooing their girl friends at the bedroom windows under cover of night. (The tradition, usually good-humoredly tolerated by the community, prescribed that the visit take place *at* and not *through* the window.) In most situations, the bedrooms were on the second floor of the houses and a ladder was needed for the visit. This semistealthy business had to proceed quietly lest disapproving parents be awakened.

The two young suitors arrived at the home of two sisters, ready to woo and see what affectionate rewards might be forthcoming. They leaned the ladder against the house and were about to ascend when they heard voices through the windows. It was the mother talking to her two daughters, informing them that some peasant's cow was about to drop a calf. Since this was going to take place in a neighbor village, the mother urged them to leave in a hurry and "do what they must do." The girls replied that they had known about the matter, had already been at the peasant's stable, but could not do it. They explained that they had found a pitchfork turned upside down at the door of the stable where the cow was to have the calf and "therefore we could not do a thing."

The would-be wooers were petrified. They suddenly understood that the mother was involving her evidently quite cooperative daughters in the practice of witchcraft, trying to send them off to cast a spell on a newborn animal. The women's plans were thwarted by the precaution of the peasant, who had protected his livestock (perhaps only during this one critical night) by the old folk ritual of placing a pitchfork upside-down at the door.

Needless to say, the would-be suitors hurriedly retreated and dismissed the thought of ever again seeing the girls.

Another peasant remembered the experience he had with his father when they were on their way to a neighbor village to consult a healer.[4] Most of their animals had not felt well for weeks, cows ceased to give milk and the mother sow was killing her piglets. On the way, they encountered an old woman who stopped them and announced "turn back and go home, she [the healer] has died." The woman was a stranger to them—an odd circumstance, since the people in the nearby villages usually knew each other. Anyway, they decided to keep on going and finally arrived at the healer who was alive and well. Upon reporting their mysterious encounter, the healer told them that witchery was behind the entire affair and assured the pilgrims that, had they turned back, most of their animals, and all of their piglets, would have perished.

The healer promised to immediately start with the curing prayers and rituals (apparently without personally visiting the location of the trouble, as normally is the rule in the *Anfangen*). She gave them herbs for the animals, admonished them to observe the three-day period of nonexchange of personal belongings, and prognosed that their animals (with the exception of one) would be well by the time they arrived back at home. Upon their return home (ca two hours later), father and son found that one more piglet had died during their absence, but that the rest of the animals were showing signs of improvement. They followed the healer's instruction and enjoyed a healthy stable in no time.

An alternative source to appeal to for alleviation was the monastery in Gössweinstein. Peasant Oldtimer remembered how demonic spirits killed one cow after the other in the stable of a Bärnfels peasant. He recalled the event vividly, dated it at 1915 and remembered that a Franciscan monk was fetched to exorcise the stable. When this was done, the remaining animals recovered and the monk was rewarded gifts of farm produce. According to Oldtimer, the monk sounded the old folk tradition and reminded the peasants to observe the three-day quarantine of exchanging personal items. It must be noted, however, that this is the *only* account where clergy allegedly endorsed folk occultism. Generally, the clergy's advice was not to believe in those "superstitions," not to go to witches but rather to come to the monastery for help and counsel.

When a priest or monk (monks enjoyed greater trust among the country folk than regular priests) was called because of trouble in the stable, the performance was called *Aussegnung*, a blessing to oust evil spirits. This represented a mild version of exorcism, but not the Great Exorcism which was reserved for humans possessed by the Devil. Unlike baptisms or funerals, no regular fee was set for the *Aussegnung*. Instead, the man of God was rewarded with food and drink plus such farm produce as fresh eggs, a chicken or a goose to share with the friars back at the monastery.

Folk Catholicism intimately blended with the occult, especially with witchcraft. For this reason, priests often were drawn into occult affairs, although officially they tried to stay out of them as much as possible. One of the priests at Gössweinstein related an experience, taking place as late as the 1950s, when a Protestant farmer tried to solicit his service in exorcising the stable. Few Protestants live in Franconian Switzerland, except along the periphery. A desperate peasant of this minority, believing in the occult as much as his Catholic neighbors, turned to the priest for help when he experienced misfortune in the stable. His cows had sickened, and his explanation centered on satanic spirits unleashed by a hateful witch. The priest denied the request, judging that as Protestants the family stood outside his spiritual purview. He nevertheless visited the family and offered mundane advice, "Clean and scrub your stable." He suspected that the cause of the animals' discomfort had derived from exceptionally unhygenic conditions.

Hexes on the Person

The spells most dreaded by the peasants were of course those affecting their minds and bodies directly. There was no doubt among them that the curse of a witch could cause them to become sick or perhaps die.

The protectiveness of the peasants started when a baby was born. They hovered over the infant to make certain that no witch could get to it. Vigilance was particularly alert during the period before the baby was christened, since it was believed that during the spiritually unshielded time a witch could win the soul of the child. The witch could accomplish this by feeding the baby or simply by stroking it. If the infant died before being baptized, it was taken to the graveyard and buried without rites. Perhaps even more feared was the possibility that a witch might exchange the healthy baby for a *Wechselbutte* or *Büttling*, an ugly and usually deformed child. (This fear, however, is of an older vintage and rarely remembered by contemporary peasants.)[5]

Even on the deathbed, a peasant was not immune to the witch's malevolence. The dying person was surrounded by relatives praying to keep away Satan and the hexes of his accomplices. After death, windows were immediately opened and a few shingles on the roof lifted to give the soul unencumbered exit. Leaving the house, the coffin was dipped three times (an appeal to the trinity of God) to ensure the soul eternal rest.

Between birth and death, the susceptibility to the witch's spells was manifold—and so was, of course, the protectionism. An old belief, for example, was that bread baked on Friday, appropriately called *Freitagsbrot*, was of sacred nature and that, as long as you carried it in your pocket, you were protected against Satan's temptation and his witches' spells.[6] Likewise, frequent prayers and regularly attending the holy mass were trusted safeguards.

The earlier-mentioned peasant of Bärnfels was emphatic that "man kann nicht jedem etwas antun," meaning that not everybody can be hurt by witchery. A strong Christian belief afforded the most effective barrier against witchcraft and the salvation was the "sweet name of Jesus." Nevertheless, he conceded, if a witch got hold of a personal item of yours, even a pious disposition might not guarantee safety and the situation called for the *Anfangen*. In addition, a vast arsenal of protective fetishes (many of them already described: blessed herbs, wax chips from church candles and the shroud used at the requiem) were available to the cautious.

In spite of the protective customs, peasants could not explain many afflictions without recourse to Satan or his witches. A mild example of the affliction with lice was described earlier. Another affliction was diarrhea. But the earlier mentioned *Gfrasch* was the prime example. The infant's convulsions were often ascribed to demonic spirits marshaled by the witch, and in some instances exorcisms were performed. Several peasants remembered when a priest or monk was hurriedly fetched to pray over the convulsing child and, in cases warranting unusual consideration, perform the ritual of exorcism. The assumption was that the child was possessed by the Devil and that some witch was instrumental in the visitation.

While the above accounts come from persons who had personally witnessed the *Gfrasch* and requested the exorcism (I am thinking particularly of an octogenarian relative who as a young wife lost a child through exactly this phenomenon), some reports are more folklore than eye witness testimony—albeit folklore in which the peasants firmly believed.

One of these reports, also recorded by Brückner,[7] deals with the ill-reputed mother and daughter who lived at the foot of the ancient fortress of Streitburg. The daughter had a naive boyfriend who failed to realize her true identity. The scheming mother scratched a secret symbol into the threshold of her front door that was to cause the first male to cross to become fatally ill. It so happened that the first male to cross was not the boyfriend but his brother who meant to deliver a message. The hapless lad soon fell ill and died. The boyfriend kept visiting, not knowing the true circumstances. But one day he found the girl in a deep trance, as if dead, and no attempt to wake her was successful. He, then, realized that something was wrong, that the girl's spirit roamed elsewhere as an evil witch and would return to the body after the nefarious mission was completed.[8] The young man fled the scene in terror never to return.

It was a common belief that, once a witch crossed the door, she must be treated courteously and waited upon. The last thing anyone wanted was to offend a witch and arouse her anger. In fact, to have a witch move into your household could be beneficial; her presence protected the family and the house against harm. One such case was reported from Gasseldorf, where a witch lived with a family for 16 years. During that time, no harm or accident happened to a member of the household. However, after the witch disappeared (or, as some think, passed away), the family became impoverished, the members contracted ailments and soon the entire family died out.

The danger descending upon a person who offended a witch and yielded a personal item to her was thought to be horrendous. Sickness and even death could result. As an example, I was told by several peasants[9] of a young girl, the 12-year-old daughter of a poor widow, who mowed a basket of grass from a narrow strip between fields. In the process she lost the whetstone; it was left lying on the ground. The girl had hardly returned home and finished feeding the grass to the goats, when she felt faint. She had to take to bed and no application of folk medicine could cure the inexplicable sickness.

When the mother queried the girl from where she had fetched the grass, she realized that she had trespassed on the property of a witch. The ill-reputed person was an elderly woman, relatively well-to-do and yet known as exceedingly stingy. To this individual the mother rushed to ask forgiveness for the offense; that the curse be lifted; and the whetstone returned. But the witch was adamant. She opened a drawer to show the frightened mother the whetstone and threatened that anyone touching her property would be punished. Then she mercilessly shoved the mother out the door.

Upon her return home, the mother found the girl near death. In desperation, she ran back to the witch and, on her knees, begged her to lift the spell. She assured the witch over and over that the offense had been committed unintentionally and would never be repeated. The witch tortured the mother with a deliberately long hesitation, then announced forgiveness, but warned that future offenses would not be pardoned. The mother hurried home with new hope and found her daughter improved. Within a day she recovered completely.

Witches could cast hexes of warts. Mr. Oldtimer again offered personal testimony. As a boy he developed warts on both hands. The *Anfangen* that was initiated included special prayers and a singularly esoteric ritual. At a presumably propitious time, pig skin was buried under a dripping rainspout; after the matter was half rotten, the debris was wrapped around the warts. The man maintained no doubt that the disappearance of the warts soon thereafter was due to the combination of prayers and the mysterious—though not exactly hygenic—poultice.

Rather than inflicting direct physical harm, the witch often would harrass people so exquisitely as to cause mental anguish and/or economic ruin. The old blacksmith of Allersdorf revealed the following examples from his youth. Two young brothers found themselves under the obligation to look through the keyholes of 12 different churches at midnight. (The reason for this obligation is obscure. Although the people of the region agree that the two lads had to do it, they could not explain why.) When they came to the sixth church, a stranger gave them a pitcher and asked them to carry it along on their trip. As they continued their nocturnal pilgrimage, the pitcher grew heavier and heavier. When they finally arrived at home, a crow flew out of it. This bird, in various disguises, returned to the house almost daily. It haunted the house. Since apparently nothing helped to rid the home of the demon—because as such the bird and its equivalents were defined—the house was abandoned and the family built a new house nearby. But the spook followed, this time in the form of the dreaded *Wütenker*. Raging hordes, roaring through the sky, finally drove the plagued family from the area.

The *Hirtenhaus* (shepherd's house) of the village of Allersdorf accommodated a motley group of impoverished folk. It had room for four persons, one for each corner of the one-room cottage. All four engaged in poaching—a hollow in the forest was their favorite hunting ground. Almost midnight one Christmas Eve, while most villagers were on their way to mass, one of the poachers stole again into the hollow. While he lay in wait, a large black dog appeared out of nowhere and silently sat on the poacher's feet. Frozen with fright, the man did not dare to make a move until the bells began to ring for the midnight mass and the dog got up and disappeared. At that time the man jumped to his feet and ran home. He was so terror-stricken that he smashed through the locked door of the *Hirtenhaus* to report to his companions. They all understood the dog as a personification of a witch or demon. Village history tells that this was the end of the poaching by the Hirtenhaus quartet. They moved on and the building was torn down in 1912.

The belief in the black dog as the incarnation of a diabolic spirit is of ancient, heathen origin. This image was strongly sculpted by the Slavs who visualized the demon Cernobog as a black canine.[10] It is interesting that many names of Franconian villages and towns are of Slavic origin, suggesting that these places started as Slavic settlements and that traces of old Slavic beliefs might linger in Franconian stories. On the literary level, black dogs as the emblem of evil demons were depicted by Agrippa and, more recently, Goethe, who incorporated the apparition into *Faust*.

No culture has a monolithic grip on all its people. The culture of Franconian Switzerland is no exception; not all Franconian peasants believe in witchcraft and the occult. The proportion of nonbelievers has considerably increased over the past few decades and in the 1950s created an uncomfortable factionalism in the village of Birkenreuth. A good number of villagers believed in witches and feared the Devil; others rejected the "superstitions" and a third group preferred a sort of agnosticism, joining neither faction.

One of the village families firmly believed that demons and witches can change into black cats or dogs and that their house was haunted by them. The conviction was shared by many who commiserated the loss of sleep and the peace of mind of the tormented family.

Nonbelievers conspired "to make capital" out of what they considered the gullibility of the believers. A ringleader, Mr. Betterknow, pretended he was not merely a believer but an exorcist and offered his services to drive out the Devil, the transubstantiated witch or whatever demon it might be. The family agreed, and at the appointed nightly hour the man and an accomplice arrived at the bewitched house. Betterknow commenced his pseudorituals. At the agreed moment, the climax of the fake exorcism, the accomplice was to pinch the black cat he had smuggled into the house inside a burlap sack. It was a perfect performance: the cat, with a shrill howl, shot out of the sack, catapulted through the window, and disappeared into the night. The family was relieved; as far as they were concerned, they had just witnessed the departure of the witch. (Some thought it was the Devil personally.) Betterknow received his reward, a sum of money, and triumphantly headed home.

In his glory, he felt like celebrating and with his companion turned in at the local inn. Over beer and *Schnaps*, the two conspirators soon divulged the hoax. But the braggadocios were to pay for their boasting. They were sued and ended up paying a painful fine.

But this was not the end of the affair. The people in the haunted house, realizing that insult had been added to injury and that the demon had not yet been ejected, resorted to more trusty authority and fetched the priest to perform an exorcism, the *Aussegnung*.

Another case tells of the peasant who was bothered by a demon whenever he worked in the barn. In various disguises—sometimes as a crow, other times as a tiny shriveled forest man—the demon would insist on helping to cut the fodder—but actually just got in the way of things. The peasant experienced a conflict; on one hand, he feared for his and his animals' safety and on the other hand, he decided it was unwise to be rude to the demon. Not knowing what else to do, he finally burned down the barn when he believed the spook to be in it. While standing there gazing at the blaze and watching the barn disintegrate, he suddenly noticed a shadow and a little figure jumped on his shoulder—it was the demon, chuckling, "We were lucky to get out of there in time, weren't we?"

Another account, documented more reliably than the previous story, dealt with a butcher who was called by a farmer of Geiselhöhe to do the annual butchering. But in the morning the man discovered the strings of his work apron finely braided and understood this as the sign of a harrassing witch. He refused to begin his work, fearing there was a hex in the air. Since all preparations had been made, however, the farmer marshaled every bit of persuasiveness to get the butcher to complete the work. Finally, with great trepidation, many heart-felt prayers and a brand-new apron, the man commenced butchering. Apparently the precautions were effective; no misfortune happened throughout a day of butchering.

9

The Dimensions
of Witchcraft

A number of common elements run through most cases of curse
and cure. Their exposure will facilitate the understanding of the
role of witchcraft among these peasant people—maybe among peasant cultures in general—and is a step toward grasping the essential
nature of witchcraft. In the next chapter, then, we shall enjoy a
fuller understanding of the meaning underlying the seemingly absurd beliefs and bizarre behavior patterns.

The following dimensions recurred significantly often in the beliefs and practices of witchcraft among the Franconian peasants.

The Devil and the Witch

As part of the heritage of medieval Christianity, the peasants
believed in the reality of the Devil and his demons and that he or
they could dwell in a person. The servant of the Devil was the
witch—a malevolent person who entered into a covenant with him.

Fear

Probably most prominent among the sentiments of the peasants
was fear. Satan and his witches were feared as real agents who
coveted the life and happiness of the innocent. Major anxieties
centered on one's life, health, farm animals and economic welfare.
Compared to these four concerns, the question of eternal life and
the welfare of the soul were surprisingly secondary.

An interesting aspect of the fear of witches was that, in spite of the repugnance they elicited, direct hostility was never shown. If one was in a situation that made interaction with a witch unavoidable, the peasants acted with civility.

Life was viewed as a dangerous journey. One never knew when disaster might strike, let alone why. This fear attached itself to nearly everything around the peasants: other persons, animals, the vicissitudes of the weather, spirits and demons, Satan and, certainly, the witch.

Explaining Misfortune by Witchery

The array of misfortunes that were explained by malevolent witching was practically endless and included illness, accidents, death, disasters (from poor harvests to bad weather), ad infinitum.

Witches in Disguise

Consistent with late-medieval and Renaissance thought, the metamorphosis of witches was a real possibility to the Franconian peasants. The person in alliance with Satan could change her or his appearance and assume, for example, the shape of a crow, a black cat, a black dog, a hare, a stranger, or a seemingly harmless neighbor.

Stigmata of the Witch

One of the surest signs that a person had made a pact with the Devil was the continual use of evil books, particularly the so-called *Sixth and Seventh Books of Moses.*

Witching Can Be Learned

Although the propensity for becoming a witch was heavily associated with family background, it was viewed as an act of free will. Regardless of intent, however, there was a prerequisite: the consultation of the books of Moses the Magician.

The volitional element is not found in all magical systems. For example, among the Azande in Africa a witch is born a witch. This is presumably determined by a special witch substance in the body. The Azande sometimes verify the presence or absence of the substance by an autopsy to settle claims that a departed was a witch and had caused damages.[1]

Secrecy

The details of the black arts, as well as the healing arts (the *Anfangen*), were secret. It seems as if only those directly practicing one or the other knew the details of the skill. As a case in point, nearly everyone knew *about* the books on magic, but very few really knew them; those who did, refused to divulge details.

Obtaining Power through Personal Items

The witch could assume control over a person and his property by introducing a piece of her personal belongings into his household. Likewise, the witch could gain power by obtaining an item of personal property from the prospective victim.

The Witch's Self-Image

Witches apparently believed in their occult status and adopted a self-image in harmony with the definition that the community extended.

Witches Can Be Identified

Witches were identified by a number of different methods: noting the mirror reflection at the location of disaster or misfortune, kneeling on a special footstool during the midnight mass at Christmas, observing who would come to the house to borrow something within three days after the occurrence of an incubus (*Hexendrücken*), or identifying who would come to beg for the lifting of the counterhex.

Voodoo Method

The casting of curses and hexes followed the age-old, and in some parts of the world still practiced, voodoo style. Esoteric formulas and rituals were followed meticulously in casting hexes of punishment and revenge.

Protectionism

People could resort to a vast array of customs and rituals to prevent incurring hexes. Among the most trusted means were: complete shunning of suspected persons; prayer; having a mass said in one's behalf; making a pilgrimage; neither lending to nor borrowing from suspect persons; burning certain herbs in the stable; whipping cattle with switches from certain bushes; feeding blessed herbs to farm animals; exercising vigilance over newborn babies and having them baptized as soon as possible.

Avenues of Relief and Salvation

Once a hex was contracted, there were three possible avenues of relief. First, a person could consult a priest or, preferably, a monk; second, the services of the *Anfangen* could be initiated; or third, the victim was free to go to the witch for the *Abbitten*, asking for forgiveness and the lifting of the curse.

Impotence of Modern Medicine

Modern medicine—veterinary medicine specifically—was believed to be ineffectual against spells and hexes. The failure of a magical cure did not deter the believer from further healing pursuits within the magic cosmos.

Social Distrust

Since any individual had the personal power to enter into a pact with the Devil, one could therefore never entirely trust anyone.

This distrust was of course heightened in the case of unrelated persons or total strangers. The concept of *böse Menschen* (evil persons) was never forgotten.

Familism

The reputation of an individual was highly colored by his or her family background. The essential character of a person was believed to run in the family. Thus, possession by the Devil or making covenants with him, being a witch or being a healer were traits associated with the entire family. The most common association was the mother-daughter witch.

Nonviolence

An interesting characteristic was the total absence of violence from the occult scene in Franconian Switzerland proper—no trials. Nonviolence was a consistent trait of witchcraft, of the reaction to the witch and to suspected persons, and of the social interaction among the Franconian peasants in general.

Sexism

Most persons engaging in magic, black or white, were women, with a female/male ratio of approximately 10 to 1. This again is not necessarily universal. Among the Azande, women occupy inferior positions and are excluded from enacting powerful witchcraft. Witchery in this African society is a male prerogative.

The overly cautious among the Franconians generalized the female preponderance and at times exhibited what clinicians might call paranoid attitudes towards women. However, this exaggerated sentiment focused only on women who were strangers or suspects. It apparently was not generalized misogyny. Cases were reported in which farmers, rather than cross the path of a woman they did not know, would make a detour, all the while muttering prayers—or, as I was told in one case, curses. Generations ago, sexism was more pervasive among the Franconians. It was, for example, customary that a mother, after having had a baby, should not be seen in public for four weeks. Also, during pregnancy she was not to fetch water from the well, since it was feared it might dry up. On the other hand, she was not to be refused anything if she asked for it.[2]

Neutrality of the Church

The Catholic Church in Franconia, roughly over the past century, stayed officially out of the witchcraft dispute. It rarely offered definite opinion, let alone action.

Fetishism and Folk Catholicism

The Church did, however, provide an array of fetishes. Without specifically recognizing or refuting their usefulness in cases of witchcraft the clergy allowed for their beneficial effects on the spiritual lives of believers. Among the fetishes dispensed by the clergy were blessed medals with religious emblems, blessed herbs and farm produce, holy water, chips from the blessed Easter candle, and so forth.

In addition, charms and fetishes of less official sanction were frequently secured by peasants. A number of supposedly sacred objects were believed to be perfect remedies against hexes. Folk Catholicism combined such objects with certain rituals. For example, chips cut at midnight from a certain wooden cross in the graveyard of Gössweinstein had the reputation of keeping demons away from the house. Such items (especially chips from the Easter candle at the basilica in Gössweinstein) were sometimes part of the healer's ritual in the *Anfangen*.

People "Know": The Role of Reputation

An intangible dimension was the attitude of "knowing" who was a witch or an evil person. In other words, the character of a person was "known," although in many cases there was no concrete evidence to justify casting an individual into such a role. *Man weiss es* ("it is known") was the key phrase often used to settle questions about the character of a person. The origin of such naive claims must be sought in the subtle process of opinion formation in small communities, governed by fear and rigid images.[3] Under duress (peasant communities usually have their goodly share of it), there is much stubborn adherence to public opinion.

The Healer/Witch Duality

The pursuit of magic branched into two irreconcilable avenues. One was the enactment of the *Anfangen* by the healer whose pious disposition and personal charisma allowed her to tap divine grace. The other was the demonomagy by the witch whose covenant with the Devil allowed her to manipulate demons. There was hardly an overlap between the realms of the two figures, reflecting the age-old dualism of good versus bad, light versus dark, God versus Satan and so forth.

A modification must be made in regard to the *Hexenmeister* (also called *Hexenbanner* in some parts of Germany) whose field of operation was the middle ground between the two charismatic figures, and I suspect him more of charlatanism than honest conviction.

The Intimate Victim

Witchcraft never struck at random. The victims always were neighbors or relatives of the person doing the witching and never strangers or persons far away. The witch usually focused on persons she hated, had quarrelled with and of whom she was envious. Vice versa, accusers and victims usually defamed on the basis of similar sentiments—hate and envy. This observation agrees with what researchers have found in other cultures.

Legal Stand-off: Private Affair

Witchcraft during recent history of Franconia has been considered a private affair not subject to criminal law. After all, it was a matter of belief and we seem to have learned that belief cannot be

134

legislated.(I am obviously talking about recent times, since as late as the middle of the 18th century witches were burned in Franconia. Würzburg's authorities condemned a witch and burned her alive in the market place as late as 1749.)[4]

However, the law has intruded into certain aspects of the magical imagination. While anyone can complain that he or she was harmed by witchcraft, to lay the blame on a specific person is another matter. It can now lead to a libel suit. Of course, the risk of being sued is slim, since by common reputation, the accused may identify with the accusation and accept it. Moreover, access to the legal system was and is almost unknown. Even if a person would like to avail himself or herself of legal help, knowing how to introduce such action is largely unknown to the peasants.

Features of the Witch

While her physical appearance was largely indistinguishable from anyone else in the village, including the healer, the witch met a number of psychological traits confirming the stereotype imposed on her by Western society. The typical Franconian witch was a middle-aged to elderly woman, using strange language (magical rhymes and expletives), quarrelsome, self-centered, stingy and deriving gratification from the misfortune of others.

But otherwise a witch was a farm woman dressed in the same drab peasant cloth as anybody else; was involved in the daily chores that kept her as busy as anybody else in the village; and was married with a family.

This summary would be incomplete without briefly mentioning the absence of certain dimensions of witchcraft—dimensions that are prevalent in many other societies' notions of witchcraft. For example, the concept of the "evil eye" is nearly missing from the modern Franconian scene.[5] Few of the peasants remember it. I heard it mentioned as a trait of a witch (or of an evil person in general) less than five times in about 100 conversations with different individuals. To the Franconian peasant it is not the telltale sign of the witch that it is to people in many other cultures. I could not determine whether this concept has always been absent from the Franconian region or whether it atrophied over the generations.

Another dimension prevalent in many systems of witchcraft beliefs deals with the familiars (i.e., animals associated with the witch), such as pigs, goats, cats or hares. While this concept did in fact exist in the history of the region—during medieval times the familiars were thought to be physical representations of demons or of the Devil himself and sometimes imputed to have sexual relations with the witches—contemporary peasants do not recall it.

Equally absent is the dimension of the witches' Sabbath or any notion of a coven. The entire question of an organized collectivity of witches apparently has no meaning to the Franconians. This was an issue of major consequence during the Renaissance witch-hunt, but for some reason nothing of this notion survived in Franconian Switzerland. The Franconian witch of the past few generations was a solitary magician.

Part of the coven activity of the witch-hunt era was the noctural flight to the satanic meetings. Again, the collective element has disappeared. An individual element has however been retained, as the belief in the individual witch's ability to ride through the sky—though not necessarily in order to meet other witches—lingers on in older peasants.

The cast of the magical stage is differently assembled in other cultures. Gustav Henningsen studied witchcraft in Denmark and Spain and discovered the belief in solitary *as well as* organized-group witchcraft, both apparently existing simultaneously. "In both countries the concept of a witch organization was a real if vague one within the popular tradition. The local witches were thought to be in contact with each other and to assemble at night for secret meetings."[6] Interestingly, in both countries witches usually gathered at a spring near the village, while in Franconia they consistently convened on mountain tops.

Also the witches' manner of going about their destructive business differed between Spain and Denmark on one side and Franconia on the other. Henningsen found that witches were believed to proceed from the meeting place to prowl through the night—singly or in groups—looking for opportunities to destroy crops, kill children and sicken cattle. But, in contrast to general theological assumption and specific folklore of Franconia, Henningsen found that witches were thought of as accomplishing their evil work quite effectively without the help of Satan.

However, the sum total of similarities in witchcraft by far outweigh the differences between the various European versions. These similarities become more apparent as we move into one and the same linguistic space; a striking example came to my attention through interviewing refugees from German-speaking East Prussia. During the past generation, the fear of the supernatural was as prevalent in the all-Protestant villages of that former German province as it was in the all-Catholic Franconian communities. And the *Sixth Book of Moses* was used just as prominently to summon demons, gain riches and cast vengeance. To balance evil, *Gesundbeterinnen* (faith healers) employed beneficial magic. The similarities include such details as the milking of blood, dying of farm animals, diseases, death and accidents—all explained as witches' hexes. Even the braiding of a horse's tail was accepted as a sign of a harassing witch. Finally, black cats and black dogs were highly suspect of being incarnations of demons and witches and, according to one personal testimony, when a man died whose lifestyle was tinted by witchery, several black cats with fiery eyes surrounded his deathbed to fetch his soul.

During research excursions in the 1970s I discovered nearly identical magical world views among the village elders of the Upper Palatinate, an almost entirely Catholic area, adjacent to Franconian Switzerland, extending along the border of Czechoslovakia. The similarities included the conviction that *weiz'n*, to spook, was a witch-induced phenomenon; that the witch consulted the *Sixth and Seventh Books of Moses*; that the *Gesundbeterin* healed by prayer and secret ritual; that *Unglück im Stall* (misfortune in the stable) was attributed to hexes; and that priests were called for the *Aussegnung* (the consecration of home or stable). Case studies I obtained in this region duplicate those I have already cited from Franconian Switzerland. Among the few differences were a different dialect and, in one instance, the functioning of a witch as a midwife— something unheard of in the villages of Franconian Switzerland.

These comparisons raise an important question: How do we account for the similarities? The answer is far more difficult than might appear at first. Two major categories take on shape when we examine the various explanations—or attempts at explanation. One represents the functional theory and sees the key to similarities in occult beliefs in the similarities of the living conditions of people— regardless whether they are culturally related or unrelated. The theory grows in persuasiveness when we examine the resemblance among rural societies with primitive technology and nonscientific world view, because the life-sustaining symbiosis developing between the farmer and his animals, the fragile dependence on the soil, the vital role of the weather, and the intimate proximity between neighbors produce similar problems and difficulties. Many anthropologists believe that it is because of such identical conditions that widely separate people have arrived at almost identical supernatural constructs, including witchcraft and the witch/healer duality.

The other category rests on the theory of cultural diffusion and, most plausibly, seems to account for the similarities of witchcraft practices in the German, if not the total European, realm. Some folklorists apply the theory to a much vaster frame and maintain that witchcraft similarities between *continents* are due to common cultural ancestry, or at least to close cultural contact. Henningsen marvels over the formal and structural resemblance and particularly over the parallels in the substance of ideas between European and African witch belief, and he finds no other explanation than that which assumes that the witch mythology of the two continents "rests on a very ancient common basis of tradition."[7]

I doubt that the question can be solved at this time; the issue must await further comparative as well as historical research. I will explore this question at greater length in Chapters Eleven and Twelve.

Gössweinstein, spiritual and economic center of "Franconian Switzerland," where an old monastery and a witch-reputed blacksmith existed side by side.

Entrance to the monastery in Gössweinstein, a dispensary of advice and exorcism for demon- and witch-fearing peasants.

Chapel of the Gössweinstein monastery; foundation laid in 1630 by *Hexenbischof* Johann Georg II of Bamberg.

Among churchgoers one can spot an occasional traditional peasant costume (Gössweinstein 1977).

A chat after church in Gössweinstein, woman in traditional dress (1977).

The dolomite village of Tüchersfeld, site of bizarre exorcism.

Typical crowded acreage, sometimes inducing boundary disputes between neighbors.

Franconian panorama with religious shrine at wayside.

Cathedral and bishopric of Bamberg, center of witch mania and witch persecution during the Renaissance.

III

The Meaning of WITCHCRAFT

Is our species crazy? Plenty of evidence.

Mankind has never lived without its possessing demons and had
to have them back! Oh, what a wretched, itching, bleeding,
needing, idiot, genius of a creature we were dealing with
here! And how queerly it (he, she) was playing with all
the strange properties of existence, with all varieties of
possibility, with antics of all types, with the soul of
the world, with death.

SAUL BELLOW

The Monkey was clever, but he was also conceited;
he had enough monkey magic to push his way into Heaven,
but he had not enough sanity and balance and temperance
of spirit to live peacefully there.

HSIYUCHI (*The Chinese Monkey Epic*)

Könnt ich Magie von meinem Pfad entfernen,
Die Zaubersprüche ganz und gar verlernen,
Stünd ich, Natur! vor dir ein Mann allein,
Da wär's der Mühe wert, ein Mensch zu sein.

GOETHE, FAUST II

10

The Essence of Magic

Witchcraft is a form of infatuation with magic. And magic consists of the belief in supernatural forces that can be manipulated to achieve pleasure, protection, riches and revenge; conversely, it can be marshaled against pain and misfortune. The belief in magic is usually accompanied by an assortment of esoteric practices—rituals, incantations, conjurations, uses of charms and so forth—that are to ensure the cooperation of the supernatural forces.[1]

Here is exposed the pragmatic slant of magic. To the practitioner, the art of magic is a down-to-earth pursuit, not a theoretical exercise. It is used to do things for us that we feel we are too weak and small to do for ourselves. The core of these feelings is man's existential insecurity and the dread of powerlessness. Humans are afraid of misfortune, disease and, most of all, death. In their never ceasing search for protection they turn to magic. Therefore, the essence of witchcraft is anchored in basic human emotions that demand practical solutions.

Experts agree on the emotional foundation of witchcraft. In fact, some writers couch the connection between emotions and witchcraft in causal terms. S. F. Nadel suggests that frustrations, anxieties and other mental stress cause the belief and practice of witchcraft.[2] Similarly, Bronislaw Malinowski sees the essence of magic and witchcraft in the "reaction to overwhelming emotion or obsessive desire which are natural responses of man."[3]

Emotional needs have a way of inventing superentities believed to protect and help humanity. This is another way of saying that mankind engages in wishful thinking. This type of thinking generates an intriguing supernatural morphology. It is difficult for humans to refrain from anthropomorphizing; therefore their Gods, divinities and spirits assume personalized shapes. Before you know it, the believers reduce high abstractions to concrete figures they can readily envision. Once this is done, humans try to make deals with them. How could it be otherwise? Life is too insecure and fragile—and death is certain. As Sigmund Freud tried to impress on us: we crave palliative remedies. And the moment we engage in bargaining with these personal superpowers, we engage in magic.

In most instances the sentiments propelling witchcraft come in small caliber. They are less lofty than theological questions dealing with eternal life; rather, they assume petty forms and manifest themselves as emotions common to all humans: greed, envy and malice. Therefore, we see that the immediate drive behind witchcraft, though eternal, is not of theological origin.

Magic comes in different versions. As stated above, witchcraft is one rendition. But there are others. Most of them can be subsumed under the occult. A good part of religious thought is nothing but an elaborately disguised pursuit of magic. Yet, there are some differences between folk magic and religion that should be clarified at this time.

In a limited and only "ideal-type" sense (the sly sociological phraseology that tries to avoid saying "stereotypical") do I agree with the anthropologists and other writers who draw sharp boundaries between various forms of human approaches to knowledge and the understanding of life. These academics define magic, religion and mysticism as if they were practices of totally different species. Indeed, as mentioned above, magic busies itself with utterly empirical and practical affairs.[4] It is used as a means to achieve concrete goals and in the process remains largely unencumbered by complex theoretical underpinnings. In magical systems, practical ends determine the rules for action, whereas in religious systems ethical rules are an end in themselves and must be obeyed for their own sakes.

The driving forces behind magic's practical endeavors are overwhelming emotions seeking quick solutions to immediate problems. On the other hand, religion focuses on a total meaning of life, on life hereafter and on a God–man relationship. It is an end in itself and presumably not a means to ends.

This other-worldliness contrasts with magic's this-worldliness. Although the peasants occasionally *talk* about the potential harm that the witch's malice can inflict on their souls, curses always deal with tangible, everyday issues: physical health, weather, safety at work, animals, prosperity and so forth.

Furthermore, there usually is a distinction in terms of complexity of creed between magic and religion. Religion invariably inundates its followers with a huge body of theoretical information called theology. In many cases this theoretical knowledge requires many years—sometimes a lifetime—of study before it can be understood and consists of innumerable concepts that are logically interrelated. Religious behavior basically consists, then, of trying to match actual behavior with the theoretical rules. Rules of behavior are thus abstracted from the rules of theology. Magic, according to most anthropologists, lacks such formal structure. It has a nontheoretical practicality for everyday life and works with a set of simple rules, using them as means to immediate goals. If one thing does not work, another can be tried, and trial-and-error procedure is perfectly acceptable.

This leads to another difference between magic and religion, the difference in the distribution of power. While the believer in magic claims power for himself or herself, the religious person relegates power to God. However, the difference is not entirely clear-cut. Religious systems have spawned privileged statuses allowing some persons more access to power than others. The evolution of such power statuses is influenced by the complex theology of some religions. It requires an expert to master theology, interpret it and mediate it to the common follower. Theology thus creates special statuses that endow the incumbents with higher power and the privilege to perform the sacred rituals. While priests, pontiffs and other religious officials claim almost exclusive access to the supernatural source and insist their mediation is imperative for the common person to establish communion with God or any deity, magic as it is practiced among rural folk allows anyone who so desires to take initiative in entering into communion with supernatural forces. In the case of the Franconian peasants, all it took to enact witchcraft was an esoteric book, a pact with the Devil and the willingness to call on demons. It was in anyone's power to do so. Besides these personal decisions, no other qualifications were demanded.

Magical power is a matter of personal charisma. Religious power is a matter of impersonal status. The witch, as well as the healer in systems of folk magic, preserves the personal autonomy that does not depend on an institutional hierarchy. This magical autonomy is a heritage from Antiquity in contrast with Christianity's rigid hierarchy that insists on mediating supernatural powers. (The current charismatic movement in the Christian churches, including the Catholic Church, signifies a break with patronizing tradition and attempts to establish a direct relationship between humans and God with no limitations imposed by mediation.)

We thus recognize a number of differences between the two modes of supernatural thinking. The major differences can be summed up as follows:

Issues	Religious Approach	Magical Approach
Basic focus	Other-worldly	This-worldly
Relationship to power	Indirect, mediated	Direct, personal
Basic attitude	Passive	Active
Social standing	Impersonal status	Personal charisma
Orientation	Abstract, theoretical	Pragmatic, empirical
Formulation	Dogma	Experiment
Means/end relationship	End in itself	Means to goals
Locus of authority	Institution	Person
Sanction system	Punishment by spiritual condemnation	Punishment by material or physical harm
	Reward by spiritual welfare	Reward by material or physical well-being

These are significant differences and they apparently prompted such anthropologists and writers as Evans-Pritchard,[5] Malinowski[6] and Judith Willer[7] to differentiate between the concepts as if they did not overlap or have common ground. This is a logical conclusion by these researchers, considering the particular groups they studied. Most anthropologists focused on tribal societies with relatively monistic orientations, such as the Azande in Africa and the island societies in Melanesia.

In spite of the differences listed above, I disagree with a sharp differentiation and see at least one identical element of great importance in magic and religion. I believe this common element is as significant as the total list of differences taken together. The quality cutting across both belief systems deals with the earlier mentioned characteristic of magic: the attempt to manipulate supernatural forces for one's advantage. More succinctly, both approaches are a quest for power. And in this respect, as Pennethorne Hughes put it, "Magic and religion are coterminous."[8]

In spite of the priestly mediation in religion that makes the individual powerless vis-à-vis the divine, the believer is free to attempt personal manipulation of the divine. While magic is not always religion, almost all forms of religion take a magical approach. This apparently, is not recognized by Judith Willer who wrote an intriguing book on the differentiation of the various approaches to knowledge. She does however allow for this overlap in the case of the ancient Greek religion.[9] The Greek example represents a sort of halfway point between magic and religion. Human manipulation was explicitly possible. Olympus teemed with gods and demigods that were as much the victims of intrigues and manipulations as they were the victimizers. And humans played an active part in the divine comedy or drama, whichever it may be.

But is the example of orthodox Christianity really different? Take for example the Catholic pantheon with its similar population of deities and semideities; there is God the Father, the Son, the Holy Ghost, the Mother of God, the innumerable saints, angels, archangels and the souls of the departed for whom the Heavenly gates were opened. All of them can presumably be influenced through prayers and/or good deeds. Many of them can be called on to function as kindly mediators with those higher up in the celestial hierarchy. In short, the Olympus of Catholicism teems with approachable entities that can be manipulated. (The manipulation can also be negative—through prayers begging God to destroy enemies, particularly those singing from a different hymn book.) The endeavor to manipulate God is explicit throughout Judeo-Christian Scriptures, and the Bible reveals the human practice of trying to barter with the Lord. The pursuit of plea bargaining is not unique to worldly jurisprudence; it was and is a favorite preoccupation among the followers of the Christian tradition. It is thinly disguised as a religious practice, while, at the core, it is a magical exercise.

A believer praying to God for protection or help in solving a personal problem attempts to manipulate a superpower just as much as a witch who calls on Mephistopheles to come and "bring forth the treasures of the earth." In the former instance we plead "give us this day our daily bread" and in the latter "bring forth the treasure" (so that we can buy the bread). What is the difference?

Some theorists maintain that the prayer of a churchman is a supplication, a form of subservient request, while the spell of a magician claims to work automatically. A prayer is not endowed with the certainty of success and will only be granted if God chooses to concede; a spell has the connotation of never going wrong, unless some detail of ritual observance is omitted or a rival magician has been invoking stronger countermagic. This highlights the noncoercive nature of Christian prayer—practical results might or might not be forthcoming. It is all a matter of the will of God.

However, in the practical life and attitudes of the religious believer this distinction is largely erased. After all, is the penitent believer who enters the confessional not assured that, after he says the imposed "penal" prayers, his sins will be forgiven? Of course, there are some additional theological implications, but in the mind of the common person these prayers do carry the guarantee of the practical result of forgiveness. The mechanical efficacy of prayers— or at least their promise to be efficacious—is increased by their recitation in a foreign tongue (Latin). In fact, the chants of traditional Catholicism were built upon the assumption that the offering of regular prayer would have a beneficial effect on the soul of the praying individual. One might say that there was a magical value to mere repetition of formulas. Masses of Christian believers still today believe that salvation and the fulfillment of earthly needs can be achieved through prayer—especially through repetitive prayers, thus adding a quantitative measure to the manipulation attempt of the supernatural power. We see, then, that trust in the mechanical efficacy of prayer, on one side, and spells on the other, show great resemblance.

Even the consequences of the two approaches are similar. The true believer of either version will meticulously select those aspects out of his life that confirm the success of the manipulation attempt. The confirmation will probably take place even if the specifically desired results fail to be seen. In such situations, rationalizations will reconcile the absence of a directly visible response on the part of the superpower. A striking example comes from the research of Leon Festinger, appropriately entitled *When Prophecy Fails*, in which a group of believers predicted the end of the world and the day on which God would inundate the Earth; the only ones who would be saved were those who were prepared and waited at a certain place for Him.[10] When the divine happening failed to occur, a reconciling rationalization emerged among the believers, eliminating nagging cognitive dissonance and establishing the convenient belief that God postponed the Second Flood because He meant for them to go forth and make more converts for the time when God would complete His plan. As astounding as it may sound, lack of actual confirmation of the announced event led to the reinforcement of the basic belief. Such are humans' mental gymnastics in the face of disconfirmatory evidence.[11]

Very often, of course, confirmation of the success of the manipulation attempt is plainly visible to the practitioners of magic or religion. This is particularly true in instances of psychosomatic reactions to beliefs. The world's biggest center of psychosomatic healing through what basically is a version of magic is undoubtedly Lourdes in southern France. Catholicism's renowned pilgrimage place has attracted hundreds of thousands of believers seeking healing of every imaginable ailment. Their belief in the grace of God, mediated through this particular spot and the blessed water of a spring, has indeed resulted in "miraculous" healings.

It is interesting to note, however, that the healings or recoveries were, without exception, limited to psychosomatic problems: ulcers, functionally impaired brains, paralysis due to psychological traumas or stress and so forth. The healings concentrate particularly in the area that used to be subsumed under the old-fashioned term "hysteria." There has not been a verified case of healing where a nonpsychiatric condition was repaired, such as, for example, a missing limb miraculously replaced or a fractured bone immediately restored.

Even medical experts have difficulty explaining in detail the path of psychosomatic healing—i.e., faith healing. We do know that the brain, programmed with a strong belief, can have an immense influence on the soma and can, through neural and endocrine processes, rectify certain types of impairments, some with surprising speed.

The lack of full understanding of these psychosomatic processes has kindled speculation in miracles. This speculation is rampant among the gullible, ignorant and those subject to an acute emotional need in believing in such miracles. Ignorance and the feeling of powerlessness perennially fuel the human dream in thaumaturgy—the belief that miracles can be wrought through tuning in to supernatural processes.

In the traditional form of folk magic, this was done by summoning demons and disembodied spirits (who could assume physical forms, such as humans or animals). This practice is consonant with the witchcraft of the Franconian peasants who believe that the proper use of magical formulas and rituals (as revealed in the Kabbalistic books) would command the services of a wide variety of demons.

Faith healing derives as much from witchcraft as from supposedly altogether different religions. The power of the magical imagination is as strong as that of the religious—and psychosomatic results have been observed in both instances. Charles Mackay, one of the first to call attention to the nature of mass hysteria and its psychosomatic effects, depicted a number of striking examples in his classic work, *Extraordinary Popular Delusions and the Madness of Crowds*.

The first example deals with two young English girls who suffered, "Terrible fits, complained of pain in the stomach . . . (and) sometimes were lame on the right side; sometimes on the left; and sometimes so sore that they could not bear to be touched . . . . Sometimes they lost their speech for days."[12] Two women were accused of bewitching the children. They were tried and convicted. After the jury pronounced them guilty, the children were nearly instantly restored to health. This was interpreted as additional proof that the charge was correct. The women were hanged.

The second example deals with an Englishman who for about two years had been afflicted with a painful abscess and had not found relief through the medicines prescribed.[13] He was persuaded to consult a witch doctor, since there was general agreement that he was under the influence of a witch. The "cunning man," as the English called their witch doctor, diagnosed that he stood under the evil influence of a witching neighbor who practiced a sort of voodoo over him. To counteract the diabolic process, the witch doctor provided certain medicines and a charm to be worn on the body. In addition, the patient was to repeat the 109th and 119th Psalms every day or the cure would not be effectual. Finally, the payment of a fee of one guinea settled the consultation. Faith healing apparently took over from there and after the patient had observed this regimen for three weeks, he actually felt better. The charm that the "cunning man" had given was later opened and found to be a piece of parchment covered with Kabbalistic characters and the signs of the planets. An interesting duel of witchery ensued hereafter, as the suspected neighbor feared vengeance magic and thus felt it necessary to consult a "cunning man" on his part.

A third example by Mackay is of borderline significance in respect to psychosomatic healing, but it illuminates other aspects of witchcraft. The setting was Bamberg, the city that used to be the most important urban and spiritual center of Franconian Switzerland. It is poignant that the Briton Mackay should resort to the Franconian locale for exemplifying the psychosomatics of the witchcraft belief. It tells of the degree of witch panic that used to ravage the region. Many women were executed for presumably causing foreign objects to lodge in the bodies of those who offended them. Needles, nails, pieces of glass, bits of wood, shreds of linen, hair, pebbles and even knives and hot cinders were the articles usually chosen. These were believed to remain in the body till the witches confessed or were executed. At that fateful moment, the objects were often spontaneously voided from the bowels, the mouth, nostrils or ears. Although this may have had little to do with faith healing, it is possible that the ejection of the foreign substance was sped up or indeed effected by the victim's bodily reaction to a signal in which he or she believed. Obviously modern physicians have often had cases of similar description, where children have swallowed or injected needles which later exited through other parts of the body. But people of past generations could not account scientifically for these phenomena and thus saw in them a cause-effect relationship synchronized with the enactment and the reversal of witchcraft. As Mackay chronicled, "Every needle swallowed by a servant-maid cost an old woman her life. Nay, if no more than one suffered in consequence, the district might think itself fortunate. The commissioners seldom stopped short at one victim. The revelations of the rack in most cases implicated half a score."[14]

Another instance of miraculous recovery took place in the United States during the past generation which involved belief in the Kabbala. While the account may have been told to highlight Jewish humor, it holds a potential as an illustration of faith healing. A young Jewish man, suffering from spinal meningitis, had been running a temperature of over 106° for almost a week. The danger of death increased rapidly. While the medical doctors stood by powerlessly, the mother requested the rabbi to change her son's name, since, according to Kabbalistic tradition, the Angel of Death was armed with a summons bearing the name of the prospective victim. The change of name was believed to confuse the Messenger of Death and abort his mission. Attended by a circle of believers, the rabbi changed the patient's name from Philip to Chayim (Life). According to the medical statement, the fever broke at almost the exact time of the ritual and Chayim recovered without serious consequences.[15]

One might argue about the validity of the psychosomatic curing in these examples. Maybe the disorders would have passed at the time the imagined lifting of the spell occurred anyway. Thus, coincidence tricked the masses into seeing confirmation of their beliefs. Who can tell for certain? And the same question applies to such religious healing as taking place in Lourdes. Maybe the numbers healed out of the masses of pilgrims would have been cured without the pilgrimage. It becomes a statistical exercise. A proportion of any group of ailing humans will recover inexplicably under almost any circumstances. If recovery occurs under conditions of special expectation, it justifies the expectation to the people and confirms the explanation they ascribe to the healing.

In spite of skepticism, I like to adhere to the idea that faith healing is a reality. I believe that as yet esoteric neural and endocrine processes encourage healing under prompting symbolisms.

In sum, I see not only a striking similarity between the magical and so-called religious attempt of humans to manipulate superpowers, I also see similarity in the consequences of believing in the success of such manipulation: it is healing through faith in either case.

Again, underlying both attempts is an identical core: the human desire to escape from suffering and misfortune. The differences between the two approaches of seeking alleviation become relatively nonessential in view of the identical core.

Nevertheless, there is merit in distinguishing between a number of different characteristics, and I think I have paid homage to them earlier.

The Franconian peasants pursued a complex mixture of magical and religious views. A reconciliation was forged between humankind's ancient desire to rule by the here-and-now magic and to draw comfort for other-worldly concerns from religion. It resulted in the fusion of pagan ideas and Christian ideals. After all, the Christian's Devil assumed a central role in Franconian sorcery, and the hexes of witchcraft could be counteracted through Christian rituals (prayer, blessings, exorcism, church attendance, Holy Communion, and so forth). Similarly, the Kabbalistic books prerequisite to witching grew out of the Judeo-Christian heritage and are therefore as much part of religion as they are of magic. But most important, Satanism, a Christian heresy, became the supreme fuser of magic and religion. In short, the fusion of religion and magic satisfies the craving for magical power as well as the yearning for eternal answers.

Mysticism, on the other hand, played a minor role in the lives of the Franconian peasants. According to many social scientists, particularly Willer, mysticism is distinctly different from religion or magic in acquiring knowledge and viewing the world. It proceeds without the benefit of rational thought or integrated logic; does not offer a body of theoretical information called dogma or theology; and is an absolutely personal experience of communing with the essence of meaning. Most important, mysticism bears no claim on power. Its fascination is not with how to manipulate, but how to derive meaning and inner beatitude. It is particularly in the area of power and manipulation that mysticism differs from magic and religion.

This time, the evidence found among the Franconian peasants supports the sociological contention that mysticism is distinct from the other modes of thinking. The meditative inclination of mysticism that makes each event such a highly personalized and unique experience (as in the classic case of Zen) is relatively alien to the Franconian peasantry. This does not mean, however, that traces of mysticism are entirely absent. Among older peasants, who somehow have come to question some of the magical and religious assumptions of their tradition, I have found some degree of mystical inclination. But such persons were few, not at all "pure" in their approach, and they cannot serve as examples of the typical Franconian approach to life.

Religious dogma has thoroughly preempted mystical contemplation. No questions were left unanswered. The massive pantheon of Christianity was overbearing and left little leeway for mystical pause. Magic as folk sorcery and magic as religious creed represent the strongest elements in the peasants' world view. These peasants' uniqueness lies in the richness of their magical and supernatural imagination.

II

Witchcraft in Historical Context

Many people might assume that the historical route is the simplest approach to the question, "why witchcraft?" since it does not call for examination of the roots of magic as anchored in universal human conditions, but simply chronicles the colorful path of magic throughout the ages. But this assumption is delusive; witchcraft's history is as opaque as the evolution of an obscure virus.

There are many attempts to bring cohesion and clarity into the study of the origin and evolution of European witchcraft, but, this not being a history book, it is impossible to explore all of them here. I therefore resort to Elliot Rose, who, in his fascinating work, *A Razor for a Goat*, describes four basic approaches to the subject.[1]

The *Bluff* school assumes that witchcraft was a fabrication of imaginative minds and dismisses the whole thing as one among the many benighted delusions of the credulous Middle Ages. Friedrich von Spee (1591–1635) bravely voiced this opinion in the midst of the worst of the witch mania. He considered entirely innocent the hundreds of condemned whom he, as a priest, accompanied to their places of execution. He published his objection—anonymously to avoid being prosecuted himself—in his *Cautio Criminalis*. Since the Age of Enlightenment, scholars have agreed that the persecution was based on misconception and that the countless victims fell prey to distorted theology, a corrupt judicial system, black superstition or pure self-deception.[2] Earlier in this century, this opinion was cogently argued by the German, Joseph Hansen, and the American, Henry C. Lea, in their erudite works on the history of the Inquisition and the witch persecution.[3] They agreed that the witch mania was based on sheer illusion. Extreme proponents of the Bluff interpretation maintain that there never was a person who tried to practice witchcraft and that the victims of the witch panic were innocent and naive targets of a popular superstitious hysteria. These skeptics pride themselves on a sober, detached mind, but they generally lack a convincing theory that comes to grips with any contrary evidence. In their behalf, I must, however, admit that during the age of the witch mass neurosis, they alone often stemmed the tide of hysteria and, by publicly expressing incredulity, saved innocent lives.

The *Knowing* school is less skeptical, knows that "things are going on," and often revels in sensational reports about Sabbaths and Black Masses. It resembles the more primitive forms of inter-denominational polemics, "such as Protestant pamphlets about the confessional and Roman Catholic pamphlets about Freemasonry."[4] Its interest is on a level that satisfies the popular thirst for the sensational, visceral and pornographic, including such phenomena as Devil worship and the sexual rituals associated with it.

The *anti-Sadducee* school not only knows, but also believes. (This school opposes the Sadducees who originally were a sect of Jews around the time of Jesus accepting only the five books of the Law and disbelieving everything not taught therein, e.g., immortality, the resurrection and the existence of angels.) Throughout the ages, staunch defenders of orthodoxy have rallied to this school and made it a widely accepted approach to the supernatural. In their cosmology, witchcraft is a very real activity dealing with real supernatural elements, and their leaders are ever prepared to argue the point militantly. This theory has a vast popular following and everyone confessing that "there may be something to the old tales of witches casting spells" is an anti-Sadducee. It is a view of witchcraft that enjoys popular revival today. (Actually, has it ever been absent from any era of modern history?)

The history of the anti-Sadducee approach is sprinkled with notable writers. Most of them are members of orthodox creeds and strikingly illustrate the old axiom that superstition thrives as a parasite on orthodoxy. A celebrated example is the late Rev. Montague Summers, an Anglican clergyman who converted to Catholicism and continued to call himself "Father." He wrote a number of books on the subject of witchcraft and concluded that it represented Satanism which deserved persecution.[5] The witch was the Devil's servant and the coven a formidable menace.

Dennis Wheatley is another anti-Sadducee who, unlike Summers, labeled his occult writings novels and enriched Western civilization, particularly his publishers, by selling over 40 million copies of his 80-odd books, including such bestsellers as *The Devil Rides Out* and *The Forbidden Territory*. His effort netted him close to two million dollars and was meant to be as a novel on Napoleon—fiction based on fact. Wheatley, who in 1977 took leave of us for the realm of ghosts, rendered a tremendous amount of penmanship spreading the anti-Sadducee slogan among those who wanted to believe witchcraft and, at the same time, be entertained. No need to add that the movie industry also made its occult contribution and cashed in on the anti-Sadducee craving of millions of Americans by delivering *The Exorcist, Rosemary's Baby, Carrie, The Omen* and other accounts of supernatural evil. While we can only speculate on how seriously the producers regarded their work, the broad masses perceived its value greater than entertainment and set attendance records.

The *Murrayite* school inspired on higher intellectual levels— apparently where fascination with history mates with belief in the romantic. Starting in the 1920s, many educated people were persuaded that Professor Margaret Murray was revealing the true history of European witchcraft. The theory possessed an enviable completeness and left hardly a question unanswered. But many historians found it highly speculative. Egyptologist Murray had a captive audience when, in the 1920s, she rose to a chair in social anthropology at the University of London and added a sophisticated addendum to the popular anthropological genre of the time, spearheaded by such works as Sir J. G. Frazer's *Golden Bough* and later by Robert Graves' *The White Goddess*.

Murray, in her first work on the subject, *The Witch Cult in Western Europe*,[6] portrayed what she chose to call Ritual Witchcraft of a highly organized pagan cult, rich with rituals of fertility and reverence for Nature. The Dianic cult expressed itself exuberantly and quite viscerally, the religious meetings exuding gaiety and group ecstasy. (Murray's description evokes memories of Durkheim's explanation of the origin of man's religiosity. The experience of ecstasy, generated through group excitement, was felt to be a religious experience, the descent of the "spirit," or God, upon the individual.[7] The witches of the pagan world, Murray claimed, formed covens of 13 and met regularly at their Sabbaths. Each coven had a leader dressed in animal disguise: the hide, hoofs, horns and skull of the bison or other powerful animals. This priest commanded his followers' worship, since they believed him to be an incarnation of a god.

Murray's main point is that, with the coming of the Christian era, the pagan ritual fell into disrepute and was tainted with Devil-worship. In fact, followers of Murray's theory believe the physical description of the Christians' Devil—hairy, hoofed, horned—derived from the coven leader's appearance. Pre-Christian gaiety was viewed as an attack on the austere values of Christian society; their meetings were construed as orgies; their leaders were seen as devils, and the delirious emotions of power and ecstasy exhibited at their rallies were believed to be a sign of possession by the Devil. According to Murray, the witches persecuted by the Christians were remnant believers of the Old Religion who remained faithful to their creed even under torture—an ironic parallel with the Christian martyrs.

Murray's theory that medieval witches worshipped a mysterious Horned-God of extreme Antiquity has been severely attacked.[8] Among her critics, Rose provides a point-by-point exposure of inaccuracies, so that, in the end, Murray's theory stands exposed as one big error. The criticisms can be summed up under four labels. First, and most importantly, Rose demonstrates that Murray misrepresented the pre-Christian Celtic religion, mistaking Roman syncretism for pure Druid religion. While the ancient Druids limited their supernatural cosmos to an animistic form, the invading and converting Romans introduced their anthropomorphisms that allowed for gods, demigods, half-men, half-goats, the Devil—all symbols we find reflected in witchcraft. In short, Murray's assumptions cannot be authenticated by reliable historians, and therefore are suspect of having been selected on the basis of a theoretical bias. The critics take Murray to task particularly for what they feel is a completely unfounded speculation on the existence of covens and the formation of a self-conscious organization. She was accused of confusing what medieval people thought happened with what really happened, and of failing to show that there actually was an ancient witch cult.

It is interesting to note in this connection that many tenets of the alleged witch cult were extremely unclear throughout the Middle Ages, but were defined and expanded during the Renaissance. For example, the concept of the witches' Sabbath was only present in rudimentary form in the witch mythology of the medieval theologians and lawyers—not fully defined until about 1600.[9]

Second, Rose believes that even if there might have existed an ancient Druid witch cult of the nature described by Murray, she failed to account for the interval between the Roman invasion of the Celtic realm with the accompanying conversion to Christianity and the early witch trials. There is no reliable evidence of continuity of an ancient cult from Antiquity to the Middle Ages.

Third, Murray's research focused only on England and Scotland. Even if her observations in that locale were to be trusted, generalizations about other regions, for example, the central-European arena of witch mania, would be of questionable validity.

Finally, Murray's selection of her "evidence" is late—based upon material dating from post-trial time, which allows for the possibility that abstract ideas about a witch cult could have penetrated public life and encouraged role playing of the Inquisition-created image of the cult's behavior—a behavior that really had no model in preceding periods.

Historian Julio C. Baroja elaborated this last point and suggested that the origin of witchcraft is largely found in the Middle Ages' confused appropriation of the beliefs of a previous era and the distorted application of them.[10] No direct physical continuation of the cult took place, and the victims of the witch scare were targets of a Christian invention. He suspects an artificial, though admirably literate, attempt to introduce the mythical personage of goddess Diana (or goddess Holda in the Germanic context) into the medieval visualization concerning witches. Baroja agrees with Murray that there was a flourishing cult of Diana among European rural people during the 4th–6th centuries, just before Christianity's assumption of power. Of particular significance were the women who lived in the forest and were viewed as priestesses. (See discussion at the beginning of Chapter Four.) Diana herself was visualized as the deity of the fields and woods—a goddess riding through the skies. This pagan figure, Baroja suggests, may have inspired Christians to see in her a devil—and the witch was born. Thus, the medieval witches were unwitting descendents of the forest priestesses, the representatives of Diana or Holda. But the succession was forced on them and therefore of mere symbolic and not affiliative nature.

This theory would explain the Christians' insistence (especially at the onset of the witch-hunt) on the witch's feminine gender. Baroja

162

tries to document the notion of the Diana-derived witches by pointing to Romanic and early Gothic art and architecture where witches
were depicted riding on more or less fantastic beasts. Such decora-
tions, he believes, referred to the Dianic cult.[11]

To this European pagan cult of certain female deities—or, more
likely, to the late medieval *belief* that there was such a cult was
added the Christians' obsession with the Devil. This concoction
created the belief in black witches. It also created a split in the
formerly unified personage of the antique sorceress who could
celebrate both good and evil. The witch came to represent only the
evil side of the sorceress. This left a void for the good (or white)
magic. The healer woman of rural societies apparently stepped into
the void and so completed the ancient wholeness. Two personages
were now required to recreate the holistic magician of Antiquity.
Thanks to the savage interference of the medieval Catholic Church,
we now have a duality—a sort of schizophrenic imagination of
magical power.

Joseph Hansen, considered a reliable historian of witchcraft, held
that the image of the witch evolved from two basic sources: the
Nordic European—emphasizing weather and animal magic and the
witches' eating of humans; and, since the 13th century, the southern and southeastern European influence, basically alien to the
Celto-Germanic style—stressing the Sabbath, nocturnal flight and
the pact (including sex) with the Devil.[12] The corrupt product that
the Inquisition concocted from the confluence of these two cultural
streams led to the witch panic and subsequent persecution.

So, we see a competition of two basically different historical
interpretations of the question of origin of witchcraft. One speaks of
physical continuation of a cult and the other of an invention, a
symbolic process. Murray's cult theory appears to be on the losing
side. Nevertheless, Murray acquired a following among such well-
known writers as Pennethorne Hughes, Hugh R. Williamson, and
Peter Haining—writers who, unlike the anti-Sadducees, present
their ideas as anthropological and historical data rather than a
religious manifesto.[13]

From a belief in the existence of a witch tradition of Antiquity to
a belief in the teachings of that tradition was a small step for many
people; Murrayites easily transformed into anti-Sadducees. This is
tempting because both groups think of witches primarily as members of a cult and accept roughly the same *external* picture of the

cult. That means they agree on what witches *did* at their gatherings—but not necessarily on what witches *were*. Among the many who have been inspired by Margaret Murray and taken the additional step to anti-Sadduceeism was Gerald B. Gardner, founder of the witchcraft museum on the Isle of Man and "master of all the witches." Gardner described the pre-Christian wicca in his books, *High Magic's Aid* (1949) and *Witchcraft Today* (1954),[14] and founded many witches' circles in England. This does not mean, however, that all Murrayites supported these groups. Peter Haining, for example, believed that they exploited superstitiousness.[15]

The clash between theorists assuming an ancient witch cult and their opponents is not all there is to the historical discussion. There is a host of additional theories, and Rose sarcastically noted, "I should be surprised if nobody has put forward a theory that would make witchcraft the last degenerate trace of spiritual sciences that came to us from lost Atlantis."[16] Among the more serious theories are those dealing with the causal role of misery, scapegoating, guilty conscience, religious strife, misogyny and the "industry" of witch persecution. Many scholars would, however, deny that these notions assume the status of etiological theories and call them supplemental theories or mere tidbits of interesting information which, though true within a limited scope, amount to no more than focusing on special aspects.

Some writers, for example, emphasize the role of communal despair of the masses during medieval times when heinous wars, the plague and other epidemics ravaged Europe. Collective misery needed scapegoats and witches often were convenient targets for venting frustrations.[17]

The 1692 Salem witch-hunt is often used as a vivid illustration of the misery-scapegoat theory. A bleak mood prevailed in Massachusetts during that period—the French waging war, Indians on the warpath, taxes intolerable, smallpox raging, pirates endangering commerce and the winter cruel. Men and women had been brought up in a narrow evangelical cosmos, assigning an important role to the Devil and his agents, the witches. Witchcraft accusations by a group of young girls snowballed into the arrest of 150 people, trials for 31, and the death sentence for all 31 (seven men and 24 women).[18]

To jump backward in time (not to mention place), we are reminded that the visitations preceding the era of the witch-hunt in central Europe included the threats of the Turks and Swedes from the outside, religious dissension, wars and the plague from the inside. At least two historians, focusing on the Franconian region, singled out the plague and ascribed to it a causative role. Friedrich Leitschuh felt that the 14th-century plague, killing about 25 million Europeans or roughly one quarter of the continent's population, was popularly interpreted as a satanic plot and fueled the witch panic. The hysteria started in France in 1470 and soon spread across the rest of the continent. Johann Looshorn reminded us that in 1611, just a few years before the peak of the witch scare, the plague raged with particular savagery in Franconia.[19]

Hannsferdinand Döbler sees another stimulating factor in the scientific progress made during the Renaissance. It was a time of scientific breakthrough when new insights into mathematics, medicine, astronomy and various natural sciences threatened old convictions raised questions about the almightiness of God, his angels, the centrality of our Earth, and the general anthropocentricity of the medieval cosmos. The feeling that traditional values needed protection generated a highly defensive reaction on the part of the conservative authorities—ecclesiastical as well as civil—and resulted in measures that included the persecution of scapegoats, helpless people branded as witches.[20]

Some researchers describe witch accusations leveled against certain segments of the population as an effective move to eliminate undesirable opposition and/or religious minorities. In at least one instance, the witch-hunt evidently served as an effective tool of the Counter-Reformation, since the Catholic authorities singled out Protestant citizens for witchcraft accusations, confiscated their property and executed a number of them.[21]

But I consider this example highly unrepresentative of the witch-hunt. Generally, the religious communities persecuted within their own ranks and rarely stepped outside. In the history of Franconia, for example, I have not come across one instance where a person other than a member of his own religious community was accused and prosecuted. Interestingly, Würzburg, with one of the most rabid persecution manias, had a relatively large Jewish community, but never a trial against a Jew. Jews escaped witch suspicion and witch persecution because they lived in their ghetto, had their own laws and judges and, as non-Christians, could not be defined as witches but only as sorcerers.[22] (During the later years of the Renaissance, they were banned from the city—but not because of witchcraft suspicion.)

Other historical data, showing that witch persecution was not a scourge that one religious community inflicted on another, come from the Lutheran camp. Luther himself believed in the reality of witches and, in 1540, at a time when in the rest of Germany the witch persecution was underdeveloped, four witches were burned in Wittenberg.[23] The tradition within the Lutheran realm was more than ably continued by the Saxon jurist, Benedict Carpsov (1595–1666), who prided himself on having signed 20,000 death sentences of witches and on having read the Bible 23 times. Carpsov, published his major work, *Practica Rerum Criminalium*, in 1635 in Wittenberg. It became the *Malleus Maleficarum* of Protestantism and responsible for the definition of one of witch persecution's greatest legal absurdities: the *Vermutungsbeweis*, "proof by surmise."[24]

There are additional theories trying to explain the excesses of the witch-hunt: Elliot Rose's is one of them. But I question the correlation he feels existed between the virulence of the witch-hunt and weak ecclesiastical discipline. Conversely, he argues that where authoritarian hierarchy was ensconced, there were no excesses. This theory is refuted by examples in the history of Franconia: Würzburg and Bamberg had unwavering ecclesiastical authority and yet the witch-hunt was at fever pitch there. One could also use the example of Saxony with Lutheran rule entrenched and the witch persecution running high. Even Sweden with its monolithic Lutheran rule had its share of the witch scare. Likewise his argument that witch-hunting grows in intensity "wherever two or more religions were struggling for the mastery"[25] (a religious supremacy of one church) appears untenable in the face of evidence we have of religious dissension in England, Hungary and Bohemia, where extreme religious disharmony existed without generating any particular zeal for hunting witches. Also during the time when the Swedes occupied Catholic Franconia and struggled for political authority, the witch-hunt decreased sharply.

Another historian advancing the religious-strife theme as cause for soaring witch persecution was Hugh R. Trevor-Roper. He generalized, "Every major outbreak is in the frontier-area where religious strife is not intellectual . . . but social."[26] His hypothesis is not supported by Franconian history. All-Catholic Franconian Switzerland and the county of almost all-Protestant Bayreuth-Ansbach existed side by side. This frontier area showed a considerably lower persecution rate than the nonfrontier areas of Bamberg and Würzburg. The city of Nürnberg and its immediate environment, the middle of a frontier area, exhibited one of the lowest prosecution rates of any Franconian city.

I am supported in my observation by Alan Macfarlane who sees the motive for witch persecution not in religious fervor and competition, but in the crises in small communities "generated by quarrels between neighbors that come from the incidents of every day."[27]

Additional refutation of Trevor-Roper's argument comes from Gustav Henningsen who studied Danish and Spanish witch trials and discovered a far greater number of cases brought to trial by ordinary citizens concerned with *concrete* witchcraft crimes than concerned with religious issues. He concludes: "Thus the witch-hunting of the Western European villages throughout the 16th and 17th centuries had very little to do with religious persecution. It was in fact entirely related to the function of witch belief in the social life of the time."[28] It may be true, however, that theology suggested a framework of rationalization to the people, but was not, in itself, the persecutory motive. Trials were usually the tail end of local social psychological issues.

Further refutation of the religious causation comes from Monter's study of the southwestern part of the Jura Mountains, Franconian Switzerland occupying the extreme northeastern spur. Monter rejects Trevor-Roper's notion as "nonsense when confronted with Jura evidence."[29] While Monter's region was certainly a religious frontier area, it seems to have had no religious strife at all. Almost identically to Franconian Switzerland, the County of Neuchâtel slumbered peacefully throughout the age of religious warfare—yet had a regular and constant flow of witch trials during the age of the mania. Another similarity between the two Jura regions appears to have been the abrupt decline of witch trials at the moment military occupation threatened or actually took place. "Under these circumstances, very few people were tried for witchcraft. Whether this was because the inhabitants knew that the hand of God and foreign mercenaries were responsible for their miseries and had no need to blame them on witches, or simply because their legal machinery was not in working order for prosecuting them, seems impossible to determine."[30] In any case, just as in the dioceses of Bamberg and Würzburg, trials abruptly declined during the worst crisis of the Thirty Years' War when the Swedes threatened and then actually temporarily occupied the bishoprics. Franconian history seems to indicate that religious conflict was a strong deterrent to and not an instigator of prosecution, while, in contrast, during undisturbed years the machinery of witch persecution ground at an all-time high.

The idea that trials were but the consequences of a dramatic form of religious persecution becomes untenable, and the reasons for their fluctuations must be sought elsewhere.

Some historians see the roots of witchcraft anchored in the profit motive. This primarily involved persons in powerful positions, such as witch finders, inquisitors, judges, priests, bishops and executioners. But it also applied to the common people. In Franconia, the denunciation of a person (neighbor, relative, public figure or whoever) would net the accuser 10 guilders for the public service of bringing a suspect to the attention of the authorities. If the suspicion "proved" justified, an additional bonus was paid the accuser from the fortune of the condemned. Defamations coming from children were equally acceptable.[31] In short, the "industry" of witch persecution had a vested interest that tended to perpetuate itself.

One voice was bold enough to lay responsibility for profiteering at the feet of the highest authority of all: the Pope. Canon Döllinger, a 19th-century Catholic cleric, assembled an arsenal of learned arguments to denounce this papal abuse.[32] Standing out amongst these alleged corruptions was the papal responsibility for the invention of Satanism. Once the invention was accomplished, anthropomorphic formulations followed to stamp mostly innocent women as allies of Satan. The helpless victims were used to confirm the Christian notion of the Devil.

Many more aspects depicting the historical evolution could be added. After all, there are thousands of volumes lining the walls of libraries throughout the world that deal with this matter. But the historical explanation is insufficient.[33] In fact, it is not an explanation. It is merely a description. According to my sociological bias, trying to understand the witchcraft phenomenon from a historical viewpoint alone is as superficial as answering the question, "Why do you have a tumor?" with, "Because it developed six months ago." Or, as Arthur Miller once said, "Life tells us more about history than history about life."

The basic "why" of witchcraft transcends historical and geographical boundaries and addresses itself to fundamental human conditions. One of the basic human conditions is the need to explain experiences. The more dramatic an experience, the more insistent the desire for an explanation. And the Franconian peasants' experiences included all the dramas that our species can muster: pain, poverty, hunger, loneliness, disease and death. It becomes the function of religion and witchcraft to explain and justify misery and insecurity in a perilous universe and, furthermore, to provide means of comfort and control. Religion gave holistic meaning and taught acceptance; witchcraft demanded power. Witchcraft manifested the age-old and never ending dream of *Homo sapiens* to wield magic to overcome misery and powerlessness. The axiom that magic takes over when control over the environment is weak poignantly applies to the Franconian peasants.

Misery has many faces. To the old peasants it was the narrowly won fight against hunger and cold and disease. It was the often lost fight against exploitation and social injustice. To the modern anomie-haunted individual, it is a sense of purposelessness that can drive him or her to despair and suicide. (Again we see a reason for the regression to the occult by modern people: the promise of power over an environment of anomie.) The reasons for turning toward witchcraft were forms of misery that differed for the older and the younger generations. Traditionally, without doubt in the case of the Franconians, witchcraft was primarily an attempt to overcome physical misery; now, particularly in the urban setting, it is an attempt to overcome psychological misery.

But, of course, this is an oversimplification. Witchcraft serves many more purposes than this statement suggests, as we shall see.

12

Witchcraft as Response to Human Needs

What is so peculiar in the human condition that creates witchcraft, or magic in general? Does the tenacious celebration of the black art indictate that it meets a necessity of human existence—social as well as individual—which must be satisfied in one way or another? Many social scientists have pondered this question, and as it is difficult, within the framework of this book, to do justice to all their ideas, briefly sensitizing the reader toward the major conclusions must suffice.

This discussion focuses primarily on the period when witches were no longer persecuted, and the functions of witchcraft in village life may have somewhat changed during the transition from persecution to tolerance. Since an examination of the shifts in the functions of witchery over the past 600 years is too vast a project for coverage here, I intend to limit my investigation to the past two or three generations. However, even within this relatively short time, belief in witchcraft has constantly declined, affecting its various functions and revealing which of them are the most persistent. Even if I were to talk about a period without change, there would be no simple depiction of the social and psychological functions of witchcraft. Its role in community and personal life is manifold, with many levels of beliefs and participation.

For example, some functions are clearly tied in with the social structure of the community, guarding it against upheaval and punishing those who would disturb peace and order. As we shall see, witchcraft as a social sanction system—justice magic, so to speak—and as boundary maintenance between good and evil are such social-structural functions; they guarantee that the community will remain a viable and ongoing process. On the other side, witchcraft takes care of a number of very personal needs, providing explanations for vexing idiosyncratic problems and unintelligible and frightening events as well as assuaging uncertainty, anxiety and fear through the imagination of personal power.

Of course, the functions aiming at the community and those aiming at the individual are never totally separated; they usually overlap and have dual purposes. For instance, witchcraft as vengeance magic has a typical hybrid function with the community as well as the individual benefiting from it: on the collective level it serves as a social sanction system encouraging orderly and cooperative interaction between members of the community; on the personal level it provides release of aggressiveness and the feeling that justice is being done—not a small feat, considering the deep satisfaction and the mental health benefits that undoubtedly derive from this. In other words, on the community as well as on the personal level, witchcraft can assure a state of equilibrium and peace.

Here, under a number of subheadings, I will discuss a medley of witchcraft functions, and, I am confident, the reader will easily recognize to which party of social existence the various functions cater—in some cases to the community as a whole; in other cases to the individual; and in probably most instances a case could be made that the function caters to both.

Explaining Natural Phenomena

One of the oldest and most enduring functions of witchcraft emerged from the desire for explanation. Anthropologists agree that the magical imagination became an institution in part because it quenches the thirst for answers to occurrences that otherwise lack ready explanation.[1] There is hardly anything more intolerable to human beings than to be persistently disturbed without being able to know why and without being able to define the situation in a manner that allows countermeasures and relief. In short, a situation of anomie deprives of meaning, and that is unbearable to humans. Witchcraft belief facilitates the labeling of unintelligible happenings and the coping with the anxieties that grow out of these events. The resulting explanations change *anxiety* (a typical reaction to unknown danger) into *fear* (the reaction to known danger), which humans can handle more adequately. The encounter with a vexing situation then proceeds with a minimum of uncertainty, and stereotyped or routine responses take care of the contingencies of life. In other words, witchcraft ultimately creates institutions and traditions—routine approaches, acknowledged by the community, that presumably solve the problems at hand.

And many problems there were! Among people such as the rural Franconians harsh environmental conditions, poverty, poor santitation, malnutrition and primitive technology prepared the soil in which witchcraft and the magical aspects of religion were implanted. Their suffering included high infant mortality, mysterious diseases (stubborn illnesses without apparent natural etiology) among themselves and their animals, inadequate medication, overwork and exposure to the elements. In addition, there were the less tangible psychosomatic impairments brought on by too much worry and too many fears. Finally, death often came without visible or intelligible cause.

One of the most lucid writers on this subject was Charles Mackay. He wrote,

> "There are so many wondrous appearances in nature for which science and philosophy cannot even now account, that it is not surprising that, when natural laws were still less understood, men should have attributed to supernatural agency every appearance which they could not otherwise explain."[2]

Many "wondrous appearances" that emerged among the Franconian peasantry were frightening and disastrous. People were unable to recognize natural causes and resorted to witchcraft explanations. Here are a number of examples, most of them mentioned earlier.

Probably the most frequent complaint about witch-caused trouble concerned the milking of blood. The scientific explanation is found in the bruising or straining of the mammary glands caused by using cows as beasts of burden. With the abandonment of beast-powered transportation, fewer such injuries occur. The peasants interpret this change supernaturally: fewer cows milk blood because fewer hexes are cast. A peasant said, "Milking blood used to to be more common because people fooled around with witchcraft and put curses on each other's animals."

The reader might opt: a misplaced correlation or rationalization, on the one side, and scientific progress on the other. However, for many peasants, this presumed correlation supports the validity of their magical beliefs.

The childhood disease called *Gfrasch* was caught up in a similar correlation and explanation. As stated earlier, the convulsions usually were symptoms of malnutrition (particularly lack of calcium), a condition that has largely been extinguished through improved nutrition. Cases of severe diarrhea, once inexplicable, now can be medically explained. Through the mass media and the availability of doctors, the peasants increasingly learned of natural causes. Another "wondrous appearance" was the miscarriage by peasant women who, by all appearances, were healthly and had no family histories of such trouble. What they did not know was that a disease from animal droppings could cause spontaneous abortion; ocular toxoplasmosis can be contracted from close association with pets or farm animals. Even if spontaneous abortion did not take place as a result of the infectious protozoa, the risk of the child being born with brain damage or other nervous system abnormalities was great. Such defects, again, were inexplicable to the rural people, and a magical interpretation was tempting.

One of the reasons why the peasants of this corner of Franconia adhered so persistently to supernatural interpretations of medical problems was the delayed availability of medical doctors and veterinarians. It was not until the 1910s and 1920s that such professionals settled in the area and then only in a few towns (such as Pottenstein and Betzenstein) which were hours away from most villages. Prior to that time, medical service (if that is the right term) was rendered either by the barber (again, only in a few towns) or by the women who knew the *Anfangen*. Veterinary service was often rendered by butchers (who boasted expertise in "internal medicine") and cattle traders. However, even after regular doctors and veterinarians were available, most peasants distrusted them and preferred the services of the folk practitioner.

The differential infection with lice can also be medically explained. One human out of two in close physical proximity may be favored because of different blood or skin chemistry—nothing "wondrous" at all if one knows the biochemical details.

Another supernatural explanation was given to the incubus, or *Hexendrücken* as the Franconians called the nocturnal oppression.

It has not been until recently that this complex psychosomatic phenomenon has been understood. In the nebulous state between waking and sleeping, the brain confuses fantasy with reality and produces impressions of haunting clarity. What apparently happens is that the body is in the paralysis of deep sleep and the brain is ready for the dream experience, but the eyes remain open. This constellation of conditions seems to convince the brain that the dream vision is concrete reality. The brain cannot accept a message as a dream if the eyes monitor openness. These visions, which psychologists call hypnagogic imagery, are suspected as the basis of certain folklores.

There seems to be surprising similarity of incubus images among different cultures. First of all, this type of experience was almost always interpreted as a supernatural experience: loved ones long since passed away, deities, angels, or, as I was told in one case, Jesus personally descended upon the sleeper. This belief has an Appalachian version wherein an elderly mountain woman in Virginia claims to suffer from an incubus with a penchant for equestrian sports: a witch frequently descends on her and rides astride her through the night. The tormented woman believes in the reality of her nocturnal excursion and in the morning shows the dirt under her fingernails as proof of having had to gallop on all fours through the woods with the witch on her back.

Researchers have found the "old hag," the witch or an ugly old woman, to be the most persistent vision. Donald Ward found that "the 'old hag' has been a common world-wide vision for years, and that it may be responsible for the tradition of the nightriding witch that still persists in many societies, especially in farm communities."[3] These incubi are usually believed to be demons that descend upon the sleeper's chest. As described in Chapter Eight, the witch incubus is part of the Franconian tradition.

The Franconian peasants misunderstood another natural phenomenon, the sink hole (or doline). A sink hole is a natural opening in the ground connected with subterranean chambers and caves, frequent in such areas of limestone formation as Franconian Switzerland. At certain times, conspicuous air currents move through the hole and a faint howl can be heard. While these are symptoms of changes in air temperature and air pressure, the natives had no scientific explanation and took them as signs of the presence of demons and witches. One such place, near the village of Elbersberg, was shunned and feared.

However, labeling the unintelligible is only one form of witch-craft's explanation. There are actually two levels of giving explanations. One, as described by the examples above, deals with explaining phenomena for which the people lacked a natural or scientific explanation. Another deals with explaining the causation of events that, in their immediacy, had a perfectly natural explanation. Villagers, for example, understood the "how" of an accident but wondered about the "why." It became a question of supernatural "motive" behind the natural occurrence. Thus, an illness could be recognized as natural, but the causation or meaning behind it as supernatural. When my grandmother suffered with a hernia, almost everyone understood what it was—a physiological disability. *But why did it happen?* Did a malicious witch weigh down the basket when she tried to lift it? Or, did God punish her for some mistake or sin?

These questions raise far-reaching issues. They suggest that even with advancing scientific insight, the functions of witchcraft do not necessarily end. The question of the ultimate "why" or "motive" cannot be answered by science. It becomes a supernatural question. Therefore, the advance of science and technology does not provide automatic immunity against the penetration of witchcraft or other magical beliefs.

Nonetheless, we may assume that the first level of magical explanations, the prima facie misinterpretation of natural phenomena, will subside with increasing scientific knowledge. Maybe the abortion-inducing micro-organism will be understood as just what it is and does—causing the loss of a baby. But who willed it? Who, in a sense, caused the cause? A witch? These questions may well remain valid ones even for people in a scientific era. Once more: there are two levels of causation—one the direct and natural, and the other the "motive" cause.

The question of "motive" leads to the highly individual nature of witchcraft. It was always a personal issue and taken as the explanation for a particular, as opposed to a general, misfortune. Although the theory of bygone eras held witches responsible for such general problems as bad weather, floods and epidemics, the scrutiny of actual events (including the trial proceedings during the era of the witch-hunt) shows that they were blamed for *specific* damages only.

Witch accusations still follow this rule among the Franconian peasants. Witchcraft answers the anguished questions, "why me?" in lieu of abstract and academic answers dealing with probability theory, statistical chance or sampling theory. Most rural people had little abstract inclination, they lacked the academic penchant for statistical thinking and asked questions of personal immediacy. A peasant might say, "I have swung the scythe a thousand times. Never did I have an accident. Why did the scythe slip today and cut my leg?" While the peasant perfectly understands the natural cause-effect relationship between the scythe and the injury, the explanation on the second level is not so simple. "Why me?" "Why today?" These are questions demanding answers; for many the answer was "because someone cast a hex."

These insistent questions seem universal in cultures lacking the modern obsession to explain by statistical principle. In such societies, the people need alternative answers, a need in keeping with the universal human desire for certainty.

To give a soothing answer becomes the function of the folk healer or the shaman. The patient who goes to a healer or a shaman wants to know, "Why am I suffering?" or "Why have I been singled out for this?" It is not uncommon for an African tribesman to have a Western practitioner set a broken arm and then visit his shaman for the "reason" behind his misfortune.[4] It is also not uncommon for the Franconian peasant to scientifically repair a broken-down wagon and then wonder why it happened and who cast the hex. In the same vein, the modern psychiatric patient asks the same type of questions and wants reasons and the lifting of pain.

In sum, then, witchcraft and sorcery function as personal explanations for personal misfortune. One writer goes so far as stressing that personal tensions and misfortunes are the *etiology* of witches.[5] Ascribing total causation of the witchcraft phenomenon to this one function may be overdrawn, however. The picture is more complex than that. Yet, it is certainly true that explantions based on witchcraft enabled the countryfolk to account for tragedies.

The belief that misfortune can result from witchcraft found relief in a contrasting parallel: the belief that fortune can be restored by a healer. Since the creator of misfortune, the witch, was human, people invented a counterfigure to satisfy their craving for controlling or reversing misfortune. The stage was now set for the drama of the two antithetical characters to begin. They now proceeded to contest each other's claim over the fate of the innumberable seekers of explanation and salvation. This drama emerged from the primordial feeling that there must be a just cosmos, ordered and coherent, in which evil can be balanced by good and suffering by solace. The moral of the play was that by reading the correct script, you could achieve security amidst danger. In the end, one way or another, you would be part of a moral order.

With this in mind, we are touching on the next function of witchcraft.

Social Sanction System

Once, when I described to my students the functions of witchcraft as a social sanction system guarding correct social behavior among the villagers, one of them mused, "Why didn't the authorities leave the belief system alone? It worked better than most formal rules of conduct, and it was nonviolent and egalitarian." The student may have had a point. Since witchcraft was a system in which anyone could participate, it erased social class, sex, age and other differences. It offered a universal system of justice that was open to all members of the community, independent of social or material power. Since witchery was never aimed at random but was a meaningful tool used to punish those who wronged, it encouraged people to be honest and helpful in their community. (It is noteworthy that these social qualities were not necessarily extended to members of other communities or strangers—in short, to "outsiders.")

An example of a community that cements its cohesiveness by exactly this type of "justice magic" are the gypsies. While there are of course numerous reasons, such as family bonds, economic security and the perils of a hostile surrounding, that explain why they strive to preserve solidarity, these ubiquitous nomads safeguard discipline within their bands by fear of punishment for disobedience or deviance—the punishment being hexes or curses. This tradition is institutionalized among the gypsies and executed by a council's formal decision to impose a hex.[6]

Among the Franconian peasants, witchcraft has never evolved to quite such formal and overtly functional status as among the gypsies, but it has contributed to social justice and social order. In a sense, it functioned as the salvation of the underdog. The belief that the poor, the destitute, the aged—and even animals—can, if treated unkindly, retaliate with witchery, is an effective protection for these otherwise powerless members of the community. Witchcraft can rightly be called *justice magic*. In other words, witchcraft served as an instrument for preserving a style of social interaction that was fair to everyone. It was an equalizer exerting control over all statuses. Magic could be used to retaliate against tyrants, be they the landlords and counts who owned the Franconian soil, or the constable in the English villages (there was none in the Franconian villages) who enforced law and order and often pressed the young men into military service.

It is, however, a negative sanction system, because fear of punishment is its core. A positive sanction sytem would be one where kindness and honesty are explicitly rewarded, and one might prefer it as a superior system. But where in the world have humans succeeded in working out such a system? Most likely, it has remained a Utopian scheme.

Perhaps the tradition of believing in magical punishment explains the nearly total absence of crime and violence among the peasants of Franconian Switzerland. Similarity to this type of pacificism was found among the Indians of the American Southwest where the conspicuous social timidity of the Zuni, Taos and Laguna has been interpreted as a consequence of their belief in witches.[7] These Indians accepted insult without fighting back and refused to defend themselves in quarrels. Because they believed that there were many witches and that their identities were uncertain, they deemed it wise to observe an inoffensive stance. This behavior is almost identical to the Franconian peasants' behavior and became explicit when villagers dealt with suspects, who were shunned rather than harmed.

Another cross-cultural example is the earlier mentioned study of the Azande by Evans-Pritchard. He found that suspicion of witchcraft usually revealed a bad conscience on the part of the person who suspected. Witches were seen as personal enemies, "And if some misfortune befalls you, you at once run through in your mind as possible witches the names of those with whom you are on bad terms, such as those who bear you a grudge for some action in the past."[8]

Since the Franconian peasants believed that, if wrong-doing occurred, magical forces could be immediately commanded by anyone, it was a more effective system of sanction than their Catholic dogma which allowed for forgiveness of evil deeds at a later time— such as confession officiated by a priest. The fear of being punished in the hereafter was greatly alleviated by the punishment being remote and, if forthcoming at all, in the far future. What's more, there always was the possibility of being officially forgiven through the sacraments of the Church. These tenets of the Catholic dogma lacked the effectiveness of witchcraft's immediate retaliation if you harmed your neighbor. As any psychologist steeped in conditioning and learning theory can tell us, the immediacy of response (in this case punishment) is far more effective in determining behavior than abstract promises or threats to be enacted later.

The unconscious establishment of witchcraft as a social sanction system is testimony to the human inclination to invent what is functional for survival. Thus the "truth" or credibility of a belief depends, at least in part, on its functionality. This means that humans tend to hold as a true belief or a "fact" something that is functional. Drawing from Franconian examples, I discovered that the folklore of the ghost guiltily lugging around the property marker he had deceitfully moved was more credible to the peasants than the story of the nymphs in the crystal springs. The first belief served a fucntion: deterrence against cheating. The second belief had no particular usefulness and was thus regarded a myth.

The peasants' belief in witchcraft was, among other things, a property-marking device, ensuring respect for individual property and safeguarding rules for borrowing, lending, trespassing, thieving and poaching. In a sense, it was a perfect reinforcement of what Robert Ardrey called the territorial imperative. In so doing, it contributed to order in human interaction.

Again, I must stress that the power to cast a curse was not limited to a "fulltime" witch but could be enacted by anyone (provided he or she had access to the witching books or knew the secret formulas). Therefore, *any* wrongdoing could result in punishment. To avoid becoming the target of a hex, it was best to mind one's own business, observe civility and be honest and helpful toward your neighbors. Such cooperation and friendly behavior assured a good measure of safety. Parents trained their children early in life to observe courteous and cooperative manners, lest they offend a witch. The identical motive in child rearing was detected in unrelated cultures. The Nyakyusa of Africa, for example, warn their children "not to be quarrelsome or boastful or brusque in their manners, lest they arouse the anger of witches."[9] If you wanted to increase the margin of safety, you observed caution with whom you traded or whom you invited into your home.

This social sanction system operated effectively even if a peasant was not in the public eye, since demons or the witch's clairvoyance could detect wrongdoing under almost all circumstances. Moreover, the traces of animism found among the Franconian peasants made for compliance with prescribed social behavior since the innate spirit in an object might react to theft or to any sort of mistreatment. We also must keep in mind an earlier mentioned tenet of Franconian witchcraft, namely, the belief that retention of another person's belonging gives the power of hex to the rightful owner. Thus a believing peasant would think twice before he or she would engage in a property violation: a perfect mechanism for enforcing honesty!

If some wrongdoing, a misdemeanor at worst, did occur (such as sickling off a basket of clover from a neighbor's pasture), it was settled through informal sanction, often through the type of voodoo magic described in earlier chapters. The offender would usually deem it prudent to come to the injured party, ask forgiveness and make restitution. That usually settled the matter.

Strong family bonds played a role in respecting the rules of witchcraft. Since wrongdoing could result in hexes detrimental not merely to the individual offender but also to his stable, household and other family members, a person had the responsibility of behaving correctly in order to avoid harm to his family or clan. Thus, we see how the fear of witchcraft reinforced familism: the individual's feeling of responsibility for the entire group kept him or her from behaving antisocially and risking harm to the family. For example, a peasant would be reluctant to steal from the neighbor's orchard because of the fear of a revenge hex that might dry up his cows and cause hardship on his children. In this way, witchcraft encouraged ethical and family-centered behavior.

The belief that the whole family might suffer through the imprudence of one member was widespread and has been observed in many folk societies. The Zulus, for example, explain misfortune by resentment growing out of quarrels and expressed in hexes. They feel justified in ascribing guilt for the quarreling to their women, because they are outsiders to the lineage.[10] While the Franconian peasants did not rationalize so narrowly and blame only women (they are bilineal, i.e., lineage is figured through father as well as mother), they did mull over the question of which family member wronged someone, offended God or generally was so sinful as to bring misfortune to the family group.

180   Witchcraft demands a price in return for its service as a sanction

system. And the cost may well balance its benefits. Fear of attracting curses because of envy by others was among the factors that impeded progress—technological and otherwise—among the Franconian peasants. This in part explains why the region has remained backwoodsy for so long. The nature of witchcraft includes a stagnation factor. The fears associated with witchcraft immobilize those who could be innovators and leaders in matters of bettering living conditions. This timidity, in conjunction with other factors, explains the destitution that characterizes the history of the peasants of this region. The region suffered from extreme poverty until recent social-welfare legislation by the West German government improved conditions.

The stagnation role of witchcraft is visible also in other cultures. Clyde Kluckhohn, the anthropologist, for example, found the Navajo unwilling to assume or continue responsibilities of leadership because of similar motivations. He cited a Navajo man with a fine record of judicial decisions in the tribal court who told his friends that he was resigning because "his father's serious illness was traceable to witchcraft activities occasioned by resentment at some of his decisions as judge."[11]

The Navajo's phobia of witchery is by no means a thing of the past, such as the 1940s when Kluckhohn made the above observation. Identical fears created problems in 1977, preventing the tribe from filling the position of tribal prosecutor and causing several hundred cases to be dismissed without official action. The belief that prosecutors invite revenge-hexes cast by those they prosecute or by the witches hired by the defendants was one of the main reasons why no one was willing to assume the post. Previous prosecutors visited medicine men every other month for ceremonial sings to ward off spells and restore spiritual harmony.

So far we have discussed witchery as it functioned as an available tool to virtually everyone in the community. But what about the person defined as a witch? There have been some witches who failed to adhere to rules of socially responsible witching. These are the cases where power corrupted. Such persons assumed a reckless attitude and used witchcraft not as a tool to maintain order but as a tool of personal malice and greed. They may also constitute cases of strict role playing where persons, once they were defined as witches, assumed a role that apparently demanded violation of the form of witchcraft that was not only tolerable but even useful to the community. In some of these cases, pathological personality traits may have been operating. Therefore the extraordinary activity of the witch and the ordinary witchery of the villagers were two different things. (More about this later.)

Boundary Maintenance

The witch has been used as an example of boundary maintenance. Social scientists refer to the abstract social boundary that separates good from bad behavior. The assumption is made that if you have a clear conception of evil behavior it is easier to visualize the parameters of proper behavior. Crime or any other form of deviance, as is theorized, may actually perform a needed service to society by uniting people in a common posture of indignation. The deviant member of the community violates rules of conduct that the others respect, and when these people are drawn together to express disapproval and outrage, they reinforce their solidarity.

The sociological celebrity who first suggested this theory was Emile Durkheim;[12] when sociologists discuss deviant behavior, they, almost without exception, feel obliged to refer to his theory. It has become regulation reference. But whether the theory reflects reality and contributes to understanding of human behavior seems to have become a distant purpose. I fear their homage to Durkheim is more stylistic than substantive. Nevertheless, I will explore the theory's pertinence to the Franconian situation—in case an additional insight might be gleaned.

The values and the behavior of the witch directly oppose those of the community. Her witchery has little to do with justice but is motivated by avarice and personal sordidness. Generalizations about the witch's behavior proclaim the opposite of respectful conduct, condemn such behavior, and by so doing assert the proper cultural values. The witch establishes an image of what people should *not* be. By counterimage, people derive standards with which they can identify. In essence, thus, the image of the witch made a contribution to the maintenance of social order. The stereotype of the witch goes into gory details describing her vices. During the peak of the witch-hunt era, she was often accused of bestiality, consorting with the Devil, being a traitor to the community and to her own clan, and also slaughtering and devouring children. Of course, the legacy of this extreme portrayal is eroded, and the modern Franconian witch's malfeasance is confined to casting hexes and generally being meddlesome.

In any case, it seems that a funciton of witchcraft lore was the affirmation of solidarity by dramatically defining atrocity.[13] In so doing, it defined the in- and the out-group. And this, after all, is the fundamental goal of "boundary maintenance." Witchcraft lore strengthened the community's consensus of what was good by describing the deviant: secret and malicious activities against the property, health and lives of neighbors. To add to the stigma, the witch was accused of such abhorrent deeds as listed above. Still today, the witch is thought of as engaging in malice for its own sake, sexual perversion, possession of forbidden books and speaking in strange tongues.

The threat of being classified outside of the boundaries accepted as community standards served as conformity pressure. Undesirable habits could be controlled by accusing a person of witchcraft. Many a peasant woman may have suppressed her inclination to be stingy, quarrelsome, isolationistic or heretical (deviating from Church dogma) because of the fear of being called a witch. People's anxiety of having witches' characteristics ascribed to them resulted in a striking polarization of the members of the community. Those classified as witches usually followed the role and behaved accordingly—there simply was no escape from consensual validation. Those classified as good villagers stayed as far away from witch connotations as they possibly could. In sum, boundary maintenance stimluated polarization of reputation and conduct.

But, there is a complication: the kind of person accused of being a witch resembled the person claiming to be victimized by her. Both tended to be boastful, meddlesome and unsympathetic toward the needs of their neighbors. The reader may recall the typical example of the Meddler family in Kirchenbirkig who alternated victimizing and being victimized. With the exception of a certain neighbor, the rest of the community was uninvolved. This showed that witchcraft—regardless of whether one was hexing or being hexed—was self-selecting; it attracted a certain type of aficionado. This client could easily change from being the victimizer to being the victim, and vice versa. Either way, he or she mainfested himself or herself as the deviant type and was punished by either being accused of or victimized by witchcraft; either way, the ambiguous person belonged to the darker side of the polarization.

Seeking Power

Many psychologists think the feeling of powerlessness is the most significant motivation of human activities. Any sort of magic, especially witchcraft, can be seen in the perspective of the quest for power. As mentioned earlier, the urgency of the quest is the essence of witchcraft.

Alfred Adler recognized the feeling of inferiority and discouragement as core elements in the neuroses of many societies.[14] Although not specifically addressing witchcraft, Adler would most likely define it within his theoretical framework as a neurotic striving for power, as a compensatory means to make misery bearable, and as a placebo for insecurity. Most of all, he would call it an inane overcompensation for ignorance. According to Adler, a sane striving for power to overcome helplessness and misery lies in the direction of greater social justice and a more objective understanding of the cause-effect relationships underlying misery.

In a similar vein, Ernest Becker looked at human life as basically a power drama.[15] Humans want to be secure, deny death and extend life; and witchcraft can be viewed as a symbolic gesture of such omnipotence. New strength comes to humans through the illusion of magic. It is the ancient Faustian dream: to buy life through whatever method, and if that should mean eternal death—a paradox emanating from self-conscious human nature. However, in the long run, Becker thought, real human strength must be drawn from the knowledge that fear is not weakness but is acceptable and lies at the heart of life.

Alas, Adler's and Becker's advice was not heard by the Franconian peasants as well as by people elsewhere in the world, who continue their fascination with witchcraft and desperately seek to alleviate powerlessness. At their stage of cultural and scientific-technological development, witchcraft evidently was the best means of generating a sense of power.

The prescientific approach to power can be observed in different societies, the similarities are striking. Above all, they do not rely on a scientific-empirical world view but on an attempt to participate in the presumed powers of nature and supernature—the two often being indistinguishable. With the exception of the talent inherent in the woman skilled in the *Anfangen*, access to supernatural power is open to everyone and rarely requires the mediation of an expert, such as priest, scientist or psychiatrist. Besides the Franconians, this is true, for example, of the Fox Indians' manitu concept:

> Power is universally available and unlimited; it does not have a unitary locus; it is everywhere, and equally available to all.
>
> The possession of power is temporary and contingent; it is not a quality permanently possessed by any human being, but can be gained and lost, possession being demonstrated by successful performance in specific situations.[16]

What are the weaknesses that stimulate preoccupation with power? It is the unreliable environment, (physical as well as social), the fragile organism and unavoidable death. Gaining control over these frailties is the aim of magic.

To experience misery and become fully aware of it takes—as most other things in life—time. This explains to some writers why the typical witch was middle-aged when she developed her demoniacal powers. Baroja, for example, thinks that a woman tended to become a witch "after the initial failure of her life as a woman; after frustrated or illegitimate love affairs have left her with a sense of impotence or disgrace. This, in turn, drives her to use improper means to achieve her ends."[17] As she grows older, her situation changes. Her sensual desires and the accompanying frustrations decrease; now she derives gratification from seeing younger women embark on the same avenue and embrace a life of inverted values. For them, evil becomes good, secrecy meaningful, normal social interaction insignificant and power all-important.

Although they probably never heard of Friedrich Nietzsche, he spoke for them when he wrote, "What is good? Everything that heightens the feeling of power in man, the will to power, power itself. What is bad? Everything that is born of weakness."[18] Nietzsche despised religion and thought it a product of slavering weakness; he preferred magic and thought it a noble expression of strong persons. While the philosophical esthetics of these ideas were probably wasted in the case of the Franconian witches, these peasant magicians apparently agreed that there was greater power in magic than in religion. Somehow they sensed that religion drains the world of power, whereas magic amplifies it in those who are daring.

The sociology of Karl Marx and Friedrich Engels would have been of similar appeal to the witches.[19] The helplessness of the masses, epigrammatized by the adage "religion is the opiate of the people," was challenged by the folk magicians. They tried to overcome the dull euphoria of the "opium," reached for the power of magic and attempted to take their fates in their own hands.

Sigmund Freud's tinting of religion as a largely impotent and delusional "palliative remedy" does not apply to witchcraft. Instead of taking solace in the hereafter, the individual with magical imagination seeks here-and-now power. The magician abhors what Freud called the common man's

> . . . system of doctrines and promises which on the one hand explains to him the riddles of this world with enviable completeness, and, on the other, assures him that a careful Providence will watch over his life and will compensate him in a future existence for any frustrations he suffers here.[20]

Freud saw this belief as patently infantile and inimical to a realistic world view. Common man is mired in the need to seek palliative remedies for a range of dismays—"life as we find it, is too hard for us; it brings us too many pains, disappointments and impossible tasks."[21] While religion inhibits the discovery and fruitful application of creative measures, magic takes corrective action. When confronted with misery, the folk magicians sense the impotence of religion and prefer the power of magic. They realize that religion merely consoles, whereas magic empowers.

Like Adler and Becker, Freud advocated a more humane and scientific lifestyle to reduce the need for erecting religious consolation as a futile monument in the first place. The lifting of religious restrictions would give us a freer hand in building a saner world. However, Freud was realistic and admitted that certain frightful events, such as disease and death, can never be overcome and therefore tend to cause acute anxieties—unless soothed and explained by religious beliefs. He therefore added a charitable note, admitting that devout believers are highly safeguarded against the risk of certain neurotic illnesses and that their acceptance of the universal neurosis (religious dogma and fear) spares them the task of constructing a personal one.[22]

Freud could have mentioned the role of magic: it shortcuts the tortuous detour of religion and offers more than a palliative remedy. Rather than merely consoling neurotic anxieties, it attacks the very problems causing the anxieties—but, of course, in the process creating others.

Channeling Aggression

Almost all communities suffer from some degree of internal tension, be it brought on by the frequently lost battles against the elements or the frustrations growing out of interpersonal relations, and aggression seems to be an effective mechanism for releasing such tension.

The witch played an important role in this context. This unfortunate role grew to a horrendous crescendo during the era of the witch-hunt and lingers in such rural communities as Franconian Switzerland. Whatever functions the witch had, she certainly served as a scapegoat. In other words, her stigma facilitated the channeling of all sorts of free-floating anger and anxiety. The epitome of scapegoating took place during the 17th century when thousands of witches were condemned and executed to purge the community of distrust and anxiety. It gave desperate emotions, generated by unusual disturbances, a focus. Public enemy number one was identified and an attempt was made to eliminate her so that all could breathe more freely. Apparently this type of communal purging is a perennial propensity of all societies and such recent witch-hunts as the Nazi persecution of the Jews and the McCarthy blacklisting of "the Reds" exemplify the social tendency of placing blame.

This tendency is sometimes described as a need for catharsis of pent-up frustrations. People suffering from suppressed anger are everready to respond explosively to a target if social consensus is achieved to legitimize the victimization. (This notion is consonant with the age-old frustration-aggression model that has been promoted by some psychologists.) How effectively and conspicuously therapeutic such release of anger can be was demonstrated by the most radical means of scapegoating: by killing. The best cure of ridding oneself of the harm a witch had inflicted was to have her prosecuted and executed. Thus, the point of many trials was not merely that they afforded the gratification of revenge, but that they positively relieved the victim. Keith Thomas cited examples in which there was immediate restoration to health of a group of children when the Warboy witches, suspected of having cast hexes, were executed. The assumption of the days of the witch scare was that "the malifice (harm) is prevented or cured in the execution of the witch."[23] The vehemence of the prosecution is thus more understandable because the trials were credited with a genuine therapeutic effect on the victim. Moreover, in those days, it was the only procedure which the theologians approved, as they prohibited all forms of countermagic.

The special applicability of witchcraft for channeling aggression arises when aggression is directed against persons whom one should normally exempt from one's wrath—such as one's neighbor or clansman. Accusation of witchcraft was a means of breaking this immunity. How else could the frustration of a neighbor reaping rich harvest in his or her orchard, while one's own dried up, be expressed? The neighbor did nothing wrong. Hating the neighbor for the riches was not a reasonable excuse, but one could hate him or her because he or she was a witch. This was an acceptable, and perhaps plausible, manner of coming out with negative emotions against a person of intimate acquaintance and gave license to disliking with impunity someone he or she should ordinarily not dislike. The insinuation of witchcraft was an expressive guise for getting back at the envied person, perhaps the only feasible way to express animosity and inflict punishment. Such accusations were often motivated by the parties' unwillingness to reconcile, and were instigated with the intent of rupturing an unrewarding relationship. Thus a legal claim was rarely the central issue, although sometimes it may have been construed that way. This principle is amply supported by examples of curses and cures among the Franconian peasants. Nearly all witch accusations were between neighbors and relatives because something went sour in the relationships themselves. The most evident example of relational malfunction and an accompanying accusation of witchcraft derived from the two brothers when they shared the common homestead and found it difficult to settle property questions (see "Intrafamilial Witchery" in Chapter Eight).

This principle was also borne out by research in other cultures. Max Marwick showed that, among the Cewa, accusations of witchcraft served the purpose of terminating relationships when they had become insupportable, "Witch beliefs and accusations of witchcraft serve to blast down dilapitated parts of the social structure and clear the rubble in preparation for the development of new ones."[24] Similarly, Philip Mayer found that the Gusii aimed witchcraft accusations to change the tenor of a relationship—usually breaking it up—while they aimed other accusations and quarrels at reconciliation after certain adjustments were made.[25] Clyde Kluckhohn found that the Navajo use witchcraft accusations to legitimize hostile feelings against persons toward whom such feelings would otherwise be forbidden.[26]

Another source of tension from which can emerge a particularly perverted aggressivity is guilt. Guilt feelings can sometimes be alleviated by channeling hostility against the very agent responsible for having created the guilt feelings. In the end, it is the aggrieved person, not the one who caused the grievance, who is held to be at fault. Such are the everyday emotional gyrations of human beings!

We have seen this principle operating in several examples cited in Chapter Eight. It was usually the person who had first violated the tradition of cooperation and charity who later claimed to be bewitched. After the Meddler woman denied the neighbor the *Back-ofen*, she found reason to label her a witch. In another episode, soon after the Meddler matriarch refused kinsmen a favor, she found cause to accuse them of witchcraft. A faction of the Small-farmer family, after having refused cooperation in common projects, accused the other of witchcraft.

This pattern reveals a serious breakdown of a major function of witchcraft: the encouragement to be cooperative and pacific. Guilt feelings are the Trojan Horse in witchcraft's functionality, can overpower the function of sociability and turn people into defamers. A large majority of documented witch cases reflect a pattern where an indigent was sent away empty handed, perhaps mumbling some malediction, and where in due course something went wrong in the household for which the slighted person was promptly blamed. The witch suspect, hence, became the doubly wronged party. Keith Thomas cites a typical case:

> Margery's neighbors were denying her the charity and help which was traditionally required. When shutting the door in her face, however, they were only too well aware of having departed from the ethical code. They knew that they had put their selfish interests before their social duty. When some minor accident subsequently overtook them or their children or animals, it was their own guilty conscience that indicated to them where they should look for the cause of their misfortune.[27]

This pattern was observed by other researchers. Alan Macfarlane's study of Essex witchcraft showed that witchcraft accusations usually aimed at women who had begged favors from the more well-to-do members of the community, had been refused, and then held responsible for wreaking revenge by witchcraft. This pattern deals with the failure in moral obligation, with the resulting guilt complex and the attempt to legitimize failure in the guilt-ridden individual. In plain words, it deals with a guilty conscience trying to whitewash itself. Consequently, one might conclude that with fewer instances of guilty conscience, there would be fewer cases of accusation of witchcraft. This is precisely the conclusion at which Macfarlane arrived when he studied the replacement of the idea of charity as a personal Christian duty by the idea of charity as primarily the responsibility of formal institutions. The researcher noticed that, concomitant with this attitude change, there was a steady decline of witch persecution in England.[28]

Sometimes an intricate twist of hostile emotions lies at the core of a person's motivation to point at others and call them witches. And it has little to do with guilt feelings. These are persons who are fundamentally alienated from their community, have lost meaningful social integration, feel hostile and project their hostility upon others. This means, their hostility tricks their perception into believing that others are just as hostile toward them. If witchcraft is part of the community's life, they may claim to be victims of curses. Kluckhohn made striking observations about the projection process among the Navajos,

> If exaggerated fear of witches arises in a person partly because he feels aggressive and thus suspects that others feel the same way toward him, witchcraft "illness" is to this extent dependent upon a loss of rapport with the society—the penalty for giving way to feelings the society does not permit.[29]

This projection-and-becoming-victim process may help us understand some of witchcraft's victims described in Chapter Eight. I am reminded of the Meddler people who showed feelings of alienation and hostility, projected these sentiments unto their neighbor and, in the final effect, felt victimized by the neighbor's curses. I see reflections of the Meddler matriarch's aggressiveness and estrangement even in her posture in a wedding picture. (See photo on page 53.) Out of the entire party, she was the only person to ignore the camera and provocatively stare at the Schneider matriarch known as a healer. In addition, she violated convention when she, as the bride's mother, failed to wear the customary kerchief.

Some writers suspect a special kind of hostility operating in witch accusations. It is the issue of misogyny. Wholesale animosity toward women could conceivably be vented by accusations of witchcraft. Wolfgang Lederer sees this motive, veiled as it might be, as a significant component of the genesis of historic witchcraft.[30] He believes that men tend to oscillate between love and fear of women and pleads for an end to the ancient hostility and the beginning of reconciliation. This plea is long overdue, for the oscillation goes back at least to the 15th century when erudite men debated not merely the role of women in the black art but their essence as creatures. Medieval scholars earnestly considered the possibility that women might be lacking in reason and therefore be more vulnerable to demonic influence. There even was serious musing as to whether women were truly human and reputable scholars concluded "mulier non homo." Medicus Johannes Hartlieb's *Buch aller verbotener Kunst, Unglaubens und der Zauberei*, published in 1456, was, among other things, a manifesto of sexist attitude and attributed the higher frequency of witchery among women to their less stable characters allowing the Devil to use them.[31]

Apart from this highly impressionistic theological-psychological opinion, it is difficult to explain the persecution of witches by general misogyny. If we really attempted such explanation, we would run into logical problems. Among them are, first, the historical fact that witch accusations were not exclusively directed against women but also aimed at an important number of men; second, that accusations were made not exclusively by men against women, but, on the contrary, mostly by women against women; and third, that just as there was the evil witch, there was the esteemed healer, thus balancing the attitude toward women—at least among the Franconian peasants. Nevertheless, Lederer's argument deserves attention and further research, if such historical questions can be adequately researched at all.

Before we leave the issue of misogyny, a related opinion should be introduced. Monter deduced from his French-Swiss study that witch accusations were projections of patriarchal social fears onto women who lived apart from the direct control of fathers or husbands: the defenseless elderly widows or spinsters.[32] While this observation does not necessarily advance a theory of *general* misogyny, it bases male hatred on a *specific* misogyny: the fear of women not under their control. Monter complements his observation by pointing out that, since this suspected group of citizens had no recourse to physical revenge or defense, it was feared that their revenge might be magical. Here, again, we see at work the guilty conscience, dreading the consequences of its own prejudice.

Finally, witch accusations have been suspected as the result of tensions and fears created through social upheavals of basically extracommunal origin. Lyle Steadman interprets the Hewa witch killings on New Guinea not so much as an act of hostility but as a symbolic gesture to warn outsiders to leave the community undisturbed.[33] He feels that such substitute killing—unconsciously aimed at outsiders who cannot be reached—explains a good part of the witch-hunt during 17th-century Europe when Reformation and Counter-Reformation forces confronted each other. At this time, the interpretation is precisely what the author says it is—a hypothesis.

We have talked exclusively about witch accusation as a form of channeling hostility. What about aggression management from the witch's point of view? The person practicing the black art can release hostility directly by casting curses on envied or hated neighbors or relatives. An annoyance might motivate her to cast a curse, which may prompt the victim to come and do *Abbitte* (ask forgiveness). The witch would most likely negotiate a settlement and lift the spell. So, in the end, social equilibrium is reestablished. In understanding the aggression-channeling function of witchcraft, the main focus, however, is the accusation of witchcraft and not the enacting of it.

We are now at the end of our discussion on channeling aggression and I must warn the reader against deriving wrong impressions. It would be naive to exalt witchcraft as a mechanism from which only salutary functions emanate. In many, if not most cases, witchcraft accusation does more to promote fear and intimidation than dissipate pent-up feelings of aggression and animosity. Witch accusations worsen social relationships. If this type of catharsis is expected to improve communal life, it is a largely unwarranted expectation. Such accusations embitter people more than placate them, and the instances where feelings of hostility are relieved are probably more than matched by instances where feelings of anxiety are aroused. These irritating side effects of witchcraft have been observed in other cultures, as, for example, among the Navajo, where the socially disruptive effects of witchcraft were evident.[34]

192

Witchcraft, at best, keeps a community on an even keel, provides enough sanctions to make it an ongoing process. In the absence of other explanatory and social-sanction systems, witchcraft may be the only or major alternative to cement the community together. As such, it is beset with the shortcomings typical of social institutions in general: sometimes they work and carry out their intent, and sometimes they fail in their constructive intent. In a sense, the forces immanent in witchcraft form a two-edged sword, sometimes cutting the Gordian knot with one easy stroke and solving the problem at hand—and sometimes worsening the problem or even slashing the unwary and innocent. Although witchcraft is in essence a system meant to avoid harm, and its implementation in form of rituals, incantations, taboos and regulations makes the believer feel at least partially protected, it creates as many fears as it alleviates.

One could argue that in many respects witchcraft creates its own balance of curses and cures, a repertoire wherein the two sides cancel each other—a useless exertion of energy. On one side a fear is created and on the other side an antidote is provided for exactly that fear. For example, a woman fearful that a neighbor has cast a spell upon her, and as a consequence suffers psychosomatic problems, might find instantaneous relief by going to the neighbor, begging forgiveness, and having the curse lifted. In such fashion, the Gordian knot is easily cut by power of witchcraft. But, one must not forget that the knot was tied by witchcraft in the first place.

Even if we look at frustration release from the witch's point of view, we have to admit that the benefits were limited. It was probably the aggressive individual who resorted to witchery, while the nonaggressive refrained from using it, experiencing it as a threat, a disruption of relationships and a source of anxiety.

13

Witchcraft, Drugs and Mental Illness

Although a full grasp of the meaning of witchcraft necessitates the larger perspective of social, cultural and theological conditions, some aspects of witchcraft have also been understood as mental pathology. Witchcraft as an outgrowth of deranged minds must be considered on at least two levels. First, the level of the personality of the witch; and, second, the level of the personalities of the witch's adversaries: the secular and ecclesiastical officials, witnesses, victims and other members of the community. These levels are, of course, interrelated. I will begin by looking at the personality of the witch and raise the question of mental illness in her behavior and self-perception.

Personality Conditions of the Witch

Behavior that is symptomatic of mental illness has often been attributed to witches, and the first to so declare and brave the popular witchcraft myth was the Rhineland physician, Johannes Weyer (1515–1588), who in 1563 published *De Praestigiis Daemonum* (About the Glitter of Demons).[1] In it, he defined witches as suffering from melancholy, feeblemindedness or hysterical-epileptic convulsions, who should not be punished—least of all, with capital punishment. Weyer would have fitted perfectly into the *Bluff* school (see Chapter Eleven) as he believed that witchcraft was pure imagination—either imagined by mentally ill persons or practiced by heretics who, he conceded, might be rightfully punished by fines

194

or temporary banishment from the community. The Englishman, Reginald Scot (1538–1599), followed suit and, in 1584, published his skeptical and sarcastically mocking work, *The Discoverie of Witchcraft*. In his opinion, "spiritualistic manifestations were artful impostures or illusions due to mental disturbance in the observer."[2]

These psychiatric views have continued throughout the ages, re-emerging in the works of the 19th-century author, Charles Mackay, and today can be found represented by such writers as Ilza Veith and R. E. Masters.[3] Mackay persuasively described the years of the English witch mania and believed that the hypochondriac and "the nervous in temperament" could easily succumb to the cultural images of the times and experience visions and specters of witchcraft. He cited the example of Isabel Gowdie whose monomaniac tendency led her to distill the whole of witch creed of her time. She voluntarily surrendered to the authorities and confessed to a long list of hideous deeds: digging up unchristened infants whose limbs were serviceable in witching rituals, riding through the air on broomsticks, helping Satan destroy his enemies' crops, changing herself into a cat or hare and proving by scars that once, disguised as a hare, she was bitten by dogs. She said that she deserved to be stretched on an iron rack and drawn asunder by wild horses.[4]

In another case, a deluded old spinster was condemned to death on her confession of bewitching the cows and pigs of neighbors. She was "insane, and actually laughed and clapped her hands at the sight of the 'bonnie fire' that was to consume her."[5]

The sorcerers' ability to transform themselves into animals, *Corporum mutatio in bestias*, is a theme among most, if not all, cultures, and ancient Greek and Roman writers such as Plato, Ovid, Pliny the Elder, Vergil, Petronius, and Apuleius, mentioned it. The myth was particularly strong among the pre-Christian Nordic-Germanic peoples, infusing it into medieval imagination. It not only fascinated the gullible, but, more importantly, effected imitation among the hysterical and mentally deranged. Although animal transformation could take many forms, the animal selected usually included those most dreaded in a given society. In Malaya, for example, humans turned into tigers; in Iceland, into bears; in Africa, into tigers, hyenas or leopards; in India, into tigers or leopards. In Europe, the most feared animal was the wolf, and therefore lycanthropy, a human fancying himself transformed into a wolf, was the most common version of *mutatio in bestias*.[6] This

195

peculiar delusion was the issue at many trials. Although I have not heard of such accounts in the Franconian Jura, William Monter, studying the southwestern Jura, presents interesting Renaissance examples.[7]

Sometimes deranged individuals would voluntarily confess to changing into wolves at night and devouring livestock. These werewolves claimed to be in the service of Satan, and Charles Mackay found an English youth who described how he "howled in excess of joy as he tore with his fangs the warm flesh of the sheep asunder." [8] Such "criminals" were thought to be too abominable to be hanged first and then burned; they were burned alive.

The belief in lycanthropy was widespread and Peuckert reports legends from various parts of Europe, including Switzerland, the Upper Palatinate and northern Germany.[9] From the latter region we hear of a witch who changed into a werewolf to hunt her neighbor's cows. When her husband came to the scene, suspecting the true circumstances and calling her by name, she reverted to human form, excepting reddish hair and glowing eyes.

Other animals that were imitated included werefoxes and man-bears. Peuckert reports Swiss legends, common among the rural folk, in which a hunter observed a weird procession of foxes marching on their hindlegs through the woods. He shot at one of them but retrieved only an abandoned frock. The interpretation was that a group of werefox witches was on the way to their bacchanalia. In another story, a hunter came across an emaciated fox tied to a tree; he released the creature, and it disappeared into the forest. Years later, the hunter was rewarded by a lady who revealed herself as the werefox whom he saved and explained that she had been punished by the Devil for a minor breach of diabolic conduct.[10]

While most reports of this type are legends (and considered as such by most people), some were derived from events where humans actually tried to imitate animals. Regardless of factuality, such stories could serve as models for behavior to channel hallucinations and mental aberrations. Today, psychiatrists define the werewolf obsession as lycorexia, involving a wolfish hunger and a fixation of being a ferocious predator. He howls, lusts for raw flesh and mimics the movements of the animal. Practically, he *is* the animal. He suffers from glandular aberrations and the mental symptoms of possession. These symptoms were horrifying to those lacking psychiatric insight; they defied any explanation other than that the deranged individual had been diabolically transformed, and that this transformation was the result of a voluntary decision. Indeed, the wolfish person himself usually believed in the condition as a supernatural phenomenon. This held true for other conditions of witchery. For example, there were many cases of witches who believed they had attended the Sabbath, although there was evidence that they had never left their beds. Such obsessions, hallucinations and visions may sometimes have been the result of advanced alcoholism, diabetes, hypoglycemia, depression, malnutrition, poisoning, psychosis and outright brain damage.

Sometimes the causes may have been what early psychiatrists defined as hysteria. Charles Richet, for example, compared the chronic cases of hysteria which Charcot studied at the famous 19th-century Paris School of Hypnotism with the demoniacally possessed.[11] The hysteria patients exhibited symptoms strikingly similar to those of the witches. For instance, patients were found to lose their sense of feeling in parts of their bodies. Most importantly, such symptoms were highly dependent upon suggestion, from others as well as from self, and had the properties of "contagious diseases." Witchcraft and cases of possession can therefore be seen as mass hysterias of a highly contagious nature.

During the years of the witch scare, participation in the hysteria could prove to have fatal consequences, for one of the witch finder's method of determining diabolic alliance was to find the telltale spot on the suspect's body that showed insensitivity to pain and would not respond to puncture, piercing or burning. Besides hysterical anesthesia, more frequently his Devil's Mark was nothing but anesthetic scar tissue that lacked nerves.

Certain individuals appear more susceptable to the dangers of demoniacal neurosis than others, and among those attracted to demonolatry are the esthetically sensitive. Baroja feels that magic and demonolatry tend to be practiced or appreciated by persons with a highly developed artistic sense, and that "more than one Protestant has been converted to Catholicism for esthetic reasons."[12] Similar susceptibility has been observed among the insecure for whom demonolatry is a haven of security, and among the maladjusted who are fanatic proponents of magic and other aspects of the occult. In these cases, the religious motive, compared to the emotional need, is insignificant.

Psychedelics may have played a role in demoniacal visions and hallucinations, and a few writers have allowed for the possibility that some aspects of the witch's perceptions were drug-induced.[13] They argued that the question was not so much one of insanity as of drug influence, and that, by pursuing this approach, much badly needed logical continuity in the history of witchcraft could be discovered. The person who thought she was a witch may, to a substantial degree, have derived her self-definition from the dream-world provided by certain European herbs. There seems to be enough reliable historical information to show that leaves from plants of the nightshade family were sometimes smoked or boiled, with the most frequent ones being Bilsenkraut (*Hyoscyamus niger*), Eisenhut (*Aconitum napellus*), Stechapfel (*Datura sanguinea*) and Tollkirsche (*Atropa belladonna*). The decoctions and ointments so often mentioned in the witch trials may have included these drugs and may explain the witches' perception of flying, attending sumptuous Sabbaths and other extraordinary things—though all the while they were in a trance fast asleep in their beds. The German pharmacologist, H. Fühner, examined these drugs, mostly alcaloids, in the 1920s, and found them to cause vertigo, distortion of vision, coma, insensitivity to pain, insensible laughter and all sorts of hallucinations. When prepared as a lotion and rubbed into the skin, they can reach the brain and cause a narcotic reaction which, indeed, can trigger the effects ascribed to witches' unguents: sedation, dreams of soaring through the sky, and images of dancing and erotic experiences.[14] The victims, upon awakening, felt certain about the reality of their dreams and refused to regard them as mere images.

Two academics were curious—and brave—enough to experiment with these drugs on themselves. Siegbert Frerkel, in 1954, followed a witches' recipe and rubbed the ointment on his chest. Soon his pupils enlarged, pulse increased and he started to hallucinate: seeing dark, distorted faces; soaring through the sky with great speed; hovering over the town; being joined by other figures on his flight through clouds; and finally all beginning to dance in a circle. Through it all, time seemed to stand still. Folklorist, Peuckert, a professor at the University of Göttingen, experimented in 1960, applying a recipe extracted from the Italian Giambattista Porta's 1568 *Magia Naturalis* and had a more or less identical experience: narcotic sleep; wild dreams; gruesomely distorted faces dancing in front of his eyes; sensation of flying through the air for many miles; and images of orgiastic feasts with grotesque sexual aberrations.[15]

While I am not doubting the personal integrity of the two experimenters, I wonder to what extent the preconceived notions of what to expect might have influenced the slant of their hallucinations. Perhaps the LSD trips among the countercultural youth of Western civilization over the past two decades are comparable to the witch-unguent experiments insofar as they produce similar neurochemical reactions, but produce different hallucinatory images due to different preconceptions.

Countercultural youth's fascination with what they believe to be magical experiences and insights is partly responsible for their tenacious infatuation with psychedelic drugs. One of modern youth's heroes in this respect is loquacious Carlos Castaneda who, over the past ten years, has successfully sold—and still is selling—five volumes in which he testifies to his magical experiences under the tutelage of an obscure Yaqui Indian *brujo* (sorcerer) Don Juan. He reports his experience of "flying" after applying an ointment prepared from the datura plant.[16] While the datura alcaloid is well capable of creating the sensation of flying, the rest of Castaneda's "report" deserves little credibility. (It is genre talk perfectly fitted to the mood of the 1970s youth scene.) It is disconcerting to see the otherwise discriminating Danish folklorist, Gustav Henningsen, cite Casteneda as an "anthropologist" and unquestioningly accept his writings as verified anthropological research.[17] Apparently he is unaware of the serious doubts that many American anthropologists hold about the authenticity of the "report." This naïveté—in contrast to his able grasp of the history of witchcraft in Europe—puts him on a par with a majority of contemporary college students who accept Castaneda uncritically and so disclose their longing to find evidence justifying their belief in magic. They refuse to recognize that Castaneda has not given one iota of evidence that shows any aspect of his "experiences" to be factual. I dwell on this point, because for the past 15 years I have lived in the Sonoran desert, the alleged setting of Castaneda's story, and must disagree with him on most every point when it comes to his description of the natural environment. With my backyard blending into a huge wilderness area (Superstition Mountains), and on merit of being an avid outdoor person, I have derived some knowledge of this environment and would argue that Castaneda invented what he claims as "observations."

Be this as it may, the principle that certain hallucinations and delusions render their own reality cannot be refuted—provided that such psychedelic experiences truly took place. In any case, psyche-delic experiences, if taken as reality, influence personal identity. The importance of such impressions is that they eventually shape self-perception. The story of the mother–daughter witches of Streit-berg may illustrate psychedelic "trips" wherein they perceived their souls flying through the night, while their bodies stayed behind (see Chapter Eight). Even the skeptic Elliot Rose concedes that, "If these ointments were really employed they might help to explain the element of honest self-delusion in the confessions."[18]

Personality Conditions of the Witches' Enemies

Some writers shifted the pathological diagnosis from the witch to her adversaries. They allowed for the possibility that the witches were perfectly sane, while accusers, judges and witnesses were paranoid and often hallucinating. Whether these writers actually turned the pathology diagnosis around or merely expanded it to include persons other than witches is of no consequence here. The importance lies in the fact that pathologies seemed to be operating in those who so often accused and condemned. The "victims" were more often responsible for witch persecution, witch belief and witch mania than the actual behavior of the witches. The condition of these people may have included classical persecution complexes, paranoid reactions attached to the scapegoats of the community. They were victims not of the diabolical witch but of the mass demonomania that devastated many communities.

This tendency can still be observed today—though with lesser consequences than a witch prosecution. Neighbors, villagers and townspeople still seriously and gullibly accept and spread rumors. Besides being a function of ignorance, this habit may also satisfy a perverse personality need. All humans, because of their abstract symbolic capability, tend to engage in rumoring and inventing. Some far exceed the normal degree and become what an early student of this behavior tendency called "mythomaniacs." Dr. Dupré described the pathological inclination in many people to lie and invent imaginary stories.[19] Mythomaniacs, even though they may initially lie deliberately, finally come to believe what they have said. Dupré found that most who fall into this habit are either children or the mentally retarded. While a child's lying does not always indicate a serious pathology, an adult's continual lying is pathologic. In children and young adolescents mythomania is frequently related to vanity, maliciousness, precocious sexual appetites, an excess of youthful imagination and the need for attention.

The deadly role of children's testimony has been amply documented throughout the history of witch-hunts. They often reveled in mythomania to please the tribunal, to satisfy a sadistic need for revenge or to wallow in imagery and exaggerations.

Mackay reminds us of the incident where Swedish children described a Sabbath at which the Devil pretended to be dead so that he could determine whether his entourage would mourn him. Indeed, the children testified, the followers set up a loud wail and each wept three tears for him. Satan was pleased, jumped up and hugged those who had shown sorrow most convincingly. This description was corroborated by the confessions of the adult witches. But the children's extraordinary imagination backfired fatally. While on the first day, 23 adults were burned for witchcraft, on the second day, 15 children were executed in the same manner. Fifty-five more children were punished by running the gauntlet, imprisonment or public whipping.[20] Today, such mythomanic children would be referred to the high school counselor—and the credulity of the parents would be laughed at.

The witch-hunt in New England was spearheaded by a score of girls who blamed witches for their alternate fits and paralyses. The first execution, an innocent woman against whom the children held a grudge only fanned their imagination and hysteria. Additional children claimed to be suffering from witches' spells; more witches were executed. When the colonists finally realized their error and stopped prosecution, the girls ceased having fits and stopped talking about being tormented by the Devil and his witches.[21]

In connection with the Salem witch panic, researchers developed an interesting theory on the role of hallucinations in identifying witches. A recently completed reexamination of 17th-century Salem speculates that the grain eaten by all eight of the afflicted girls came from the same fields. The climatic conditions during the key year of 1692 presumably favored the growth of ergot, an hallucinogenic fungus mainly found on rye. The active ingredient of ergot is lysergic acid amide (basic to LSD) and the researchers suggested that it may have caused psychotic symptoms in the girls. Since ergot was not identified until 1800 (by Dr. John Stearns), the community may have diagnosed its toxic symptoms as possession by the Devil.[22]

This conclusion is, however, challenged by other researchers who feel that the symptoms of the hysterical girls were not those of convulsive ergotism. They point out that abrupt endings to large-scale witch manias were the rule rather than the exception, and that the true explanation is to be sought in community processes and role-playing.[23] (They, as well as I, consider the ergot theory as more colorful than trustworthy.)

Most researchers think that the behavior of only a small number of witches and witch-hunters can be understood as personal insanity, let alone as chemically induced delusions and hallucinations. They see the meaning of witchcraft inextricably intertwined with social processes and cultural symbols. I believe this is particularly true of witchcraft among the Franconians. These peasants followed the tradition of witchcraft as intelligently and naturally as the traditions of Catholicism, farm technology and kinship patterns. The basic meaning of witchcraft thus lies not in mental disturbance but in cultural symbolism.

Witchcraft as Cultural Symbolism

The witchcraft-insanity equation as applied to the personalities of the witches or her victims and persecutors, has fallen into disrepute among modern scholars. While in a few cases it may reveal an element of truth, social scientists generally reject the equation as superficial name-calling that tends to obscure the more complex social processes and cultural symbols involved.

Thomas Szasz, for example, attacks the fundamental postulates of psychiatry and portrays the modern health industry as another form of the Inquisition.[1] He maintains that the medical establishment unfairly judges believers in alternative world views as aberrant or insane. In essence, Szasz and other so-called "radical therapists" call for a "schizophrenia liberation" whereby respect and freedom be granted to those preceiving the world in unconventional terms. Alas, this gesture is valuable only as a token of the larger fact that occult beliefs must be approached on their own terms. It is relatively useless, however, in grasping the essence of the occult.

I see greater usefulness in concentrating on the cultural symbols with which witchcraft behavior aligns. In a sense, witches and their accusers alike were intelligent and aware of what they were supposed to do—and ultimately be. To me, the symbolic prompting and symbolic interacting make up the most valid framework for grasping the meaning of witchcraft. However, I admit to a judgmental attitude insofar as I charge inhumane and unrealistic cultural symbolizing with the cause of pathological conditions on the cultural, social and individual levels. Symbols, then, are most basic. At this time, I turn to a group of cultural symbols that I see as pathogenic.

If a given culture provides a blueprint for a role, there will always be individuals whose particular personality traits make them rally to that role. This is true as well of the various roles inherent in witchcraft: witch, victim, accuser, prosecutor and so forth. Symbols thus function as organizers and sponsors of behavior. And how powerful the organizing strength of symbols can be was illustrated earlier when I spoke of religion and magic and resulting behavior, including some astonishing psychosomatic symptoms.

It is therefore entirely plausible that perfectly sane people, indeed quite sensitive and intelligent individuals, should come to embrace cultural suggestions, identify with them and, thus, over a period of time, step forth as witches or their victims. There are records of people whose ignorance, despite intelligence, allowed them to wonder whether they had the personal mark of the Devil. Being sensitive, they mistook their own fears for the objective truth of witchcraft. What today we would construe as a superstitious and unrealistic fear was to them, under conditions of largely uncontested cultural symbols, a sign that they actually were either witches or victims. An example from the era of the witch-hunt describes an honest woman who "because she was called a witch, believed that she was, asked the judge upon the bench whether a person might be a witch and not know it?"[2] Another suspect, an impoverished weaver, confessed that he was a witch; being asked why, replied, "Because he had seen the Devil dancing, like a fly, about a candle."[3] These examples indicate no mental pathologies, but merely simple-minded attempts to understand cultural images and organize their experiences accordingly. If we must impute pathology, it should be done on the cultural and not the personal level.

In another example, an old, ugly hag coincided with the community's witch stereotype and perhaps even exploited the role in which she was cast. Her appearance was so repulsive that she was invariably regarded as a witch by all who knew her. She was extremely stooped; had unusually bright eyes ("malicious," it was said); wore a red cloak; and supported herself on a crutch—in short, she was the *beau ideal* of a witch. She seemed to savor the reactions she elicited in others, reveled in witchcraft accusations, and liberally cursed those who offended her.[4]

The same innocuousness emerges in records concerning the witch persecutors. Most witch finders probably were fundamentally honest people who believed in witches and in their own ability to find them. A typical example was Matthew Hopkins, a prominent witch finder during the Essex witch mania. This man went around administering various tests that supposedly revealed the identity of a witch. Among them was the "swimming test" in which hands and feet were tied together crosswise. The suspect was wrapped in a blanket and laid on her back in a pond or river. If she sank, she was innocent (though usually dead); if she floated (as she might if laid carefully on the water), she was found guilty and tried accordingly. Who is to say that the Witch-finder General, as Hopkins was called, was devious? He probably was as much as believer in the cultural symbols as anyone else. The uniformity of "confessions," visions and apparitions points to the power of religious symbolism as it permeated the populace of an era, instead of to Murray's putative witch organization.

It all boils down to belief in cultural symbols. Taking these symbols as suggestions, they function perfectly as autosuggestions. *What appears to be a pathology is basically a belief.* Witches believed they had certain powers; the people believed that witches had them; *so they worked.* This is an underlying principle in all magical beliefs and their often stupendous effectiveness. Exactly the same principle operates in the miracles of all Churches, and in that context, it is usually seen as the *legitimate* use of power. In the context of witchcraft, it is seen as the *illegitimate* use of power.

Heterosuggestion is grounded also in the use of symbols, and is the belief that others have power over you. A great majority of "spells" fall precisely into this class of suggestions. They work because cultural symbols reinforce them. So we see the results in terms of the "evil eye," the role of the "moribund person," sexual inhibition and demonic possession.

Seeing witchcraft in the context of symbolic interaction makes us aware that it was a self-reinforcing phenomenon. Whether hunter or hunted, both supported a system of symbols that made up the belief in witchcraft. There is no doubt that one of the reasons why witchcraft has survived in Franconian Switzerland was this circular reinforcement, extended by those who endorsed and those who condemned it. This process was particularly effective because it was left undisturbed and operated in a region largely cut off from the influences of the larger German culture. Franconian peasants accepted mental constructs that may not have matched reality. But this is beside the point. The point is that, once set in motion, those constructs elicited corresponding behavior and perpetuated themselves.

The constructs contained role definitions. And roles, once defined, generally tend to gain a momentum of their own and are apt to overpower the unwary and uninformed.

Learnedness Does Not Protect against the Power of Roles

There is little that affords immunity except the type of existential cynicism that acknowledges human susceptibility to any sort of role and keeps an ever wary vigil as to the chances of this tendency turning into perversion or inhumanity. The learned person, as we have encountered him throughout the history of the witch panic, often served as a striking example: he was a pedant fanatically clinging to an absurd premise and, with typical meticulousness, following the premise to its flawlessly logical conclusion. Legions of *mallei maleficarum* prove the point.

This principle applies to all types of witch-hunts. The McCarthy panic in the United States is an example. Once the reality of the Great Conspiracy was established and believed by sufficient numbers of people, logical deductions took place and the witch-hunt was on. The widespread fear of a secretive crime helped many investigators mount the political and legislative saddle. Such officials gained acclaim as saviors of the country and could proceed with a minimum—some would say, no—regard for due process of law. Presumption of innocence was thrown overboard; guilt by association was established; reputation was destroyed by mere accusation; and traditional legal safeguards were rejected as fettering effective prosecution. And all this, not in a backward but in one of the most civilized states of our age, not in the newest and untried democracy but in one of the oldest. When journalists described this happening as a "witch-hunt," they were for once not hurling sensational or inappropriate language, but using an acceptable analogy.

Other examples include the Nazi persecution of the Jews when millions were considered enemy number one of the state, defined as the Great Conspiracy and systematically destroyed. The Great Cultural Revolution of Communist China branded a large portion of the population as reactionaries who posed a serious threat to the people and needed to be liquidated.

206

The common sociological dimensions running through the various witch-hunts, including the Renaissance prototype, include the proclamation of the Great Danger, the focus on scapegoats, the attempt to confine or eliminate the threat, and either the bypassing of due process of law or the issuance of new legislation to facilitate prosecution.

One of the most insidious consequences of the witch-hunt is the psychological effect it tends to have on the victim. During many witch trials the accused person suffered a complete reversal of identity. When the hopelessness of the situation became evident and pain and frustration unbearable, he surrendered the old identity and adopted the one imposed by the persecutors. This "brainwashing" effect was probably most conspicuous among the non-Aryan inmates of the Nazi concentration camps who adopted an inferior and guilt-ridden self-image, and the witch suspects in the hands of the Inquisition who combined the most perverse side of their imagination with what they already knew about the role of the witch. They would fabricate the type of confession, or actually imitate behavior, that they thought was expected of them. The threat of torture was always looming over those not conforming to these expectations. Thus, why not make it easier for oneself, evade extra agony and adopt the expected role. Moreover, compliance and voluntary "confession" might save them from the gas chamber or the stake—at least so they hoped. Retaining one's normal identity under such trying circumstances was probably the exception rather than the rule. The personal report of a remarkable exception reached us through a letter smuggled out of *Hexenbischof* Johann Georg II's witch prison. In 1628, the burgomaster of Bamberg, Johannes Junius, endured torture for so long that at last even the jailer grew compassionate and begged him for God's sake to confess something. A few days before being burned at the stake, Junius succeeded in getting a letter to his daughter in which he said,

> Many hundred thousand good nights, dearly beloved daughter, Veronica. Innocent have I come into prison, innocent have I been tortured, innocent must I die. For whoever comes into the witch prison must become a witch or be tortured until he invents something out of his head and—God pity him—bethinks him of something. . . .[5]

But this amazingly clear-minded attitude is probably the exception among the persons cast into such abysmal situations. Usually, if a human being is isolated for a considerable time from all receptors and reinforcers confirming his identity, and if he is, by both violent methods and sympathetic persuasion, constantly pressed to confess his crimes, it is not only likely that a false confession will be obtained, but that the accused will identify so much with the fake confession that he betrays his true personality and begins to doubt who he really is. The habit of the Inquisition (as well as the Gestapo or the Chinese thought-police) to keep the charge secret for months before it was revealed and to permit the prisoner to converse only with his interrogators, who ceaselessly exhorted him to confess the "truth," was enough to effect brainwashing. Indeed, the research by Robert J. Lifton on thought reform in China established a universal and timeless picture of what goes on in all types of brainwashing—applicable to the Renaissance witch trials as well as to this century's concentration camps. Compare, for example, the thinking of a Catholic priest while he was locked in a Chinese prison accused of anticommunist activities, and recognize the identical psychological pressures:

> They will have their false confession. But I don't want to make a false confession. Maybe there is a way to say something that is not totally untrue to satisfy them—but what? . . . I have said the truth. They don't want the truth. I've only one way to escape: to guess what they really want. . . .[6]

Lifton divides the process of brainwashing into a number of main steps: (1) the assault upon identity; (2) the establishment of guilt; (3) the self-betrayal; (4) the breaking-point—total conflict and the basic fear; (5) leniency and opportunity to redeem oneself; (6) the compulsion to confess; (7) the channeling of guilt; (8) re-education and the logical dishonoring of the past identity and all others who adher to it; (9) progress and harmony; (10) final confession: the summing up; (11) the ultimate birth of a new identity.[7]

The identical "confessions" obtained during the Renaissance witch trials must be understood as the result of identical psychological pressures exerted on the victims. If we fail to understand this social-psychological process, we fall easy prey to theories like the one by Margaret Murray who interprets the identical confessions as proof of the existence of an organized witch cult and its members' truthful reports of what was going on in it. The operation of this psychological process becomes apparent from many Renaissance trials where the accused confessed to "crimes" that were entirely illusory, and in the process abandoned their real personalities. Several examples emerge from the lengthy trial held before the burning of witches by the Spanish Inquisition at Logrono in 1610. One of them deals with a 40-year-old Pyrenees woman who died after 18 months of imprisonment and confession of the most improbable things, showed profound repentance and conducted herself like a faithful Catholic. When on her deathbed, she implored God's forgiveness with copious tears.[8]

The essence of these events is that symbolic meanings prompted both persecutors and victims to play certain roles and that these roles became substantial parts of their personalities.

Heinous torture in witch prosecution must be seen in a similar light and, whether we like it or not, understood as a meaningful act. The use of torture could usually not be attributed to the inquisitors' penchant for personal sadistic impulse, but more frequently to the belief of doing a righteous and necessary thing. Theological opinion of the Renaissance even assumed that torture hurt Satan or the possessing demon, and it was meant to drive him out so that the person, once freed from him, could and would speak the truth.[9] The use of torture was therefore the behavioral implementation of a theological premise.

But on the practical level this may have been different. My perusal of historical data revealed little evidence that torturers and executioners would pause to ponder theological doctrine. I doubt that they sighed with relief when they effected "confessions" and that they joyfully congratulated the tortured for good riddance of the Devil. It rather seems that the craftsmen of torture and execution went about their "job" with theological indifference and personal insensitivity.

It is interesting that the legalization and popularity of torture was brought from the Mediterranean countries to central and northern Europe. Torture used to be alien to the Germanic tradition and was hardly known until introduced by the Romans, culminating in the Renaissance Inquisition.[10] The Romans thus based torture, at least in part, on theological reasoning, and it is significant to recognize how the spread of this reasoning contributed to the spread of torture. New symbols resulted in new behavior.

The core of the witch persecution was really a matter of believing in Satan, and, in pinpointing a motive for torture, we are closer to the truth if we ascribe it to the judges' and executioners' conviction of carrying out their duties than to their sadism. As long as the belief in an incarnate Satan continues to be a facet of Christian cosmology, the existence of witches will remain a logical adjunct relatively immune to attack by science. All it would take to revive witch persecution is a mating of ecclesiastical dogma with civil penal law—and anyone daring to declare witchcraft irrational or superstitious would be branded an atheist, heretic or a witch herself. Definitions make the world of witches a real world, and the symbolic interaction deriving from these definitions and evolving within this world would assume a status as entrenched, respected and "natural" as any other firmly held belief.

Once symbols are firmly established—in roles, rituals and beliefs—one of mankind's most fascinating mental gyrations takes over: our perception of the world around us becomes narrow and selective and we see and hear only what we are prepared for. Witchcraft offers poignant and often fatal examples. After a person is perceived a witch, any aspect of her behavior becomes "proof" that the perception is correct. If such a woman is independently wealthy or just self-sufficient, she is suspected of nightly metamorphosis into a cat roaming around stealing; if she is a beggar, she is thought to be after some personal item to put a hex on the owner; if her window is dark at night, she is said to be out committing sorcery; if her window is lit, she is assumed to peruse witchery books. Should someone defend the suspect, the defender himself or herself can become a suspect and be thought of as an accomplice; should someone accuse the suspect, and the accuser be unpopular, the accuser can become a suspect and be thought of as trying to use the accusation to divert attention from his or her own witchery.

Symbols are constructs that often exhibit a perplexing contagion. The penetrating contagion can be illustrated by the consensus concerning the minute details inherent in the role of the witch. Through all of Europe during the witch-hunt era, people understood that the witch bore the mark of the Devil, belonged to a coven, worshipped Satan and worked with evil potions and ointments. The populace displayed an amazing agreement that witches possessed these and other traits.

Margaret Murray took this consensus to be the reflection of the witches' organized cult, of Ritual Witchcraft. Accordingly, the mark of the Devil was a tatoo signifying membership in the cult, the coven the group of devoted cultists, "Satan" the priest clad in animal hides, the potions and ointments were herbal medicines and psychedelic drugs and so forth.

But symbolic interactionists and many historians suggest that this consensus probably was less a summary of facts and more the persuasiveness of symbols that, through complex social psychological processes, emerged during the Middle Ages. The witch creed, instead of being based on fact, was probably purely symbolic or delusional.

The contagion of symbols is furthered if they are written. The written form helps symbols and meanings survive. Here we must acknowledge the role of the "secret books" as they are found in many different cultures. For example, the *Books of Moses* spread and perpetuated witchcraft among the Franconian peasants, testifying to the significant role of treatises on demonolatry. The written word sometimes aids, or even causes, the revival of traditions just when, had they not been written, the tradition might have died out completely. I am thinking of the current revival of voodoo among black Americans who look for guidance in the same Kabbalistic books as the Franconians of past generations.

Those courting the occult are well advised to proceed with caution when they accept symbols in order to construct a belief. The often lacking factual base of a belief or assumption may be of minor significance in this context; after all, the essence of belief is that truth is inferred and not proven. What is of major significance here is the understanding of the potential consequences of symbols: while they have the power to heal and foster humanity, they also have the power to destroy and foster inhumanity.

15

Witchcraft and Theology

Those wedded to Christian orthodoxy experience no difficulty in defining witchcraft: it is as real as it is heretical. The meaning of witchcraft is deeply anchored in Christian dogma, and since the religious postulates out of which the meaning grew have not changed in substance over the ages, the validity of the belief in witchcraft has remained fundamentally undisturbed. If orthodox Christians fail to act on still valid Church dogma, it is mainly because they lack large social support, not because they lack belief in the evils of witchcraft. It is conceivable that they would be willing to take punitive action if they had sufficient power.

This traditionalism is not a quality found only among semiliterate peasants, but is often present among the erudite scholars who indulge in myopic deductions from archaic Church premises. To them, the meaning of witchcraft harbors no ambiguity: it is the work of Satan and his witches, purely and simply.

One of the premises of traditional Christian thought is the existence of the Devil. Once this premise is accepted, it is a small step to also accept the role of his servants and agents, the witches. Since God has granted Satan uncanny powers, it is absolutely plausible—within this theological scheme—that he may possess humans, use them to do his evil deeds and even transform them into a variety of animals. The claim of metamorphosis, sometimes voluntarily and sometimes involuntarily confessed by witches, presents an example of theological logic. Many a learned doctor of divinity gravely proclaimed the possibility of such transformations, believing them to manifest the power of the Devil—and divine permission. These gentlemen contended that "confession" was sufficient evidence, thereby revealing a total ignorance of the psychiatric phenomena of delusions, hallucinations and other symptoms of mental disturbance. Today, individuals who imagine themselves transformed into animals are sent to the hospital instead of to the stake. Orthodox erudition also lacked sociological insight, and failed to recognize role-playing.

But even today, the scientific attitude is rivaled by non- or prescientific thought. What's more, the rivalry has penetrated into the realm of erstwhile objective science; many scientists are beginning to waver in their trust of objective consciousness and the empirical approach to knowledge.[1]

What prevents contemporary traditionalists from reacting to witchcraft claims on the basis of theology instead of modern medicine? It certainly is not lack of belief in the possibility of Satan's incarnation. One might ask, then, what would happen if they had authority to enforce their theological assumptions? A chilling thought!

The modern tolerance of witchcraft is nothing more than an issue of social power and not of some kind of philosophical maturity accumulated by Homo sapiens over the past 1000 years. Decriminalization of witchcraft is shielded by little more than a thin armor of modern legislation. This is weak protection, since it is not entirely commensurate with popular belief. Charles Mackay reminded us that the roots of witchcraft are still alive and that "another King James VI might make them vegetate again; and more mischievous still, another Pope like Innocent VIII might raise the decaying roots to strength and verdure."[2]

To scale the sweeping historical perspective down to contemporary Franconia, what are the theological attitudes of the region's clergy toward witchcraft? (Obviously, we do not need to raise the question as to what it used to be. The record of the bishops and their henchmen of the Bamberg diocese speaks clearly.) The priest of the town of Pottenstein is representative. Across a desk covered with scriptures written in half a dozen languages (including ancient Hebrew, Latin and Greek), he assured me that just as there is a benediction there is a malediction; that Satan is real and has real power; that humans can carry out Satan's wishes; and that it is inconsequential what name we give to such individuals—"witches" will do. The priest knew of the so-called *Sixth and Seventh Books of Moses* and considered their inclusion in the *Index* wise since, he reiterated, the diabolic malediction they teach has as much substance as the divine benediction by the priest.

The theological premises that prevailed during past centuries are still with us. The only thing that has changed is the power to implement them and carry them through to logical consequences in daily life—logical consequences that might include punitive action against those practicing "witchcraft." We can only speculate how such official power would have influenced the turn-of-the-century Franconian scene of witchcraft and the power to persecute witches. Admittedly, it sounds hyperbolic, but it is conceivable that in this century official power might have created a witch-hunt with resulting witch trials not unlike those of the Renaissance. While formal prosecutions have not been practiced for more than two centuries, the beliefs, rumors and character asassinations associated with witchcraft were alive during the early decades of this century.

There is no need to limit ourselves to the Franconian peasants and their clergy when we look for contemporary examples of medieval theological thinking. Robert Balch, who is currently studying beliefs in witchcraft and satanism in the northwestern United States reports that, ". . . many Christians are literally terrified of witchcraft and satanism. Because they are so obsessed with fear, they actually open themselves to the risk of demonic possession."[3] He describes what is commonplace in much of the United States: that demonic possession is a reality to the world of Pentecostalism—a world in which Satan exists as an actual being, in which demons are real entities, and in which all forms of human misery are attributed to Satan and his demonic agents.

A theologian who made his view widely known (he wrote at least 17 books between 1933 and 1958) was Montague Summers.[4] He speaks of Bodin and of Institor and Sprenger, the authors of the *Malleus Maleficarum*, with reverence, as if they contributed to the elevation of humanity. Conversely, he liberally criticizes those accused of witchcraft and calls them impious, damnable and abominable. Medieval laws and edicts, even the most questionable ones, are in his opinion still defensible.

However, I must emphasize that the above examples are by no means representative of modern Christian theology. There is wider divergence of opinion among modern theologians than among those of the past. To many contemporary theologians, the witch-

214

hunt was a deplorable mistake and they try to psychologize the theological premise from which the mistake derived. In such fashion they maintain Evil, Satan, and the Witch as abstract constructs that, they assure us, should not be taken literally. To them, these figures have merely symbolic value and are helpful in labeling human sinfulness and fallibility.

But there are no such things as "merely" symbolic values. Symbolic they may be, but the consequences of human belief in them are very real. Human folly throughout history testifies to the perennial temptation to seek concrete incarnations for abstractions, and symbolic values can swiftly metamorphose into physical entities.

Before we leave the subject of Christian theology and its impact on—or, rather, its creation of—witchcraft, I would like to discuss how Catholicism and Protestantism differ on this issue. For this purpose I generously draw from Keith Thomas' major work, *Religion and the Decline of Magic*.[5]

Catholics as well as Protestants based their antiwitch orientation on Mosaic law, primarily the famous passage in Exodus 22:18, "Malificos non patieris vivere" ("Thou shalt not suffer a witch to live"), and also Leviticus 20:6, 27, where mediums, witches and wizards are threatened with banishment or death through stoning. From this broad Scriptural foundation sprouted forth ecclesiastical treatises condemning witchcraft, with the 1486 *Malleus Maleficarum* surpassing all of them. This supreme manual of witch persecution influenced the Imperial law of the Holy Roman Empire, the 1532 *Constitutio Criminalis Carolina*, allowing the death penalty for a number of specific offenses contained in the general crime of witchcraft. The capital offenses included blasphemy, sodomy (including copulation with the Devil), sorcery (as defined by the Bamberg penal code of 1507) and adultery (applied to married witches, since they presumably had sex with the Devil). It recommended death through fire for harmful sorcery (harmless sorcery was to be punished according to the judges' discretions) and sexual perversions (bestiality, homosexuality, lesbianism). This legislation could be supplemented by local law and the traditions of local rulers, as long as they did not contradict the essence of the *Carolina*. Thus, the legal attitude covering the crime of witchcraft was based on both sacred and secular sources: the Bible, Church tradition, and the Imperial and local laws.

These sources formed, more or less, the point of departure for

Catholics and Protestants alike, with both camps convinced of the evil of witchcraft. The common Christian cosmology had the Devil as one of the central figures, a necessary counterfigure to the all-perfect Christian God—since, otherwise, how could evil be explained in the world if God was good? (The early Hebrews did not have to face this question, for they could attribute evil to the influence of other rival deities. With the introduction of monotheism, evil had to be explained by a Devil, who was permitted by God, in order to sustain the notion of an omnipotent divinity.) Luther proclaimed in the 1520s that, "Sorcerers and witches are the Devil's whores who steal milk, raise storms, ride on goats or broomsticks, lame or maim people, torture babies in their cradles, change things into different shapes. . . ."[6]

Certainly, this tirade differed little from those delivered by Catholic clergy, but changes soon developed between the two Christian religions. As Thomas saw it,

> If the distinction between magic and religion had been blurred by the medieval Church, it was strongly reasserted by the propagandists of the Protestant Reformation. From the very start, the enemies of Roman Catholicism fastened upon the magical implications, which they saw to be inherent in some fundamental aspect of the Church's ritual.[7]

Luther and Calvin shifted their theological guidance from ecclesiastical tradition to a greater reliance on the Scriptures and on faith. In their adherence to the principle of *sola scriptura* they came to emphasize the role of the Devil and the reality of the witch's pact with the Devil. (They proceeded to understand Exodus 22:18 without benefit of Erasmus' exegesis of the original Hebrew text that would have allowed a different interpretation of what the Bible meant by "wizards and witches.") Ecclesiastical practices, as well as old folk magic, to ward off the Devil and his witches were condemned as superstitions, even blasphemies, and to a large extent became alien to Protestant life. As a consequence, Protestantism rejected the practice of exorcism and blessings, since it did not believe that clergymen had the power to *command* a spirit to depart. Only God was thought to have that power and all that men could do was to entreat God to show mercy by taking the Devil away. The same disbelief in the powers of men and the Church was reflected in the abandonment of old folk customs that focused on the concept of the *geweiht*, the beneficial consecration offered by the medieval

Church and generously applied to homes, stables, animals, farm produce and objects functioning as talismans to ward off evil. Protestants saw protection in abstract faith and went without tangible procedures and reassuring rituals for dealing with instances of possession or witch-caused harm. They went as far as removing the incantatory aspects of formal prayer and changed from Latin to the vernacular. Thomas cites an example where it was decided to delete the prayer for delivery from violent death on the grounds that it was a particularly obnoxious conjuring of God.[8]

We can only guess at the extent of the psychological discomfort that must have resulted from the liturgic sterility failing to give sensory succor to people who actually believed in the activities of the Devil.

Concurrent with the decline of ecclesiastical protection among Protestants went a decline of certain aspects of witchcraft. Monter found that the new doctrine did not grant witches as much power as Catholicism. In the French-Swiss Jura, the hail-making witch was a typical pre-Reformation phenomenon that drastically declined in Protestant areas, but remained a common phenomenon in Catholic areas. Protestant authorities tended to give natural disasters, particularly hailstorms, a "Providentialist" (stemming from God's will and guidance) interpretation, which was reflected in the extreme rarity of a witch confessing to causing hailstorms. But "Providence" did not affect the Catholic governments of the Jura; there were large numbers of confessions to hail-making before as well as after the Reformation. Similarly, the belief in werewolves decreased with the influence of the Reformation. But Protestants readily and early (in the 16th century) accepted the *signum pacti*, the Devil's Mark, since they accentuated the role of the Devil and the witch's pact with him. Although without great initial interest, Catholicism finally accepted the significance of this characteristic of witches in the 17th century.[9]

In the meantime, Catholics continued to take advantage of the rich repertoire of rituals and sacraments that they could employ to rid themselves of the Devil and the curses of witches. The Catholic hierarchy, especially the authors of the *Malleus Maleficarum*, assured their followers that the Church could dispense many efficacious remedies for protection against witches: holy water, the sign of the cross, holy candles, church bells, consecrated herbs, sacred medals worn on the body, consecrated rosaries and the seven sacraments (of which Protestantism retained only baptism and the Lord's Supper). These were the means through which the loyal Catholic could secure immunity or cure from diabolic injuries. The Franconian healer working the *Anfangen* is the folk dispenser of these medieval religious remedies.

The Reformation relied on Scriptures, placed trust in religious faith, acknowledged God's Providence and dismissed the old mechanical protections as empty symbols, lacking any efficacy. The bleakness of the new religion increased by denying the importance of guardian angels and the intercessionary power of saints—all the while stressing the reality of Satan and the scope of his worldly dominion. It is therefore not surprising that Protestants who felt helpless when confronting witchcraft retained old Catholic formulas. I recall the Protestant farmer who begged a priest of Gösswein-stein to exorcize his stable, and Protestant northern Germans and East-Prussians who have adhered to the medieval rituals of making the sign of the cross over the hexed butter barrel, speaking the "sweet name of Jesus" to drive the Devil out and even have *Gesund-beterinnen* (faith healers) in their communities. A recent example comes from the village of Mailach, not far from the western edge of Franconian Switzerland, where in 1960 Protestant farmers were found to occasionally employ the Catholics' holy water and holy incense to exorcize their stables as soon as they interpreted a sick animal as the work of a witch. This partial adherence to ecclesiastical magic can be explained either by a continuous observance of such rites since pre-Reformation time or by later cultural diffusion whereby Protestants readopted Catholic customs.

Protestantism, it seems, forced its followers into an intolerable position by asserting the reality of witchcraft and yet denying the availability of effective protection or cure. Actually, the situation was not quite as pessimistic as it sounds, for steadfast *faith* in God was an infallible shield against Satan's onslaught on the *soul*, while leaving relatively unprotected bodies and goods. In fact, Satan's purpose in molesting material possessions was to weaken people's faith and seduce them to deviate from the right path in hope of relief. The real goal of Satan was to capture souls, and the person who used magic to defend himself against the Devil's (and his witches') material attacks might gain temporary relief, but incur eternal damnation.

Finally, Protestantism's otherworldly consolation included encouragement for trust in Providence. Calvinism carried it to its logical conclusion and submitted to its followers the concept of predestination—but with a twist whereby those blessed with material success were ipso facto characterized as being of the Elect. This, certainly, must be one of mankind's most ingenious rationalizations—allowing the rich to enjoy their riches and forcing the poor to resign. However, there was a possible way for the poor to acquire Elect status: to get rich and ipso facto acquire the "sign." And how could one get rich if one started out poor? Through *work*. According to Max Weber in his fascinating book, *The Protestant Ethic and the Spirit of Capitalism,* this was the birth of the spirit of capitalism.[10] In any case, it was a comfortable doctrine for the well-to-do, and those who found it uncomfortable could always be reminded of Providence and the inscrutable will of God. This doctrine had a self-confirming quality and could never be faulted: if the wicked experienced adversity, it was God's punishment; if the righteous were smitten, it was God testing them.

With the Reformation thus arose a crisis in ritual protection and things had to be figured out in much more abstract terms. During pre-Reformation time, a person could protect himself by observing the prescriptions of the Church and, by ecclesiastical magic, inhibited and delayed witch persecution. But the Reformation shattered this barrier and caused ecclesiastical magic to crumble. The social system felt it now necessary to initiate legal action against a danger which, for the first time, threatened to get out of hand.[11] While this does not explain witch persecution in all areas, Thomas feels that it is a strong point for its development in England. In other parts of Europe the reason for the rise of persecution was not so much the actual Reformation as the immediately preceding debunking of ecclesiastical magic by intellectuals who doubted the efficacy of Church magic. Nevertheless, the persecution in both cases derived from the undermining of the remedies of the medieval Church: on the Continent it was a pre-Reformation process, and in England it was the Reformation.

Whatever other causes of the persecution one might list, Thomas is convinced that,

religious beliefs as such were a necessary pre-condition of the prosecutions. Theologians of all denominations upheld the reality of the Devil's assaults and Protestants denied the possibility of any effective ecclesiastical defense against them. The way was thus left open for the people to take action against the witches from whose *maleficium* they believed themselves to have suffered.[12]

How have these broad religious-historical currents affected Franconian Switzerland? I believe they largely bypassed it, and the longevity of witchcraft among the peasants of the region was greatly furthered by leaving the protective methods of medieval Christianity undisturbed. The seclusion of the area played a decisive role in preserving medieval customs, and the Franconian peasants see in their Church a limitless source of supernatural aid applicable to most of the problems they encounter in everyday life. It offers blessings to safeguard important daily activities, and exorcisms and protective rituals to drive out demons and ward off witches' spells. To these peasants, religion is not an abstract creed, but a practice— definable as a mode of behavior. The religious behavior of the Franconian peasants, from the Middle Ages to almost this day, differs little in this respect from the religious practices of primitive tribes: religion was important to them not because of its formalized creed, but because its rites were vital ingredients of everyday life, helping them to get on with work, responsibilities, fortune and misfortune. Religion dignified such significant occasions as birth, marriage and death by providing reassuring or comforting rites of passage. And in the case of evil, it helped with rituals of exorcism, blessings and other ceremonies—many of them of mixed pagan-Christian origin.

The undisturbed medieval practices may also account for the fact that the interior of Franconian Switzerland was spared witch prosecution. Perhaps the undiminished medieval Church magic afforded enough protection and communal acquiescence to find it unnecessary to introduce official action. These protective techniques were left intact until this, or the preceding, generation. Now they are rapidly declining. To the older peasants, the Devil is still allergic to holy water, blessed herbs and a *geweihten* talisman. To the younger generation, these things are of uncertain value, since the existence of the Devil has become uncertain. Most likely we presently see the last generation for whom religion and magic were an indivisible whole. Modernity has finally caught up with Franconian Switzerland and we witness the triumph of formal religion over practical magic.

220   Just as undisturbed ecclesiastical magic explains the marked

peacefulness in the villages of Franconian Switzerland, disturbed ecclesiastical magic explains, at least in part, why the areas surrounding Franconian Switzerland suffered one of Europe's most savage witch-hunts. The vehemence may have been incited by the questioning of the efficacy of the protective techniques. This disturbance deprived the communities—Catholic as well as Protestant—of psychological security, opening the door to formal persecution.

The continuing religious-historical dynamics call for an addendum to Thomas' theory. Either because of the unbearable liturgic sterility that Protestants inherited from the Reformation, or because of new developments (their discussion is beyond the frame of this book), some Protestants have tried to reforge a sense of magic and fervently attempt to manipulate supernatural powers to grant them the things they desire. I am thinking of the Pentecostal churches and the charismatic movements especially in the United States. Their adherence to religious magic is matched by their respect for the reality of folk magic, including witchcraft. I would venture the guess that today just as many Protestants as Catholics believe in witchcraft but that their protective techniques still differ: Protestants believe in prayer and faith healing, and Catholics still cling to the fringes of ecclesiastical magic. The former is a *demanding and manipulative magic* directly addressed to God; the latter still embraces rituals of *immanent magic*, with the magical power residing in the ritual itself, thus definable as mechanical magic. Protestants must rely on the willingness of God, His Providence, and can only try to appeal to Him; Catholics, on the other hand, can rely on rituals that are endowed with certain efficacy. This, of course, is only true in areas untouched by doubt; and, I repeat, one of Europe's last strongholds of mechanical magic, Franconian Switzerland, is now experiencing a decline of magic.

16

The Vagaries of Magic

For the new generation of Franconians, witchcraft is largely the lore of a tradition of superstitions. Many of the young are either embarrassed when reminded of the beliefs and practices of their forefathers, or, more often, show ignorance of these things. I made it a habit to ask the children of my relatives and of other villagers whether they knew the meanings of such words as *Wütenker*, *feurige Männlein*, *Milchhexe*, and so forth. *None* knew what these terms meant: they had never heard the words. Even among members of my generation, the children of the current elders, knowledge of such terminology is dwindling. I was therefore tempted to entitle this chapter, "End of an Era," but had second thoughts. While it is true that it is the end of an era for the Franconian peasants to whom much of this book is dedicated, it is not true for the larger cultural setting.

This larger cultural setting begins with the Franconian flatlands that surround mountainous Franconian Switzerland. Although Franconian Switzerland is politically a part of the larger province of Franconia, the religious and cultural processes of the various parts are not necessarily identical. The distinct outcropping of the Jura mountains provides a geographic seclusion that has supported cultural integrity. This explains why folk culture, including witchcraft, fluctuates between this enclave and adjacent regions. For example, witchcraft in Franconian villages to the west of Franconian Switzerland have made national, if not international, news over the past two decades. In addition to the earlier described 1976 case of fatal exorcism in the diocese of Würzburg, the Mailach witch-hunt deserves some attention. The village of Mailach lies approximately 20 miles off the western edge of Franconian Switzerland (see map in Chapter Two) and, in 1960, it experienced a witch scare worthy of the Renaissance. Sixty-four-year-old Elisabeth Hahn was generally regarded as a witch; she met the stereotype: spinster, poor (one cow, a flock of chickens, a few acres of land), shrivelled and stooped, isolated, friendless—except for three dogs, which were imputed to be her familiars "with whom she slept." The villagers shunned her, children threw rocks at her and a hostile neighbor threatened to beat her to death because of hexes he felt she cast on him. One day, this neighbor set fire to her house, killing most of her animals, badly burning her and totally destroying her home. Investigations and court hearings ran into mute neighbors who "hadn't seen anything"; and had it not been for the arsonist himself who self-righteously admitted that he had intended to drive out the "witch," it would have been difficult to convict the man.[1] This example reminds us that the belief in witches is still prevalent in the areas surrounding Franconian Switzerland; however, it also reminds us that such incidents have ceased to occur in the Jura mountains proper.

If we expand the cultural environment and look at Germany at large, we notice sustained belief in witchcraft and continued practice of it: "Germany still has more witches of the traditional kind than almost any other country."[2] A survey revealed that about 10,000 witches of a variety of black and white magic are still practicing in West Germany. Over the past two decades, close to 100 lawsuits dealing with witchcraft occurred each year. Altötting in Bavaria was the place of a 1973–1976 fight by a padre to exorcize a devil, who called himself Pluto I, in the 33-year-old daughter of a peasant. In Hamburg, during the 1950s, a 70-year-old woman and her 40-year-old assistant practiced "in-patient" exorcisms for 15 marks a day, including room and board.[3] In the late 1950s, Professor Peuckert reported that *grimoires*, like the *Sixth and Seventh Books of Moses*, were reprinted and immediately sold out.[4] He felt that the mid-century interest in the mythic-magical was a rebellion against the rational climate in our western societies. Döbler reported, mostly from northern Germany, that a typical town of 40,000 had numerous *Gesundbeterinnen* and seven *Hexenbanner*. To ban the effects of witches' hexes, the latter pseudosorcerers asked fees of up to $30. Most incidents of exorcism involved *Pech im Stall*, where farmers complained about ominous sicknesses among their animals.[5] A national poll during the mid 1970s established that 8 percent of the West German population believed in the existence of the Devil and witches; 16 percent were not certain, but believed in supernatural experiences not explicable by science. A similar poll during the same decade found that 11 percent of the adult West Germans believed in a physical Devil, 7 percent believed in exorcism of the Devil or demons, and in Bavaria (which includes Franconia) 9 percent believed in such exorcisms.[6]

The larger cultural setting includes American culture. The growing American trend, in harmony with the counterculture, is a revival of occult traditions. Among college youths the occult is "in" and the trustworthiness of reason is "out." A short while ago it seemed somewhat daring for an academic to profess belief in God; nowadays it is quite fashionable to believe in leprechauns and astrology. Certainly, a professor doing so would immediately conquer the hearts of the majority of his students. The current American scene teems with figures who publicly promote the idea of witchcraft. Raymond Buckland, an anthropologist, and his wife Rosemary are coven founder and high priestess who created the first national museum for witchcraft in Bay Shore, Long Island, New York; Sybil Leek is witchcraft's first TV star; and Louise Huebner, the "official witch of Los Angeles," wrote *Power through Witchcraft* in 1969, claiming to be a 6th-generation witch. Numerous young people are interested in coven membership; many observers suspect that their interest is based less on witchcraft as a religion than as a vehicle for sexual license.

The revival of witchcraft must be divided into two different traditions. One of them deals with the black witch, the Satanist of the Middle Ages and the Renaissance, whose contemporary protagonist is best illustrated by the dilettante who participates in the urban Satanic coven. The other tradition deals with the white witch; she allegedly was a member of the wicca cult—or Old Religion. In 1975, in the state of Washington, once a month 13 "daughters of wicca" gathered to their Sabbath. In the light of candles they formed a circle, nude, enveloped by the scent of sweet incense, singing Latin psalms that were to heal the sick and exorcize the souls of the dead. These women believed they could determine the weather, cause machines to stop and personally levitate. The high priestess of the group explained that they are fighting a continuous battle with black witches, lest the daughters of Satan get the upper hand and use their powers to gain financial advantages.[7] This is a new emphasis. But, then, this is the United States and, as everything else, the old is quickly adapted to new conditions and concerns. A bank account is as important today as the peasants' stables in the Middle Ages. California witnessed the first public marriage of witches in 1977. The world press recorded details: the long rust-colored dress of the bride, the satin-robed groom, incongruously holding a sword in his hand, the wicca temple with circle and superimposed reversed triangles (pentagram), a buffalo head— symbol of the Horned-One—on the wall of the large hall, a witches' broom leaning casually in a corner, and the bride assuring reporters that, ". . . witches are normal people and not some kind of Devil worshipers. Witchcraft is a religion to us, thousands of years old, a way of life, of love and harmony with Nature." Added the groom, "We are a part of God and don't believe in Satan. You know, Christians burned witches, but a witch never threw a Christian on the pyre."[8] One might add that without belief in Satan, such humanity is no feat. Anyway, the marriage was legal and, sometime, we may expect a real witch baptism.

We can observe a fascination with magic throughout Western civilization in general. Rather than being in the wake of a romantic and occultist era, Western societies stir with the resurrection of the occult. Witchcraft is on the rise.

Thus, it is a strange phenomenon—like a *déjà vu* in the theatre of the absurd—to see that, at a time when exotic vines of the occult creep in all directions, the ancient magic of the peasants of Franconian Switzerland is dying. Their religion has increased in formal doctrine and decreased in practical magic. Like weary wanderers after a tortuous and centuries-long road, our peasants finally come to rest at crossroads where they dumbfoundedly observe hordes of strangers scrambling down the path they have just covered.

By abandoning their magical imagination they lost the last defense against scientific objectivism. But, how long before the objective consciousness encountered at the crossroads will inflict disillusionment and loneliness on these exiles from the world of magic? How long before they will have forgotten the road their ancestors traveled seeking freedom from fear and from the oppression of capricious supernaturalism? Soon they may long to turn back, join the surging masses who head toward the dark mansions their fathers vacated, and re-enter the realm of the occult.

But if such reversal is in the offing, so far it has failed to give notice. No new mythology is on the horizon; and there are no tangible symptoms that would allow us to reasonably speculate on what is going to replace the old folk magic. Maybe there will not be a substantive replacement at all, at least not for a long time and anomie will prevail. If the Franconians are left with spiritual void, when will we recognize the symptoms that typically accompany such vacuity—such symptoms as increases in crimes, interpersonal quarrels and legal squabbles? But such symptoms are not noticeable at this time either. Maybe it is too early to see the effects of the dying folk magic. And what's more, maybe the Franconians *are* embracing a new mythology of sorts: the objective consciousness. Their surge toward the scientific world view may have temporarily soothed the loss of a deeper sense of magic and functioned as a palliative for ideational deprivation.

The question remains: What will happen after the newly found intoxication with science and objectivity wears off?

Elsewhere, certainly, the surge goes the other way. The widespread revival of the occult mirrors distrust in the objective consciousness and the scientific world view. Contemplating what has been achieved with A-bombs, pollution and destructive chemicals makes the promises of astrology, spiritualism, witchcraft and the rest of the occult exceedingly attractive. Powerlessness dismays the anonymous masses of our equally anonymous technocracy and drives them into the arms of a magical orientation that promises personal power and significance. Reluctance to assume responsibility for the poisonous fruits of our technology is most conspicuous among the young. They turn their backs on the frightening responsibility and grope for a new, mystic and magical lifestyle. They seek an alternative to being slaves to technocracy. The counterculture that shook Western societies during the 1960s and early 1970s was vivid testimony to the *Zeitgeist* of the late-20th century. It was a time of blind rejection of objective and scientific principles matched by the blind acceptance of subjective and occult ideas. Theodore Roszak chronicled the spirit of the counterculture when he wrote that the uniqueness of the movement, in contrast to previous youthful upheavals, was youth's preoccupation with the occult and the mystic. The fascination with the occult appeared so all-consuming that Roszak was goaded into making a sweeping diagnosis. He saw the culture disjuncture of the dissent between the generations "As great in its implications as the cleavage that once ran between Greco-Roman rationality and Christian mystery."[9]

Is Roszak's assessment more hyperbolic than realistic? No one can tell for certain. History usually implements new ideas slowly and almost imperceptibly, unless we speak of a revolution. But the counterculture was not an abrupt revolution. New notions, some of them radical, were infused into the fabric of the larger society—notions not yet well defined and continuing to stir. The least one can say is that these notions threaten to turn American society and perhaps the whole of Western civilization in some relatively uncharted directions. Rather than revolutionary change, I would expect a tumultuous process of evolutionary change that includes a greater acceptance of the occult as an alternative reality. I use the word "tumultuous" advisedly. Though the changes may be evolutionary, their unfolding is bound to be unsettling to persons and institutions alike.

While I see healthy elements in the on-rush of the new era, I also detect dishonesty and immaturity under the guise of youthful idealism. As John W. Aldridge warned, we may have been "brainwashed by the doctrine that whatever is young is right."[10] The adults' awe of youthfulness and youth's largely unchecked and frequently eloquently disguised hedonism has created a hushed audience in the United States; what the young express is often taken all too seriously. So it happened that modern youth's eager pursuit of the occult is making a noticeable impression on the elders. What is not fully recognized is that the occult is often but a guise for the hedonistic refusal to approach the necessary tasks in life in the tedious and laborious manner that is necessary for successful completion. The scientific method is not an easy route, it demands hard work and self-discipline. How much easier look the promises of the occult and the cooperation of presumed supernatural powers, when a leisurely reading of the horoscope reveals what and what not to do on a given day, who is a compatible companion or mate; and which career is suitable to one's temperament.

From such widespread and seemingly harmless occultism it is a small step to the belief in witchcraft. After all, how soothing to hedonism is the fancy that some magical formula might result in riches, security, personal identity and sensual pleasure when hard work, traditionally imposed on such achievements, now appears superfluous. Work appears anachronistic—magic the promise of a new era.

227   As mentioned earlier, there are understandable reasons why some

modern youth feel drawn so strongly to the promises of the super-natural. To put it briefly, the natural—or whatever man has done with it—has assumed an uncontrollable and frightening appear-ance. Ecological disasters and international conflicts have disillu-sioned the young and motivated them to search for solutions in another realm—the supernatural.

Alas, many counterculture people fail to realize that escape from responsibility in our technocratic juggernaut is nearly impossible and decidedly unwise; it is particularly unwise if another slavery is substituted. An alternative slavery threatens to be naive belief in the occult and the ready access to supernatural powers.

I see an alternative to the slavery of either technocracy or the occult in the type of humanism that upholds personal freedom and personal dignity, and demands self-responsibility. But personal free-dom is a heavy burden and the human longing to escape from it is legendary. Because we crave servitude and long for subjugation to authority above and beyond our human frailty, we seem to wander forever in the labyrinth of magic.

It is because of this futile meandering that history is not a straight road guiding humans to a grand terminal; rather, the path leads us in endless circles that have not been visible to the eye.

The vicissitudes of magic must be seen as an element of this endless labyrinth in which humans search for "the right way." Our Franconian peasants have just emerged from one run in the maze and can be seen resting at a crossroad, while most of the rest of Western mankind scurry with frantic urgency into vacated runs.

The credulity with which modern people, even scientists, rush headlong toward the occult is mind-boggling. In their haste to make the technocratic age more palatable, they embrace the messages and promises of a motley melange of the occult: the chariots of the Gods, karma, astrology, tarot cards, transcendental consciousness, the Bermuda Triangle, astral projection, Edgar Cayce, extraterres-trial visitors, pyramid power, Carlos Castaneda, past-lives therapy, necromancy, Immanuel Veliskovsky, the Loch Ness monster and, again, witchcraft. It is symptomatic that our age should witness the largest world witchcraft congress: the 1975 rallying of several thou-sand witches, wizards, masters of various occult arts and parapsy-chologists—in Bogota, Colombia. The international participants included those who claim to have contact with "the beyond" and can summon up the spirits of such personalities as Noah, Nero,

Messalina (wife of the Roman Emperor Claudius), Juan Peron, and John F. and Robert F. Kennedy.

It is also symptomatic of our age that astrology continues its inroads: about 85 percent of our daily newspapers carry daily columns; at least six universities teach the subject; one out of every four Americans believes in astrologers' forecasts, and three out of four know their sign. Faith in the reliability with which stars influence their lives is especially high among the young people: 38 percent of those 18–24 say they believe in astrology, as compared with 16 percent of those 30–49 and 21 percent of those 50 and older.[11]

The boundary between who is an occultist or a scientist has become blurred in recent years. There is a virtual paperback explosion of works on the bizarre and mystic; many of the authors are nothing but speculative occultists hiding under the cloak of science. Under exclusion of a number of important scientific guidelines, these pseudoscientists proceed with premises that are totally unverified and create a construct that appears internally consistent. Many people are impressed by this consistency and never notice its absurdity in the real world context. I see a great danger in accepting speculations and absurd assumptions as "facts," and sense a deadly parallel to the pseudoscience of racial superiority that reached heinous culmination with the Nazis. The danger lies in the convincing presentation of an argument that spins out a seemingly scientific rationale but conceals the fact that the initial premises are unfounded, highly biased and totally irrational.

Many of these occultists undoubtedly are honest persons who intend to pursue knowledge. But many of them are literary vultures who descend on the carrion of past inanities to sell them as life-enhancing nutrients to the lost, ignorant and insecure. These mystifiers, charlatans, exhibitionists and deluded visionaries have chosen their time shrewdly—they are cashing in at the beginning of what to me appears to be a new Era of Romanticism.

What most concerns me is not so much the masses' pursuit of the occult and other intangibles, but their confusion in distinguishing among different kinds of pursuits. This confusion also covers up the unwitting dishonesty concerning the motivation for the pursuit. Some of the occult probing can be seen as a legitimate pioneer effort to push back the frontier of knowledge and to accrue fresh insights. This is pioneering of a sort and has a legitimate place in the ongoing search for truth. But much of the occult pursuit is less a thrust for knowledge than a craving to console lost, lonely and hurt emotions. And in so doing, it usually confuses the gratification of irrational, often infantile, emotional needs with a committed search for knowledge.

To clarify their position and dissociate themselves from pseudo-scientists, a group of scientists decided to make a public declaration. In 1975, nearly 200 of them—including Nobel Prize winners—published a combined statement in the *Humanist* denouncing astrology as a sham. They warned that astrology seduces its followers to trust in Fate or Luck rather than in their own achievements, work and intelligence. The assumption that the manifold roots of personality formation can be ignored and that the labor necessary to understand this formation can be substituted for by 12 facile categories is as preposterous as it is puerile. Actually, it is genuinely infantile, reflecting undisciplined insistence on easy, as well as romantic, explanation. Most of all, the scientists disputed astrology's claim to be free of conflict with a scientific orientation. While religion deals with the supranatural and with ultimate meaning, a realm usually given respectful berth by science, astrology follows the characteristic presumptiousness of magic and deals with things of *this* world; this means that it usurps the stuff that is clearly subject to scientific inquiry—the empirical-logical explanation. From astrology's point of view, a lottery outcome is not the result of the law of probability, but of one's relation to the stars; a birth defect has nothing to do with genetics, but is the dire consequence of mismatched astrological signs of one's parents; an unsuccessful attempt at higher education is less a signal of low intellect or insufficient exertion than proof that the field of study was incompatible with one's astrological sign, ad infinitum. Hence, it is fair to say that the more people invest in astrology or other forms of magic, the less they rely on, appreciate and, ultimately, tolerate science.

Science, thus, is put on the defensive. To regain public understanding of and trust in science, astrology's usurpation and lack of base become the proper targets of disapproval by the scientific community. But rebuke alone is not a wise strategy; greater effectiveness may be achieved by educating people to understand *why* they so persistently want to believe in astrology and in magic in general. We must give astrology believers insight into their motivations and help them to see the reasons people seek reassurance from the stars.

230

But emotion may prove stronger than reason. When Prometheus cried out, "How weak is science confronted with Destiny!", he coined the shibboleth of our time—perhaps of all times. The late-20th century mood endorses it literally, busies itself with the elusive quest of Destiny and tries to fathom it through the occult.

The origin of mankind's insistence on knowing Destiny and achieving immortality is of considerable obscurity to many scholars. An unusually clear and challenging statement was offered by Arthur Koestler.[12] He believes that man's question about life after death creates problems with which our minds cannot cope: the question is far beyond the reasoning faculties of our species.

In computer language, we would have to concede that we are not programmed for the task and either must remain silent on the question or else go haywire. The stories of the various civilizations are the result of programs that went haywire. Since our minds cannot even begin to comprehend that our consciousness emerged from nothingness and returns to nothingness, our imagination runs berserk and populates the before-and-after life with souls, ghosts and divine, as well as diabolic, guardians of our immortality. These invisible presences constitute the spiritual populace with whom mankind tries to barter and bargain. Many of the spiritual powers are considered malevolent and need to be placated by grotesque rituals, including human sacrifices and the butchering of heretics.

This supernatural menagerie is central to all forms of magic. Since supernaturalism has remained fundamentally unchanged and probably never will change much, the human craving for magic will never abate. While the variations of the theme are ever changing, the basic tune stays the same.

The background of mankind's mania for magic can be elaborated further. If we had no concept of death, our great works of literature would have been unwritten, cathedrals and pyramids would not have been built, and the art of religion and magic would never have emerged. The creativity and pathology of the human mind are but two sides of the same coin.

Increasingly, experts see a neurophysiological explanation behind man's timeless madness and creativity. They hold the rapid expansion over the last million years of the human neocortex responsible for a faulty coordination between this cortex—the "thinking cap" that enables rational and abstract thought—and the so-called reptilian part of our brain, the archaic structure that we share with other animal species and which emits our emotional reactions. This evolutionary discord has resulted in a sort of "schizophysiology," a separation of reason from emotion that lies at the core of the human dilemma. The older and mightier partner of this divided "computer" is emotion, and whenever there is a conflict, the reasoning half of the brain is coerced to invent rationalizations for the senior partner's appetites.

This is a neurophysiological approach to explain mankind's incessant inventions and delusions that try to remove the sting from death, nothingness and powerlessness. The so-called spiritual pursuits of mankind are a compelling and methodical madness. They include the weirdest notions about the afterlife. While the neocortex cannot escape the realization of death, the old brain passionately refuses the idea of personal nonexistence and clings to the emotion of survival as a self-evident phenomenon. The cowed junior partner, the abstract neocortex, is then charged with providing mental constructs that fill the postmortem void with a fictitious scenario. This mindscape is populated with deities and demons; it is the playground of witches and wizards.

The purpose of briefly discussing these aspects of human nature is to lay bare a larger perspective on witchcraft, to see magic in the light of the basic human dilemma and to follow the vagaries of the occult more alertly. Most importantly, the fluctuations should never be understood as an evolutionary ascent to higher and truer insight, but as a ceaseless process of appeasing archaic emotions.

It is with this perspective in mind that we must view the experience of the Franconian peasants. Their abandoning of magic is not really the end of an era, and their retreat from the occult is only a temporary interlude within the larger *Zeitgeist*. Like first-generation Americans who reject the Old World heritage to move toward a more adequate adjustment in the New World, the offspring of the witchcraft-believing generations of Franconians reject their immediate heritage. But give them time. In another one or two generations, the descendents will proudly reclaim their "precious," almost lost heritage and join, belatedly but with equal fervor, the general surge of Western people toward the occult.

232

Notes

Chapter 3

1. W. I. Thomas, *Primitive Behavior* (New York: McGraw-Hill, 1937), p. 8.
2. The manifold ways in which the fear response acts on the soma was emphasized by Theodore R. Sarbin: "The sympathetico-adrenal system comes into action, exercising control over the viscera and blood vessels. The various internal changes render the organism ready for physical action (struggle or flight). If this state of extreme perturbation continues *without motoric charge*, death may follow." In "Role Theory," Gardner Lindzey, ed., *Handbook of Social Psychology* (Reading, Mass.: Addison-Wesley, 1954), p. 235.
3. Definition of "legend" in Jean L. McKechnie, ed., *Webster's New 20th Century Dictionary* (New York: World Publishing Co., 1962), I, unabridged, p. 1035.
4. The term may have derived from the Germanic *Wodans Heer* or possibly from the German *wütende Heer*, i.e., raging army; Karl Brückner, *Am Sagenborn der Fränkischen Schweiz* (Wunsiedel, Germany: G. Kohler Frankenverlag, 1929), I, p. 111, II, pp. 104–105. Also see Otto Höfler, *Kultische Geheimbünde der Germanen* (Frankfurt, 1934), I, p. 73, who reports the comparable Wild Hunt or cavalcade of the dead, in Thuringia and Swabia.
5. It is noteworthy that in the summer of 1976, while I was completing data collection for this book, an official case of exorcism ended tragically in the bishopric adjacent to the Franconian Switzerland. The victim of the presumed satanic possession was the 22-year-old student Anneliese Michel. Her symptoms included hallucinations, spasms, writhing, speaking in "devilish tongues" and other signs construed by her deeply religious (Catholic) family as possession. Bishop Josef Stangl of Würzburg entrusted two priests, experienced in such matters, with performing the Great Exorcism from the 17th-century *Rituale Romanum*. A desperate fight, lasting for several months, ensued between the exorcists and the presumed Satan in the body of the girl. End result: the girl died. A medical doctor was called after the exorcism victim had died of starvation. Anneliese, formerly strong and 5.8 ft., weighed a mere 70 lbs. at her death. She and her exorcists tried through fasting, and other means, to drive out the devil who manifested himself in five different personifications. In retrospect, her disorder was diagnosed as partly epilepsy and partly playing the role of the possessed. The two exorcising priests and the victim's parents were charged with negligent homicide and, in 1978, received prison sentences. The moral of the story: we don't need to chronicle the uneducated peasants of Tüchersfeld of 1915 to find exorcism applied to epilepsy; it is still done in the Space Age. See "Exorzismus," *Spiegel* 30 (August 2, 1976):60–62; AP Report,

July 14, 1977; "Sechsmonatige Haftstrafen im Exorzismus-Prozess," *Franken-post* (April, 22/23, 1978):8.

6. Besides the oral tradition, this story can also be found in Brückner, *Am Sagenborn der Fränkischen Schweiz*, II, p. 270.
7. Ludwig Helldorfer, *Gössweinstein: Burg, Amt, Kirche, Gemeinde* (Gössweinstein: Selbstverlag Marktgemeinde, 1974), pp. 868–870.
8. Brückner, *Am Sagenborn*, II, pp. 83–84.
9. Ibid., p. 85.
10. Ibid., p. 46.

Chapter 4

1. Karl Brückner, *Am Sagenborn der Fränkischen Schweiz* (Wunsiedel, Germany: G. Kohler Frankenverlag, 1929), II, p. 250. J. Franck, "Geschichte des Wortes Hexe," in Joseph Hansen, *Quellen und Untersuchungen zur Geschichte des Hexenwahns* (Hildesheim: Olms, 1901), pp. 614–70.
2. Two representative sources that elaborate on this view are Raymond Buckland, *Witchcraft from the Inside* (St. Paul, Minn.: Llewellyn Publications, 1975) and G. B. Gardner, *The Meaning of Witchcraft* (New York: Samuel Weiser, 1971).
3. Henry C. Lea, *A History of the Inquisition of the Middle Ages* (London, 1888), p. 493. Also see discussion in Julio C. Baroja, *The World of Witches* (Chicago: The University of Chicago Press, 1973), p. 250.
4. Brückner, *Am Sagenborn der Fränkischen Schweiz*, p. 250. Peter Haining, *Hexen* (Hamburg, Stalling, 1977), p. 53.
5. Henry Institor Kraemer and Jacob Sprenger, *Malleus Maleficarum*(Edition of Lyon, France, 1584), part III.
6. Jean Bodin, *De la Demonomanie des Sorciers* (Paris, 1580), II, chapter IV.
7. Rossell H. Robbins, *Encyclopedia of Witchcraft and Demonology* (New York: Crown Publishers, Inc., 1959), p. 7.
8. Baroja, *The World of Witches*, p. 92.
9. Robbins, *Encyclopedia of Witchcraft and Demonology*, p. 43.
10. Ibid., pp. 555–557; also see Brückner, *Am Sagenborn*, p. 254.
11. Robbins, *Encyclopedia of Witchcraft and Demonology*, pp. 35–37.
12. The word, in this context, is often also spelled Sabbat. Historians, such as Elliot Rose, *A Razor for a Goat* (Toronto: University of Toronto Press, 1962), p. 169, maintain that the origin of the word is identical with the Hebrew Sabbath and has assumed the broader meaning of a holy day of some regularity. They oppose the "Murrayite delusion" of other writers, such as Lucy Mair, *Witchcraft* (New York: McGraw-Hill, 1969), p. 226, who would have us believe that the word derived from the French *s'ébattre*, to rejoice. Both camps agree however that Sabbath does not derive from the Basque *Esbat*, but believe the reverse to be true, with the Basque term being a back-slang derivation from Sabbath.
13. Johann Georg Godelmann, *Tractatus de magis, veneficis, et lamiis* (Frankfurt, 1601), tract. II, chapter IV.
14. H. C. Erik Midelfort, *Witch Hunting in Southwestern Germany 1562–1684* (Stanford, Calif.: Stanford University Press, 1972), p. 135.
15. Ibid., p. 137.
16. Lyle Steadman, *The Killing of Witches: A Hypothesis*, unpublished research paper, Arizona State University, Department of Anthropology, 1977.
17. Midelfort, *Witch Hunting in Southwestern Germany 1562–1684*, p. 185.
18. E. William Monter, "Patterns of Witchcraft in the Jura," *Journal of Social History* 5 (Fall 1971):15.

19. Charles Mackay, *Extraordinary Popular Delusions and the Madness of Crowds* (New York: The Noonday Press, 1974; originally published in London, 1841), pp. 515, 526.
20. Friedrich Merzbacher, *Die Hexenprozesse in Franken*, 2nd ed. (Munich: Beck, 1970), p. 186n.
21. E. William Monter, *Witchcraft in France and Switzerland* (Ithaca, N.Y.: Cornell University Press, 1976), p. 186.
22. Ibid., p. 136.
23. Baroja, *The World of Witches*, p. 186.
24. Anton S. LaVey, *The Satanic Bible* (New York: Avon Press, 1969), p. 25.
25. Friedrich Merzbacher, *Die Hexenprozesse*, p. 116n.
26. Robbins, *Encyclopedia of Witchcraft and Demonology*, p. 42.
27. Lea, *A History of the Inquisition of the Middle Ages*, p. 1163.
28. Ibid., pp. 1177–1178.
29. Robbins, *Encyclopedia of Witchcraft and Demonology*, p. 36.
30. Lea, *A History of the Inquisition of the Middle Ages*, pp. 1173–1179.
31. See a comparison of legal procedures that tries to explain the difference in the quality as well as quantity of witch-hunting between England and the Continent: Elliott P. Currie, "Crimes without Criminals; Witchcraft and its Control in Renaissance Europe," *Law and Society Review* 3 (August, 1968):7–32.
32. Friedrich Merzbacher, *Die Hexenprozesse in Franken*, pp. 49–50. Hannsferdinand Döbler, *Hexenwahn* (Munich: Bertelsmann, 1977), pp. 295–296.
33. Brückner, *Am Sagenborn*, p. 254.
34. Döbler, *Hexenwahn*, p. 296.
35. Ibid., p. 291.
36. Monter, *Witchcraft in France and Switzerland*, p. 65.
37. Ibid., p. 66.
38. Ibid., pp. 106–107.
39. Hartmut H. Kunstmann, *Zauberwahn und Hexenprozess in der Reichsstadt Nürnberg* (Nürnberg: Stadtarchiv, 1970), I, pp. 199–200. Merzbacher, *Die Hexenprozesse in Franken*, p. 60.
40. Merzbacher, *Die Hexenprozesse in Franken*, pp. 57–58.
41. Ibid., pp. 54–55.
42. Mackay, *Extraordinary Popular Delusions*, p. 563.

Chapter 5

1. Charles Mackay, *Extraordinary Popular Delusions and the Madness of Crowds* (New York: The Noonday Press, 1974; reprinted from the 1841 edition), p. 561.
2. Karl Brückner, *Am Sagenborn der Fränkischen Schweiz* (Wundsiedel, Germany: Kohler Frankenverlag, 1929), II, pp. 250–261.
3. Ibid., pp. 252–253.
4. Hannsferdinand Döbler, *Hexenwahn* (Munich, Bertelsmann, 1977), p. 29.
5. Will-Erich Peuckert, *Geheimkulte* (Heidelberg: Pfeffer, 1951), pp. 128–129.
6. Jeffrey B. Russell, *The Devil* (Ithaca, N.Y.: Cornell University Press, 1977), pp. 93, 215, 253.
7. Alfred Wittmann, *Die Gestalt der Hexe in der deutschen Sage* (Bruchsal: Kruse & Söhne, 1933), pp. 67–69.
8. Melvin M. Firestone, "Sephardic Folk-Curing in Seattle," *Journal of American Folklore* 75 (October–December 1962): 305.
9. Hermann Frischbier, *Hexenspruch und Zauberbann, Ein Beitrag zur Geschichte des Aberglaubens in der Provinz Preussen* (Berlin: Enslin, 1870).

10. Johann Kruse, *Hexen unter uns? Magie und Zauberglauben in unserer Zeit* (Hamburg: Hamburgische Bücherei, 1951), p. 11.
11. Hugo Zwetsloot, *Friedrich Spee und die Hexenprozesse. Die Stellung und Bedeutung der Cautio Criminalis in der Geschichte der Hexenverfolgung* (Trier, 1954), p. 44.
12. Monika H. Wilson, "Witch-Beliefs and Social Structure," *American Journal of Sociology* 56 (1951): 308.
13. Bennetta Jules-Rosette, *African Apostles, Ritual and Conversion in the Church of John Maranke* (Ithaca, N.Y.: Cornell University Press, 1975), p. 206.
14. Oldfield Howey, *The Cat in the Mysteries of Religion and Magic* (London, 1930).
15. Russell, *The Devil*, pp. 126, 170, 217.
16. Peuckert, *Geheimkulte*, p. 287.
17. Brückner, *Am Sagenborn*, p. 254.
18. Johann Bächtold, *Handwörterbuch des deutschen Aberglaubens* (Berlin: De Gruyther & Co., 1942), III, cols. 1863ff., VI, cols. 293–351.
19. Kruse, *Hexen unter uns?*, pp. 15ff.
20. Wilson, "Witch-Beliefs and Social Structure," p. 307.
21. Brückner, *Am Sagenborn*, pp. 34–38.
22. Bächtold, *Handwörterbuch*, III, cols. 1863–67; VI, col. 329.
23. Frischbier, *Hexenspruch*.
24. Kruse, *Hexen unter uns?*, p. 37.
25. Ibid., pp. 26–29.
26. A. Macfarlane, "Witchcraft and Conflict," in Max Marwick, ed., *Witchcraft and Sorcery* (Baltimore: Penguin Books, 1970), p. 296.
27. Kruse, *Hexen unter uns?*, p. 13.
28. E. William Monter, "Patterns of Witchcraft in the Jura," *Journal of Social History* 5 (Fall 1971): 16.
29. Kruse, *Hexen unter uns?*, p. 10.
30. Bächtold, *Handwörterbuch*, VI, col. 351.

Chapter 6

1. A minority opinion was voiced about the question of the witch's power to withdraw her hex. Mr. Oldtimer, the peasant of Bärnfels who told me about personal witchcraft experiences, did not think that the witch had the power to withdraw the hex once she cast it. It required a person skilled in the *Anfangen* to lift the curse. This belief assumed a hierarchical order of supernatural forces: a higher power was needed to correct a lower power. The lower power, such as witchcraft, could not correct itself; it required divine power over the Devil's power to undo evil. On the basis of this hierarchical philosophy, the effectiveness of *Abbitten* (asking to undo a hex) was limited. Even if a witch wanted to comply, her diabolical hands were tied. Maybe this hierarchical view was fostered by the peasant's conviction that a person skilled in the *Anfangen* (a semi-Christian tradition believed to have divine power) could achieve the healing regardless whether the witch liked it or not.

I must emphasize that the opinion of the witch's impotence to withdraw her hexes was a minority of one; I do not know whether this logic had more followers in previous epochs.

2. That a witch was empowered to deactivate her spell was generally agreed on and corroborated by research in another part of the Jura mountains. "Among the people of the Jura, belief in the witch's power to cure her *maleficia* survived after the witch trials ended, just as it had probably preceded them." E. William

Monter, *Witchcraft in France and Switzerland* (Ithaca, N.Y.: Cornell University Press, 1976), p. 183.
3. Julio C. Baroja, *The World of Witches* (Chicago: The University of Chicago Press, 1965), p. 240.
4. Johann Kruse, *Hexen unter uns?* (Hamburg: Hamburgische Bücherei, 1951), pp. 37ff.
5. Mark Zborowski and Elizabeth Herzog, *Life Is with People* (New York: International Universities Press, 1962), index.
6. Charles Mackay, *Extraordinary Delusions and the Madness of Crowds* (New York: Noonday Press, 1974), p. 560.
7. E. E. Evans-Pritchard, *Witchcraft, Oracles and Magic among the Azande* (Oxford: Oxford University Press, 1937).

Chapter 7

1. Will-Erich Peuckert, "Das 6. und 7. Buch Mosis," *Zeitschrift für deutsche Philologie* 76 (1957):174.
2. Readers who desire a more reliable version of the Kabbala are advised to consult Adolphe Franck, *The Kabbalah—The Religious Philosophy of the Hebrews* (New York: University Books, 1967); Rabbi Levi Isaac Krakovsky, *Kabbalah: The Light of Redemption* (Brooklyn, New York: The Kabbalah Foundation, 1950); A. E. Waite, *The Holy Kabbalah* (New York: University Books, no date of publication indicated).
3. Montague Summers, *A Popular History of Witchcraft* (New York: Causeway Books, 1973), p. 77. (Originally published by Kegan Paul, London, 1937.)
4. Ibid.
5. Ibid., p. 78
6. E. William Monter, *Witchcraft in France and Switzerland* (Ithaca, N.Y.: Cornell University Press, 1976), p. 189.
7. Summers, *A Popular History of Witchcraft*, p. 96.
8. Peuckert, "Das 6. und 7. Buch Mosis," pp. 163–187.
9. Summers, *A Popular History of Witchcraft*, pp. 81–82.
10. See a dissenting view arguing that the witch craze did not stop with the Carpathian Mountains as it is generally believed: Zoltán Kovács, "Die Hexen in Russland," *Acta Ethnographica Academiae Hungaricae* 22 (1973):53–86.
11. Johann Bächtold, *Handwörterbuch des deutschen Aberglaubens* (Berlin: De Gruyther & Co., 1942), VI, col. 591.
12. Hannsferdinand Döbler, *Hexenwahn* (Munich: Bertelsmann, 1977), p. 305.
13. Ibid.
14. Will-Erich Peuckert, *Verborgenes Niedersachsen* (Göttingen: Schwartz & Co., 1960), pp. 123–148.
15. *The Sixth and Seventh Books of Moses or Moses' Magical Spirit-Art* (Translated from the German, Printed in the USA, anonymous editor and publisher, no date of publication); Henri Gamache, ed., *Mystery of the Long Lost Eighth, Ninth, and Tenth Books of Moses* (Highland Falls, New York: Sheldon Publication, 1967).
16. To do justice to the originators of voodoo, it must be said that voodoo developed as a religion among Haitians, as a mixture of Dahomean tradition and Christian belief and in no way was a secret company of witches or sorcerers.
17. See, for example, the study of a South African Bantu tribe by J. D. Krige, "The Social Function of Witchcraft," in Max Marwick, ed., *Witchcraft and Sorcery* (Baltimore: Penguin Books, 1970), pp. 237–251.
18. Gamache, *Mystery of the Long Lost Eighth, Ninth, and Tenth Books of Moses*, p. 80.

19. Ibid., p. 81.
20. Ibid., p. 102.
21. Ibid., p. 99.
22. Ibid., p. 97.
23. *The Sixth and Seventh Books of Moses*, p. 113.

Chapter 8

1. This account has been related to me in various versions. One of them can also be found in Karl Brückner, *Am Sagenborn der Fränkischen Schweiz* (Wunsiedel, Germany: Kohler Frankenverlag, 1929), II, p. 259.
2. Hans Wolf, *Gössweinstein: Gestern, Heute, Morgen* (Gössweinstein: Marktgemeinde, 1976), p. 16.
3. An example is the animistic cosmos of the Fox Indians. They make little distinction between the material and nonmaterial, the organic and inorganic, between animal and human. All varieties of phenomena can assume manitu power. See Walter B. Miller, "Two Concepts of Authority," *American Anthropologist* 57 (1955): 279.
4. In this account, the word used to refer to the healer was *Abhelfer*, a helper, instead of the more customary reference to the person who knows the *Anfangen*. Questioned about the difference, the reporting peasant deemed the expressions synonymous. Nevertheless, he continued to use consistently the phrase *Abhelfer* throughout this account but used the term *Anfangen* in all other accounts. My interpretation is that a healer remaining in his or her own home when performing the healing prayers and rituals was thought of as an *Abhelfer*, while the healer performing at the location of trouble was doing the *Anfangen*.
5. A literary treatment of this belief can be found in Ludwig Helldorfer, *Gössweinstein: Burg, Amt, Kirche, Gemeinde* (Gössweinstein: Selbstverlag Marktgemeinde, 1974), p. 825.
6. Brückner, *Am Sagenborn der Fränkischen Schweiz*, I, p. 123.
7. Ibid., pp. 34–38.
8. The similarity with which some unrelated cultures have been found to view certain characteristics of the witch is astounding. Of the Azande was reported that they "generally think of a witch sending his soul on errands by night when his victim is asleep." E. E. Evans-Pritchard, *Witchcraft, Oracles, and Magic among the Azande* (Oxford: Oxford University Press, 1937), p. 33. In a similar vein, it was reported that in Sudanese and Nigerian tribes "the shadow-souls of witches roam about and attack victims, while their bodies remain asleep at home, thus deceiving any ordinary attempt at proving, or disproving, these mystic activities." See S. F. Nadel, "Witchcraft in Four African Societies," *American Anthropologist*, 54 (1952): 18.
9. Brückner, *Am Sagenborn*, II, pp. 259–260.
10. Charles G. Leland, *Gypsy Sorcery and Fortune Telling* (New York: University Books, 1964), p. 62.

Chapter 9

1. E. E. Evans-Pritchard, *Witchcraft, Oracles, and Magic among the Azande* (Oxford: Oxford University Press, 1937).
2. Ludwig Helldorfer, *Gössweinstein: Burg, Amt, Kirche, Gemeinde* (Gössweinstein: Selbstverlag, Marktgemeinde, 1974), p. 825.

238

3. A study of opinion formation in small communities, studying the creation of witchcraft rumors, was completed by Robert W. Balch, *The Creation of Demons: The Social Reality of Witchcraft and Satanism in Western Montana*, unpublished research report, University of Montana, Missoula, Montana, 1975.

4. Charles Mackay, *Extraordinary Popular Delusions and the Madness of Crowds* (New York: The Noonday Press, 1974), p. 556.

5. A recent example of the "evil eye" concept was reported by Melvin M. Firestone, "Sephardic Folk-Curing in Seattle," *Journal of American Folklore* 75 (October–December 1962):301–310. Another example was the long tradition of the "evil eye" among the Jews of the *shtetel*.

6. Gustav Henningsen, *The European Witch-Persecution* (Copenhagen: Danish Folklore Archives, 1973), pp. 8–9.

7. Ibid., p. 10.

Chapter 10

1. Some primitive societies do not distinguish between supernatural and natural forces. Magic in such cultures is a strictly here-and-now phenomenon with exclusively empirical implications. See, for example, E. E. Evans-Pritchard, *Witchcraft, Oracles, and Magic among the Azande* (Oxford: Oxford University Press, 1950), pp. 21–39.

2. S. F. Nadel, "Witchcraft in Four African Societies," *American Anthropologist* 54 (1952):18.

3. Bronislaw Malinowski, *Magic, Science and Religion and other Essays* (Garden City, New York: Doubleday and Company, 1955), p. 80.

4. Some social scientists consider the empirical trait of magic important enough to see similarity between magic and science. Magic is seen as empirical testing without recourse to the laws and principles drawn up by science. If an attempt were made to construct science with no consideration than the purely empirical connections, the result would be the same as working in a system of magic. See Judith Willer, *The Social Determination of Knowledge* (Englewood Cliffs, New Jersey: Prentice-Hall, 1971), p. 31.

5. Willer, *The Social Determination of Knowledge*

6. Ibid.

7. Ibid.

8. Pennethorne Hughes, *Witchcraft* (Baltimore, Maryland: Penguin Books, 1970) p. 216.

9. Willer, *The Social Determination of Knowledge*, p. 57.

10. Leon Festinger, et al., *When Prophecy Fails* (Minneapolis: University of Minnesota Press, 1956).

11. Examples of the endeavor to maintain images once established can be found in all areas of life, not merely in the religious sphere. See an illustration from political life: Hans Sebald, "Limitations of Communication: Mechanisms of Image Maintenance through Selective Perception, Selective Memory, and Selective Distortion," *Journal of Communication* 3 (September 1962):142–149.

12. Charles Mackay, *Extraordinary Popular Delusions and the Madness of Crowds* (New York: The Noonday Press, 1974; originally published in London, 1841), pp. 516–517.

13. Ibid., 561.

14. Ibid., 531.

15. Morris N. Kertzer, *Tell Me, Rabbi* (New York: Block Publishing Co., 1976). pp. 131–132.

Chapter 11

1. Elliot Rose, *A Razor for a Goat* (Toronto: Toronto University Press, 1962).
2. Wilhelm G. Soldan, *Geschichte der Hexenprozesse* (Stuttgart, 1843)
3. Joseph Hansen, *Quellen und Untersuchungen zur Geschichte des Hexenwahns und der Hexenverfolgung im Mittelalter* (Hildesheim: Olms, 1901) and *Zauberwahn, Inquisition und Hexenprozess im Mittelalter und die Entstehung der grossen Hexenverfolgung* (Leipzig und München, 1900); Henry C. Lea, *A History of the Inquisition of the Middle Ages* (New York: Macmillan, 1888).
4. Rose, *A Razor for a Goat*, p. 9.
5. Examples of his writings: Montague Summers, *History of Witchcraft and Demonology* (London: Kegan Paul, 1926); *Geography of Witchcraft* (London: Kegan Paul, 1927); *Popular History of Witchcraft* (London: Kegan Paul, 1937).
6. Margaret Murray, *The Witch Cult in Western Europe* (Oxford: Oxford University Press, 1921).
7. Emile Durkheim, *The Elementary Forms of Religious Life* (New York: Macmillan, 1915).
8. Examples: Rose, *A Razor for a Goat*; Lucy Mair, *Witchcraft* (New York: World University Press, 1969); G. L. Burr, "A Review of Murray's 'Witch Cult in Western Europe'," *American Historical Review* 27 (1922), no. 4; Keith Thomas, *Religion and the Decline of Magic* (New York: Scribner's, 1971), pp. 514–517, 525.
9. Gustav Henningsen, *The European Witch-Persecution* (Copenhagen: Danish Folklore Archives, 1973), p. 12.
10. Julio C. Baroja, *The World of Witches* (Chicago: The University of Chicago Press, 1965), pp. 65, 243–244.
11. Ibid., p. 66.
12. Hansen, *Quellen*.
13. Pennethorne Hughes, *Witchcraft* (Baltimore: Penguin Books, 1970); Hugh R. Williamson, *The Arrow and the Sword* (London: Faber, 1947); Peter Haining, *Hexen* (Hamburg, Stalling, 1977); Arne Runeberg, *Witches, Demons and Fertility Magic* (Helsingfors, 1947).
14. Gerald B. Gardner, *High Magic's Aid* (London: Rider, 1949) and *Witchcraft Today* (London: Rider, 1951).
15. Haining, *Hexen*, p. 9.
16. Rose, *A Razor for a Goat*, p. 18.
17. John Demos, "Underlying Themes in the Witchcraft of the 17th-Century New England," *American Historical Review* 75 (June 1970):1311–1326. Bronislaw Malinowski, "Magic, Science and Religion," Robert Redfield, ed., *Magic, Science, and Religion and other Essays* (New York: Doubleday, 1954).
18. Rossell H. Robbins, *The Encyclopedia of Witchcraft and Demonology* (New York: Crown Publishers, 1963), pp. 429–448.
19. Friedrich Leitschuh, *Beiträge zur Geschichte des Hexenwesens* (Bamberg, Hübscher, 1883), pp. 7–9; Johann Looshorn, *Die Geschichte des Bistum Bamberg* (Bamberg, 1906), VI, p. 33.
20. Hannsferdinand Döbler, *Hexenwahn* (Munich: Bertelsmann, 1977), pp. 253–254.
21. Karl F. Vierordt, *Geschichte der evangelischen Kirche in dem Grossherzogsthum Baden* (Karlsruhe, 1847–1856), pp. 68, 127.
22. Friedrich Merzbacher, *Die Hexenprozesse in Franken*, 2nd ed., (Munich: C. H. Beck, 1970), p. 87.
23. Ibid., p. 57.
24. Döbler, *Hexenwahn*, p. 193.
25. Rose, *A Razor for a Goat*, p. 25.
26. Hugh R. Trevor-Roper, *The European Witch-Craze of the 16th and 17th Centuries and Other Essays* (New York: Penguin Books, 1969), p. 143.

27. Alan D. J. Macfarlane, *Witchcraft in Tudor and Stuart England* (New York: Harper Torchbooks, 1970), pp. 91–99.
28. Henningsen, *The European Witch-Persecution*, p. 14.
29. E. William Monter, "Patterns of Witchcraft in the Jura," *Journal of Social History* 5 (Fall 1971):9.
30. Ibid., pp. 10–11.
31. Merzbacher, *Die Hexenprozesse*, p. 112.
32. Ignaz Döllinger, *El Pontificado* Spanish translation by Demetrio Zorrilla (Madrid, no date), pp. 171–180.
33. To be fair to many of my colleagues in history, I must modify this sociological prejudice. Many historians have shown that narrative history is not mere chronicle but constitutes a mode of analysis. A careful examination of the history of ideas and concepts, tracing their inception and the reasons for evolving and changing, certainly offers valid commentary about human nature. Examples of successful attempts at the history of ideas and an explanation of its methodology include Jeffrey B. Russell, *The Devil. Perceptions of Evil from Antiquity to Primitive Christianity* (Ithaca, N.Y.: Cornell University Press, 1977), chapter 2; Keith Thomas, *Religion and the Decline of Magic* (New York: Scribner, 1971).

Chapter 12

1. Including, besides those mentioned earlier, Clyde Kluckhohn, *Navaho Witchcraft* (Boston: Beacon Press, 1962); J. H. Beattie, "Sorcery in Bunyoro," J. F. Middleton and E. H. Winter, eds., *Witchcraft and Sorcery in East Africa* (Boston: Routledge and Kegan Paul, 1963).
2. Charles Mackay, *Extraordinary Popular Delusions and the Madness of Crowds* (New York: The Noonday Press, 1974), p. 464.
3. Reported by Sherida Bush, "Hags, Ghosts, and Demons of the Night," *Psychology Today* 10 (Nov. '76): 34.
4. Herbert Rappaport, "The Tenacity of Folk Psychotherapy: A Functional Interpretation," paper presented at the Annual Meeting of the Eastern Psychological Association, New York, 1976.
5. A. J. D. Macfarlane, *Witchcraft in Tudor and Stuart England* (New York: Harper Torch Book, 1970).
6. Jan Yoors, *The Gypsies* (New York: Simon & Schuster, 1967).
7. Elsie C. Parsons, "Witchcraft among the Pueblos: Indian or Spanish?" *Man*, 27 (1927): 106–128.
8. E. E. Evans-Pritchard, *Witchcraft, Oracles and Magic among the Azande*, (Oxford: Oxford University Press, 1937), p. 170.
9. Monika H. Wilson, "Witch-Beliefs and Social Structure," *American Journal of Sociology*, 56 (1951): 308.
10. Max Gluckman, *Politics, Law and Ritual in Tribal Societies* (New York: Oxford University Press, 1965), pp. 223–224.
11. Kluckhohn, *Navaho Witchcraft*, p. 121.
12. Emile Durkheim, *The Division of Labor in Society*, trans. George Simpson (Glencoe, Ill.: The Free Press, 1960).
13. Clyde Kluckhohn and D. Leighton, *The Navaho* (Cambridge, Mass.: Harvard University Press, 1946), p. 179.
14. Alfred Adler, *The Practice and Theory of Individual Psychology* (New York: Harcourt, Brace, 1927).
15. Ernest Becker, *Escape from Evil* (New York: Free Press, 1976).
16. Walter B. Miller, "Two Concepts of Authority," *American Anthropologist*, 57 (1955): 282.

17. Julio C. Baroja, *The World of Witches*, (Chicago: Chicago University Press, 1965), p. 256.
18. Friedrich Nietzsche, *The Portable Nietzsche* selected and translated by Walter Kaufmann (New York: The Viking Press, 1954), p. 570.
19. Karl Marx and Friedrich Engels, *On Religion* (New York: Schocken Books, 1964).
20. Sigmund Freud, *Civilization and Its Discontents* (New York: Norton, 1962), p. 21.
21. Ibid., p. 22.
22. Sigmund Freud, *The Future of an Illusion* (Garden City, New York: Doubleday, 1964), p. 72.
23. Keith Thomas, *Religion and the Decline of Magic* (New York: Scribner's, 1971), p. 545.
24. Max Marwick, "The Social Context of Cewa Witch Beliefs," *Africa* 22 (1952): 232.
25. Philip Mayer, "Witches," Max Marwick, ed., *Witchcraft and Sorcery* (Baltimore: Penguin Books, 1970), p. 56.
26. Kluckhohn, *Navaho Witchcraft*.
27. Keith Thomas, *Religion and the Decline of Magic*, p. 555.
28. Macfarlane, *Witchcraft in Tudor and Stuart England*.
29. Kluckhohn and Leighton, p. 243.
30. Wolfgang Lederer, *The Fear of Women* (New York: Harcourt Brace Jovanovich, 1968).
31. Joseph Hansen, *Quellen und Untersuchungen zur Geschichte des Hexenwahns und der Hexenverfolgung im Mittelalter* (Hildesheim: Olms, 1901), p. 132. Hartlieb's original Middle-High-German statement rationalizing the greater frequency of women engaged in witchcraft was "Daruff antworten die maister, das gewonlich die weib leuchter sind an irem gemüt und gelauben, darumb so mist sich der teuffel vester zu in dan zu den mannen."
32. E. William Monter, *Witchcraft in France and Switzerland* (Ithaca, N.Y.: Cornell University Press, 1976), p. 124.
33. Lyle Steadman, *The Killing of Witches*: A Hypothesis, unpublished research report, Department of Anthropology, Arizona State University, 1977.
34. Kluckhohn and Leighton, pp. 240–252.

Chapter 13

1. Ulrich F. Schneider, *Das Werk "De praestigiis daemonum" von Weyer und seine Auswirkungen auf die Bekämpfung des Hexenwahns*, jur. diss., Bonn 1951.
2. Rossell H. Robbins, *The Encyclopedia of Witchcraft and Demonology* (New York: Crown, 1963), p. 454.
3. Ilza Veith, *Hysteria: The History of a Disease* (Chicago: University of Chicago Press, 1965); R. E. Masters, *Eros and Evil: The Sexual Psychopathology of Witchcraft* (New York: Matrix House, 1966).
4. Charles Mackay, *Extraordinary Popular Delusions and the Madness of Crowds* (New York: The Noonday Press, 1974), p. 501.
5. Ibid., p. 526.
6. The earlier-mentioned anti-Sadduccee, Montague Summers, collected demonological reports on the werewolf phenomenon. In spite of his well-known theological bias, the work is valuable as a listing of literary sources. *The Werewolf* (London: Kegan Paul, 1937).

7. E. William Monter, *Witchcraft in France and Switzerland; The Borderlands during the Reformation* (Ithaca: Cornell University Press, 1976), pp. 145–151.

8. Mackay, *Extraordinary Popular Delusions*, p. 538.
9. Will-Erick Peuckert, *Geheimkulte* (Heidelberg: Pfeffer, 1951), pp. 118–120.
10. Ibid., p. 121.
11. Charles Richet, *L'homme et l'intelligence. Fragments de Physiologie et de Psychologie* (Paris, 1887), pp. 261–394.
12. Julio C. Baroja, *The World of Witches*, (Chicago: University of Chicago Press, 1965), p. 247.
13. Ibid., pp. 254–255. Bernard Barnett, "Witchcraft, Psychopathology and Hallucination," *British Journal of Psychiatry* 61 (1965): 439–455. H. Fühner, "Los Estupefacientes," *Investigacion y Progreso* 4 (March 1930): 37. Peter Haining, *Hexen* (Hamburg: Stalling, 1977), p. 33.
14. Fühner, "Los Estupefacientes." Also see A. J. Clark who reported that, "The combination of a delirifacient like belladonna with a drug producing irregular action of the heart like aconite might produce the sensation of flying." In Margaret Murray, *The Witch Cult in Western Europe* (Oxford: Oxford University Press, 1921), p. 280.
15. Hannsferdinand Döbler, *Hexenwahn* (Munich: Bertelsmann, 1977), pp. 24–25.
16. Carlos Castaneda, *The Teachings of Don Juan. A Yaqui Way of Knowledge* (Los Angeles: University of California Press, 1968), pp. 91–92.
17. Gustav Henningsen, *The European Witch-Persecution* (Copenhagen: Danish Folklore Archives, 1973), p. 6.
18. Elliot Rose, *A Razor for a Goat* (Toronto: Toronto University Press, 1962), p. 42.
19. E. Dupré, *Pathologie de l'imagination et de l'emotion* (Paris, 1925).
20. Mackay, *Extraordinary Popular Delusions*, p. 551.
21. Ibid., pp. 551–554. Rossell H. Robbins, *The Encyclopedia of Witchcraft and Demonology*, pp. 429–448.
22. Linnda R. Caporael, "Ergotism: The Satan Loosed in Salem," *Science* 192 (April 2, 1976): 21–26.
23. Nicholas P. Spanos and Jack Gottlieb, "Ergotism and the Salem Village Witch Trials," *Science* 194 (December 24, 1976): 1390–1394.

Chapter 14

1. Thomas Szasz, *The Manufacture of Madness: A Comparative Study of the Inquisition and the Mental Health Movement* (New York: Harper & Row, 1970).
2. Charles Mackay, *Extraordinary Popular Delusions and the Madness of Crowds* (New York: The Noonday Press, 1974), p. 504.
3. Ibid.
4. Ibid., p. 559.
5. Rossell H. Robbins, *The Encyclopedia of Witchcraft and Demonology* (New York: Crown Publishers, 1963), pp. 292.
6. Robert J. Lifton, *Thought Reform and the Psychology of Totalism. A Study of "Brainwashing" in China* (New York: Norton, 1961).
7. Ibid.
8. Gustav Henningsen, *The European Witch-Persecution* (Copenhagen: Danish Folklore Archives, 1973), p. 18.
9. Friedrich Merzbacher, *Die Hexenprozesse in Franken* (Munich: Beck, 1970), pp. 139–140.
10. Ibid.

Chapter 15

1. See, for example, Eleanor L. Hoover, "Mystical Portents," *Human Behavior*, 6 (March 1977): 14; and "Science: No Longer a Sacred Cow," *Time*, 109 (March 7, 1977): 72–73.
2. Charles Mackay, *Extraordinary Popular Delusions and the Madness of Crowds* (New York: The Noonday Press, 1974), pp. 563–564.
3. Robert W. Balch, *The Creation of Demons: The Social Reality of Witchcraft and Satanism in Western Montana*, unpublished research paper, Department of Sociology, University of Montana, 1975, p. 38.
4. See, for example, his work *Witchcraft and Black Magic* (London, 1946).
5. Keith Thomas, *Religion and the Decline of Magic* (New York: Scribner's, 1971).
6. Nikolaus Paulus, *Hexenwahn und Hexenprozess, vornehmlich im 16. Jahrhundert* (Freiburg, 1910), pp. 20–66.
7. Thomas, *Religion and the Decline of Magic*, p. 51.
8. Ibid., p. 62.
9. E. William Monter, *Witchcraft in France and Switzerland* (Ithaca, N.Y.: Cornell University Press, 1976), pp. 153–159, 166.
10. Max Weber, *The Protestant Ethic and the Spirit of Capitalism* (New York: Scribner's, 1930).
11. Thomas, *Religion and the Decline of Magic*, p. 398.
12. Ibid., p. 501.

Chapter 16

1. Reinhard Federmann and Hermann Schreiber, *Botschaft aus dem Jenseits* (Tübingen: Erdmann, 1968), pp. 129–134.
2. Peter Haining, *Hexen* (Hamburg: Stallings, 1977), p. 104.
3. Ibid.,). 114.
4. Will-Erich Peuckert, "Das 6. and 7. Buch Mosis," *Zeitschrift für deutsche Philologie* 76 (1957): 187.
5. Hannsferdinand Döbler, *Hexenwahn* (Munich: Bertelsmann, 1977), p. 309.
6. Ibid., p. 312.
7. Ibid., p. 317.
8. Ibid., p. 321.
9. Theodore Roszak, *The Making of a Counter Culture* (New York: Doubleday, 1969), p. 51.
10. John W. Aldridge, *In the Country of the Young* (New York: Harper's Magazine Press Book, 1970), p. 75.
11. Amitai Etzioni, "Seeking Solace from the Stars," *Human Behavior* 7 (April 1978): 16.
12. Arthur Koestler, *Life after Death* (New York: McGraw-Hill, 1976).

Bibliography

Adler, Alfred, *The Practice and Theory of Individual Psychology* (New York: Harcourt, Brace, 1927).

Aldridge, John W., *In the Country of the Young* (New York: Harper's Magazine Press, 1970).

Apuleius, *The Golden Ass*, translated by Robert Graves (New York: Penguin Books, 1950).

Ardrey, Robert, *The Territorial Imperative* (New York: Atheneum, 1966).

Bächtold, Johann, *Handwörterbuch des deutschen Aberglaubens* (Berlin: De Gruyther & Co., 1942).

Balch, Robert, *The Creation of Demons: The Social Reality of Witchcraft and Satanism in Western Montana*, unpublished research paper, Department of Sociology, University of Montana, 1975.

Barnett, Bernard, "Witchcraft, Psychopathology and Hallucination," *British Journal of Psychiatry* 61 (1965):439–455.

Baroja, Julio C., *The World of Witches* (Chicago: The University of Chicago Press, 1973).

Beattie, J. H., "Sorcery in Bunyoro," in J. F. Middleton and E. H. Winter, eds., *Witchcraft and Sorcery in East Africa* (Boston: Routledge and Kegan Paul, 1963).

Becker, Ernest, *Escape from Evil* (New York: Free Press, 1976).

Bodin, Jean, *De la Demonomanie des Sorciers* (Paris, 1580).

Brückner, Karl, *Am Sagenborn der Fränkischen Schweiz* (Wunsiedel, Germany: G. Kohler Frankenverlag, 1929), vols. I and II.

Buckland, Raymond, *Witchcraft from the Inside* (St. Paul, Minn.: Llewellyn Publications, 1975).

Burr, George L., "A Review of Murray's 'Witch Cult in Western Europe'," *American Historical Review* 27 (1922), no. 4.

Bush, Sherida, "Hags, Ghosts, and Demons of the Night," *Psychology Today* 10 (November 1976):34.

Caporael, Linnda R., "Ergotism: The Satan Loosed in Salem," *Science* 192 (April 2, 1976):21–26.

Carpsov, Benedict, *Practica rerum criminalium*, Wittenberg 1635.

Castaneda, Carlos, *The Teachings of Don Juan. A Yaqui Way of Knowledge* (Los Angeles: University of California Press, 1968).

Castaneda, Carlos, *Journal to Ixtlan. The Lessons of Don Juan* (New York: Simon & Schuster, 1972).

Clark, A. J., addendum in Margaret Murray, *The Witch Cult in Western Europe* (Oxford: Oxford University Press, 1921).

Currie, Elliott P., "Crimes without Criminals; Witchcraft and Its Control in Renaissance Europe," *Law and Society Review* 3 (August 1968):7–32.

Demos, John, "Underlying Themes in the Witchcraft of 17th-Century New England," *American Historical Review* 75 (June 1970):13311–13326.

Döbler, Hannsferdinand, *Hexenwahn* (Munich: Bertelsmann, 1977).

Döllinger, Ignaz, *El Pontificado* Spanish translation by Demetrio Zorrilla (Madrid, no date).

Dupré, E., *Pathologie de l'imagination et de l'emotion* (Paris, 1925).

Durkheim, Emile, *The Elementary Forms of Religious Life* (New York: Macmillan, 1915).

Durkheim, Emile, *The Division of Labor in Society*, translated by George Simpson (Glencoe, Ill.: The Free Press, 1960).

Etzioni, Amitai, "Seeking Solace from the Stars," *Human Behavior* 7 (April 1978):16.

Evans-Pritchard, E. E., *Witchcraft, Oracles and Magic among the Azande* (Oxford: Oxford University Press, 1937).

Federmann, Reinhard, and Hermann Schreiber, *Botschaft aus dem Jenseits* (Tübingen: Erdmann, 1968).

Festinger, Leon, et al., *When Prophecy Fails* (Minneapolis: University of Minnesota Press, 1956).

Firestone, Melvin M., "Sephardic Folk-Curing in Seattle," *Journal of American Folklore* 75 (October–December 1962):301–310.

Francisci, Abbot M. Adam, *Generalinstruktion von den Trutten* (Brandenburg, 1691).

Franck, Adolphe, *The Kabbalah—The Religious Philosophy of the Hebrews* (New York: University Books, 1967).

Franck, J., "Geschichte des Wortes Hexe," in Joseph Hansen, *Quellen und Untersuchungen zur Geschichte des Hexenwahns* (Hildesheim: Olms, 1901), pp. 614–670.

Frazer, Sir James G., *The Golden Bough* (London: Macmillan, 1911).

Freud, Sigmund, *Civilization and Its Discontents* (New York: Norton, 1962).

Freud, Sigmund, *The Future of an Illusion* (Garden City, N.Y.: Doubleday, 1964).

Frischbier, Hermann, *Hexenspruch und Zauberbann. Ein Beitrag zur Geschichte des Aberglaubens in der Provinz Preussen* (Berlin: Enslin, 1870).

Fühner, H. "Los Estupefacientes," *Investigacion y Progreso* 4 (March 1930):37.

Gamache, Henri, ed., *Mystery of the Long Lost 8th, 9th, and 10th Books of Moses* (Highland Falls, N.Y.: Sheldon Publication, 1967).

Gardner, G. B., *High Magic's Aid* London: Rider, 1949); *Witchcraft Today* (London: Rider, 1951); *The Meaning of Witchcraft* (New York: Weiser, 1971).

Gluckman, Max, *Politics, Law and Ritual in Tribal Societies* (New York: Oxford University Press, 1965).

Godelmann, Johann Georg, *Tractatus de magis, veneficis, et lamiis* (Frankfurt, 1601), tract. II.

Goethe, Johann Wolfgang von, "Faust," in *Goethes Meister-Werke* (Berlin: Oestergaard, 1925).

Graves, Robert, *The White Goddess* (New York: Octagon Books, 1948).

Haining, Peter, *Hexen* (Hamburg: Stallings, 1977).

Hansen, Joseph, *Quellen und Untersuchungen zur Geschichte des Hexenwahns* (Hildesheim: Olms, 1901).

Hartlieb, Johannes, *Buch aller verboteter Kunst, Unglaubens und der Zauberei*, Bavaria, 1456.

Helldorfer, Ludwig, *Gössweinstein: Burg, Amt, Kirche, Gemeinde* (Gössweinstein: Selbstverlag Marktgemeinde, 1974).

Henningsen, Gustav, *The European Witch-Persecution* (Copenhagen: Danish Folklore Archives, 1973).

246

Höfler, Otto, *Kultische Geheimbünde der Germanen* (Frankfurt, 1934).

Hoover, Eleanor L., "Mystical Portents," *Human Behavior* 6 (March 1977):14.

Oldfield, Howey, *The Cat in the Mysteries of Religion and Magic* (London, 1930).

Huebner, Louise, *Power through Witchcraft* (Los Angeles: Nash, 1969).

Hughes, Pennethorne, *Witchcraft* (Baltimore: Penguin Books, 1970).

Jules-Rosette, Bennetta, *African Apostles, Ritual and Conversion in the Church of John Maranke* (Ithaca, N.Y.: Cornell University Press, 1975).

Junius, Johannes, letter to his daughter, in Rossell H. Robbins, *The Encyclopedia of Witchcraft and Demonology* (New York: Crown Publishers, 1963), p. 292.

Kertzer, Morris N., *Tell me, Rabbi* (New York: Block, 1976).

Kluckhohn, Clyde, *Navaho Witchcraft* (Boston: Beacon Press, 1962).

Kluckhohn, Clyde and Dorothea Leighton, *The Navaho* (Cambridge, Mass.: Harvard University Press, 1946).

Koestler, Arthur, *Life after Death* (New York: McGraw-Hill, 1976).

Kovács, Zoltán, "Die Hexen in Russland," *Acta Ethnographica Academiae Hungaricae* 22 (1973):53–86.

Kraemer, Henry Institor and Jacob Sprenger, *Malleus Maleficarum* (Edition of Lyon, 1584).

Krakovsky, Levi Isaac, *Kabbalah: The Light of Redemption* (Brooklyn, N.Y.: The Kabbalah Foundation, 1950).

Krige, J. D., "The Social Function of Witchcraft," in Max Marwick, ed., *Witchcraft and Sorcery* (Baltimore: Penguin Books, 1970), pp. 237–251.

Kruse, Johann, *Hexen unter uns? Magie und Zauberglauben in unserer Zeit* (Hamburg: Hamburgische Bücherei, 1951).

Kunstmann, Hartmut H., *Zauberwahn und Hexenprozess in der Reichsstadt Nürnberg* (Nürnberg: Stadtarchiv, 1970).

LaVey, Anton S., *The Satanic Bible* (New York: Avon, 1969).

Lea, Henry C., *A History of the Inquisition of the Middle Ages* (London, 1888).

LeBon, Gustave, *Psychologie des Foules* (Paris: Olean, 1895).

Lederer, Wolfgang, *The Fear of Women* (New York: Harcourt Brace Jovanovich, 1968).

Leitschuh, Friedrich, *Beiträge zur Geschichte des Hexenwesens* (Bamberg: Hübscher, 1883).

Leland, Charles G., *Gypsy Sorcery and Fortune Telling* (New York: University Books, 1964).

Lifton, Robert J., *Thought Reform and the Psychology of Totalism. A Study of Brainwashing in China* (New York: Norton, 1961).

Looshorn, Johann, *Die Geschichte des Bistum Bamberg* (Bamberg, 1906).

Macfarlane, Alan, J. D., *Witchcraft in Tudor and Stuart England* (New York: Harper, 1970).

Mackay, Charles, *Extraordinary Popular Delusions and the Madness of Crowds* (New York: The Noonday Press, 1974).

Mair, Lucy, *Witchcraft* (New York: McGraw-Hill, 1971).

Malinowski, Bronislaw, "Magic, Science, and Religion," in Robert Redfield, ed., *Magic, Science, and Religion and Other Essays* (New York: Doubleday, 1954).

Marwick, Max, "The Social Context of Cewa Witch Beliefs," *Africa* 22 (1952):232.

Marx, Karl, and Friedrich Engels, *On Religion* (New York: Schocken Books, 1964).

Masters, R. E., *Eros and Evil: The Sexual Pathology of Witchcraft* (New York: Matrix House, 1966).

Mayer, Philip, "Witches," in Max Marwick, ed., *Witchcraft and Sorcery* (Baltimore: Penguin Books, 1970), pp. 45–64.

Merzbacher, Friedrich, *Die Hexenprozesse in Franken*, 2nd edition (Munich: Beck, 1970).

Middleton, John F. and E. H. Winter, eds., *Witchcraft and Sorcery in East Africa* (Boston: Routledge & Kegan Paul, 1963).

Midelfort, H. C. Erik, *Witch Hunting in Southwestern Germany 1562–1684* (Stanford: Stanford University Press, 1972).
Miller, Walter B., "Two Concepts of Authority," *American Anthropologist* 57 (1955):279.
Monter, E. William, *European Witchcraft* (New York: Wiley, 1969).
Monter, E. William, "Patterns of Witchcraft in the Jura," *Journal of Social History* 5 (Fall 1971):1–25.
Monter, E. William, *Witchcraft in France and Switzerland; The Borderlands during the Reformation* (Ithaca, N.Y.: Cornell University Press, 1976).
Murray, Margaret A., *The Witch Cult in Western Europe* (Oxford: Oxford University Press, 1921).
Nadel, S. F., "Witchcraft in Four African Societies," *American Anthropologist* 54 (1952):15.
Nietzsche, Friedrich, *The Portable Nietzsche*, selected and translated by Walter Kaufmann (New York: Viking Press, 1954).
Parsons, Elsie C., "Witchcraft among the Pueblos: Indian or Spanish?" *Man* 27 (1927):106–128.
Paulus, Nikolaus, *Hexenwahn und Hexenprozess, vornehmlich im 16. Jahrhundert* (Freiburg i. Breisgau, 1910).
Peuckert, Will-Erich, *Pansophie* (Stuttgart: Kohlhammer, 1936).
Peuckert, Will-Erich, "Dr. Johannes Faust," *Zeitschrift für deutsche Philologie* 70 (1947–48):55–74.
Peuckert, Will-Erich, *Geheimkulte* (Heidelberg: Pfeffer, 1951).
Peuckert, Will-Erich, "Das 6, und 7. Buch Mosis," *Zeitschrift für deutsche Philologie* 76 (1957):174.
Peuckert, Will-Erich, *Verborgenes Niedersachsen* (Göttingen: Schwartz & Co., 1960).
Porta, Giambattista, *Magia naturalis* (Naples, 1589).
Rappaport, Herbert, "The Tenacity of Folk Psychotherapy: A Functional Interpretation," paper presented at the Annual Meeting of the Eastern Psychological Association, New York, 1976.
Redfield, Robert, ed., *Magic, Science, and Religion and Other Essays* (New York: Doubleday, 1954).
Richet, Charles, *L'homme et l'intelligence. Fragments de Physiologie et de Psychologie* (Paris, 1887).
Robbins, Rossell H., *Encyclopedia of Witchcraft and Demonology* (New York: Crown Publishers, 1959).
Rose, Elliot E., *A Razor for a Goat* (Toronto: Toronto University Press, 1962).
Roszak, Theodore, *The Making of a Counter Culture* (New York: Doubleday, 1969).
Runeberg, Arne, *Witches, Demons and Fertility Magic* (Helsingfors, 1947).
Russell, Jeffrey B., *Witchcraft in the Middle Ages* (Ithaca, N.Y.: Cornell University Press, 1972).
Russell, Jeffrey B., *The Devil* (Ithaca, N.Y.: Cornell University Press, 1977).
Sarbin, Theodore R., "Role Theory," in Gardner Lindzey, ed., *Handbook of Social Psychology* (Reading, Mass.: Addison-Wesley, 1954).
Schneider, Ulrich F., *Das Werk "De praestigiis daemonum" von Weyer und seine Auswirkungen auf die Bekämpfung des Hexenwahns*, jur diss., Bonn, 1951.
Scot, Reginald, *Discoverie of Witchcraft* (London, 1584; reprinted by Centaur Press, 1964).
Sebald, Hans, "Limitations of Communication: Mechanisms of Image Maintenance through Selective Perception, Selective Memory, and Selective Distortion," *Journal of Communication* 3 (September 1962):142–149.
Sixth and Seventh Books of Moses or Moses' Magical Spirit-Art, translated from German, printed in the USA, anonymous editor and publisher, no publication date.

Soldan, Wilhelm G., *Geschichte der Hexenprozesse* (Stuttgart, 1843).

Spanos, Nicholas P. and Jack Gottlieb, "Ergotism and the Salem Village Witch Trials," *Science* 194 (December 24, 1976):1390–1394.

Spee, Friedrich von, *Cautio criminalis* (Frankfurt, 1632).

Steadman, Lyle, *The Killing of Witches: A Hypothesis*, unpublished research report, Department of Anthropology, Arizona State University, 1977.

Summers, Montague, *History of Witchcraft and Demonology*, 1926; *Geography of Witchcraft*, 1927; *Popular History of Witchcraft*, 1937; *The Werewolf*, 1937; *Witchcraft and Black Magic*, 1946 (all with Kegan Paul, London).

Szasz, Thomas, *The Manufacture of Madness: A Comparative Study of the Inquisition and the Mental Health Movement* (New York: Harper and Row, 1970).

Thomas, Keith, *Religion and the Decline of Magic* (New York: Scribner's, 1971).

Thomas, William I., *Primitive Behavior* (New York: McGraw-Hill, 1937).

Trevor-Roper, Hugh R., *The European Witch-Craze of the 16th and 17th Centuries and Other Essays* (New York: Penguin Books, 1969).

Veith, Ilza, *Hysteria: The History of a Disease* (Chicago: The University of Chicago Press, 1965).

Vierordt, Karl F., *Geschichte der evangelischen Kirche in dem Grossherzogthum Baden* (Karlsruhe, 1847–1856).

Waite, A. E., *The Holy Kabbalah* (New York: University Books, no date of publication).

Weber, Max, *The Protestant Ethic and the Spirit of Capitalism* (New York: Scribner's, 1930).

Weyer, Johannes, *De praestigiis daemonum*, Basel, 1563 (Paris 1885 reprint).

Wheatley, Dennis, *The Devil Rides Out* (London: Hutchinson, 1963).

Wheatley, Dennis, *Forbidden Territory* (London: Hutchinson, 1963).

Willer, Judith, *The Social Determination of Knowledge* (Englewood Cliffs, N.J.: Prentice-Hall, 1971).

Williamson, Hugh R., *The Arrow and the Sword* (London: Faber, 1947).

Wilson, Monika H., "Witch-Beliefs and Social Structure," *American Journal of Sociology* 56 (1951):308.

Wittmann, Alfred, *Die Gestalt der Hexe in der deutschen Sage* (Bruchsal: Kruse & Söhne, 1933).

Wolf, Hans, *Gössweinstein, Gestern Heute, Morgen* (Gössweinstein: Marktgemeinde, 1976).

Yoors, Jan, *The Gypsies* (New York: Simon & Schuster, 1967).

Zborowski, Mark and Elizabeth Herzog, *Life Is with People* (New York: International Universities Press, 1974).

Zwetsloot, Hugo, *Friedrich Spee und die Hexenprozesse. Die Stellung und Bedeutung der "Cautio Criminalis" in der Geschichte der Hexenverfolgung* (Trier, 1954).

Author Index

Subject Index